SOCIAL CARE
THE COMMON KNOWLEDGE BASE
A Pic 'n' Mix Guide

**By: Siobhan Maclean and
Rob Harrison**

Kirwin Maclean Associates Ltd

SOCIAL CARE
THE COMMON KNOWLEDGE BASE
Pic 'n' Mix Guide

By Siobhan Maclean and Rob Harrison

FIRST EDITION: 2010   **ISBN: 978-1-903575-67-3**

A catalogue record for this book will be available from the British Library

Kirwin Maclean Associates Limited, 47 Albion Street, Rugeley, Staffs
All Rights Reserved

ISBN: 978-1-903575-67-3

Printed in Great Britain by:
Kirwin Maclean Associates Limited, Rugeley, Staffordshire

CONTENTS

WHAT IS A COMMON KNOWLEDGE BASE ALL ABOUT?

A great deal of work is taking place in social care designed to "professionalise" the work force and the term the "professionalisation agenda" is now in regular use in the field. This professionalisation of social care is important for a range of reasons, particularly to ensure that service users are receiving the best possible support available.

It is widely acknowledged that a core knowledge base is a key component of a profession. See for example Eraut (1994), Rafferty (1996) and Hawamdeh (2009). Clarifying the common knowledge base of social care is therefore a vital aspect of the professionalisation of social care.

This book seeks to outline key aspects of the professional knowledge base. In selecting what should be included we have looked towards recent debates about the developments of social care which are well summarised by Pat Higham (2005:1) when she suggests:

"..... a new definition of professionalism based on:

- *promoting the social model of intervention in partnership with people who use services and carers.*

- *working with other professionals and support workers*

- *intervening to protect vulnerable people when appropriate*

- *promoting human growth and developing individual capability*

- *building on awareness of structural oppression, power, service users rights and responsibilities and social inclusion."*

We have also carefully reviewed the whole range of qualifications in the sector (both vocational and academic) considering the range of knowledge referred to in each qualification.

We have also considered concepts around different types of knowledge and the inter-relationship of knowledge, skills and values as follows.

In drawing together the knowledge covered in this book, we hope that the book will act as a useful guide for everyone in the social care sector. The idea of the guide is that it can be used in very much a pic 'n' mix way – so that readers can dip in and out of the sections and the knowledge covered.

Different Types of Knowledge

In 2006 Cameron and Boddy drew on a range of research studies which considered the knowledge and education required for effective social care practice. They noted a distinction between three forms of knowledge:

➢ *"Tacit knowledge. Sometimes referred to as practice wisdom, this is the knowledge derived from experience and from personal qualities.*

➢ *Functional knowledge. This is the knowledge which might be specifically required to perform defined tasks to an agreed standard. This is the kind of knowledge which has historically featured most heavily in competence based qualifications.*

> ➤ *Professional knowledge. This type is knowledge of described as combining 'professional skills (including specific competences) and practical experience with a strong theoretical underpinning."* (Boddy and Statham 2009:13)

In bringing together the content of this book, we have tried to include aspects of each type of knowledge. However, it is only when individual workers interpret the meaning of the knowledge within their own practice that the professional knowledge base will become meaningful.

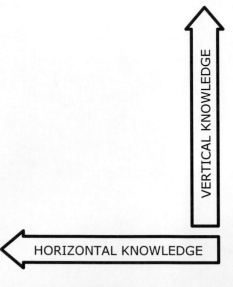

Knowledge can also be seen in terms of horizontal and vertical knowledge (Maclean and Caffrey 2009). This is a concept drawn from information technology, where horizontal knowledge and vertical knowledge can be defined in a range of ways. In terms of social care, we would define vertical knowledge as knowledge which is specific to a particular profession – for example, social care, nursing, social work etc. As such, it is knowledge which all social care workers will share – regardless of the service user group they work with (for example, knowledge about values, the principles of social care practice etc.) Horizontal knowledge on the other hand is specialised knowledge about a particular service user group. This knowledge will not be specific to social care workers but will be shared by a range of different professionals working with a particular service user group. For example, there will be specific knowledge about dementia shared between psychologists, nurses, doctors, care staff and others working with people with dementia.

The knowledge covered in this book, by its very nature (the common knowledge base) is mostly 'vertical' knowledge. In our view it is important that all staff working in social care have this knowledge as it provides the basis of the professional identity of social care. However, horizontal knowledge is also important. Inquiries into failures in social care and social work have consistently highlighted the fact that workers from different professional backgrounds have not effectively challenged or questioned each other. It is only in having a firm horizontal knowledge base (that is knowledge which is relevant to particular service user groups) that social care workers can effectively challenge other professionals. Social care workers therefore need to be proactive about developing their horizontal knowledge.

Knowledge, Skills and Values

It is widely recognised that good social care practice is made up of knowledge, skills and values (see for example, Dalrymple and Burke 1995 and Maclean and Caffrey 2009).

Dalyrymple and Burke (1995) provided the following framework of anti-oppressive practice in health and social care:

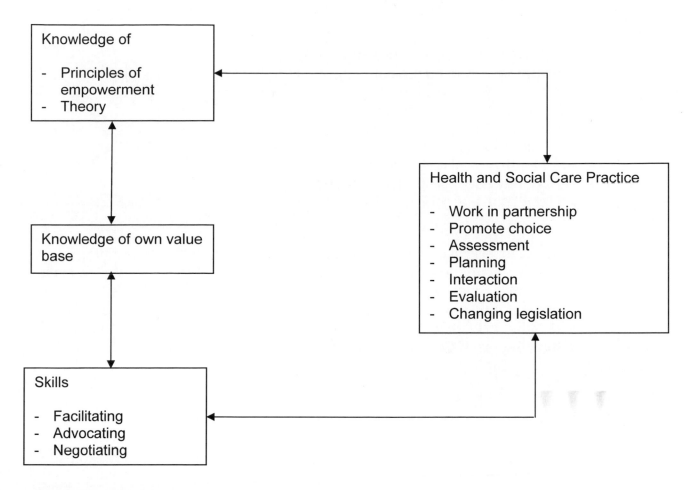

This framework clearly demonstrates the relationship between knowledge and skills and how these inter-relate to produce effective professional practice.

In considering the ways in which social care workers can promote people's rights in practice Maclean and Maclean (2005) provide the following table:

Knowledge of	Skills in
• Legal rights • Agency policies and procedures • Charters of rights e.g.: patients charter • Complaints procedures • Key principles such as advocacy and empowerment	• Listening to people • Supporting people to express themselves e.g.: choices • Negotiating (e.g.: around tensions which may arise) • Advocating on behalf of people • Supporting people to do as much for themselves as possible

Again this highlights the links between knowledge and skills. Qualifications in social care recognise the way in which knowledge impacts on skills and the fact that knowledge is a vital component of effective professional practice. By its very nature a book of this kind can only provide a reader with knowledge but wherever possible we have considered how this knowledge can be utilised to aid skill development.

Making Use of Knowledge

With the increased professionalisation of social care the importance of knowledge is becoming more apparent in the qualification framework used in the sector. For example, within the QCF there are some purely knowledge based units. However, it is not having knowledge which is important. The most important aspect of knowledge is what the social care worker *does* with that knowledge and how they use it. After all a walking encyclopaedia doesn't make a good social care practitioner.

Tutors and assessors for social care qualifications should recognise this by creating learning environments where the delivery and assessment of knowledge enable the social care practitioner to make concrete links between the knowledge and its application in practice. Knowledge should never be taught purely theoretically but in an environment where learners are able to work together to develop their ideas and to discuss their own experiences so that they have the opportunity to explore, debate and challenge knowledge.

Qualifications in the field recognise this and regularly refer not only to the candidate "knowing" something but "knowing how to ….." "understanding" "explaining". This means that candidates not only need to demonstrate they know something by for example, describing a piece of knowledge but that they can also demonstrate how they make use of this knowledge in their practice.

An Explanation of Imagery Used in this Book

We have called this book a pic 'n' mix guide not just because we liked the look of the sweets on the cover but because it's the type of book that readers should dip in and out of when they are looking for information on a particular area. However, the imagery of pic 'n' mix has been "blended" with images of a building process. This is because the common knowledge base for social care is really still "under construction". As the sector 'professionalises' it is also building its knowledge base and its qualification structures.

SECTION A: THE VALUE BASE

Social care is underpinned by a number of core values. This is essentially what has become known as our professional "value base".

But what does the value base refer to? To a layperson the word "value" conjures up images of bargain hunting or financial efficiency in services. However, in terms of social care the value base is essentially about a code of conduct which defines the way in which we should work with people.

The word values could be replaced by the word beliefs. What we *value* is what we believe is important. The professional value base is the foundation upon which all our work is based.

1: AN INTRODUCTION TO VALUES

The Importance of Values

The value base is essentially the foundation on which good social care practice is based. That said, values issues can often be forgotten or taken for granted. As Timms once said *"A man's values are like his kidneys: he rarely knows he has any until they are upset."* (Timms 1983:16). The importance of values in social care should never be forgotten and every social care worker needs to integrate the value base into all of their work.

The Nature of Values

There are four different forms of values:

Personal Values

It is generally accepted that our personal values are influenced by a number of factors. The factors which influence and shape our personal value system might include:

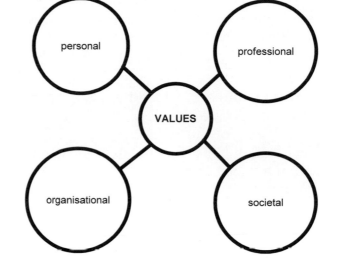

➢ Our background and upbringing (often referred to as socialisation)

➢ Personal experiences

➢ Education

➢ Religious beliefs

➢ Cultural background

Because we are all individuals and these factors will be different for everyone, then all individuals have a different set of personal values.

Professional Values

Social care is said to have a professional value base. Whilst the professional value base does not replace each individual's personal value base, professional values do over-ride personal values in terms of the way in which we work with people. All workers must adhere to professional values.

Organisational Values

It is increasingly recognised that organisations themselves have different values. Where they are driven by performance targets and funding requirements, organisational values may be in conflict with the professional value base, which can cause problems in practice for many social care workers.

Societal Values

Society values certain things and devalues others. This links very closely to an understanding of oppression and discrimination as societal values are generally based on

---

the idea that certain groups of people are more important than others. Societal values may well be influenced and or expressed through the mass media.

Examining Professional Values

Choosing to work in the field of care does mean that we need to adopt a set of professional values. These are the values of social care. Whilst the professional value base does not replace each individual's personal value base, professional values do over-ride personal values in terms of the way in which we work with vulnerable people.

Shardlow (undated) states:

"To ask 'what are the values of social [care] work?' is to miss the point. Even though phrases such as the value base suggest that there is something firm and fundamental upon which to build the edifice of social [care] work, there is no single set of values that commands universal assent among practitioners."

However, others argue that there is a clear set of professional values which forms the basis of social care practice.

As far back as 1961, Biestek defined seven principles underpinning a positive relationship between a social care worker and a service user (in his terms, a "client"). These are often taken as the social care value base:

1.   Individualisation: the service user being treated as an individual.

2.   Purposeful expression of feelings: the service user having the opportunity to express feelings.

3.   Controlled emotional involvement: the service user should have a sympathetic response from an interested professional who adopts a certain level of emotional involvement.

4.   Acceptance: the service user should be seen as a person of worth.

5.   Non judgemental attitude: the service user should not be judged by the worker.

6.   Self determination: the service user should make choices and decisions.

7.   Confidentiality

Building on Biestek's writing, many people see the principles of social care work (as covered in section B) as the value base of social care.

Generally speaking though, it is currently accepted that the value base of social care is outlined in the Code of Practice for social care workers which states that social care workers must:

➢ protect the rights and promote the interests of service users and carers

➢ strive to establish and maintain the trust and confidence of service users and carers

➢ promote the independence of service users while protecting them as far as possible from danger and harm

➤ respect the rights of service users whilst seeking to ensure that their behaviour does not harm themselves or other people

➤ uphold public trust and confidence in social care services

➤ be accountable for the quality of their work and take responsibility for maintaining and improving their knowledge and skills

(GSCC 2002)

Value Conflicts

The subject of values is complex and conflicts can often arise. Sometimes, this is a natural consequence of experiencing new situations and working with different people. In order to deal with dilemmas and conflicts in a professional manner it is important to recognise conflicts in values and work constructively to resolve them.

The word "values" itself indicates that the beliefs and ideas which people hold can be integral to our own sense of self as our personal values can include ideas about:

➤ what we feel is fundamentally important

➤ how we value and treat others

This is why conflicts between personal and professional values and conflicts between colleagues about values issues can be so painful and challenging.

To illustrate this there may well be conflicts between personal and professional values. Everybody's personal value base is unique to them and since the professional value base is common to all social care staff there will sometimes (if not often) be conflicts between these.

One helpful way of looking at these is outlined in the following illustration:

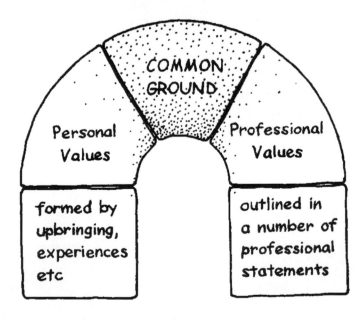

When our personal values are in conflict with our professional values we need to find some common ground in order to manage the conflict. This is clearly represented by the shaded area of the illustration (a bridge between personal and professional values).

The consequences can be serious if, for example, colleagues cannot find this common ground. Values conflicts and differences of opinion around how care is best provided can be one of the most challenging aspects of working in social care, as well as one of the hardest issues for managers of services to manage. This is partly because the consequences of "getting it wrong" for users of services can be so serious and damaging.

When working with the value systems covered it can be useful to draw something up which shows where the "common ground" may be. For example:

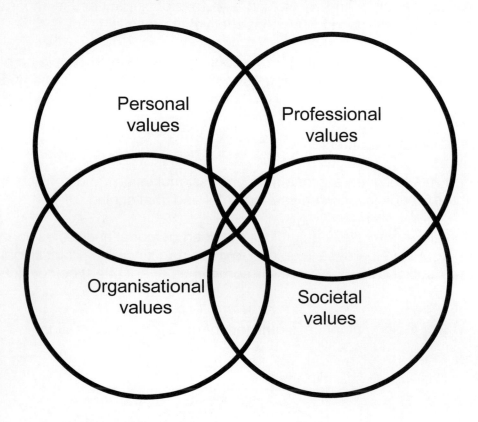

At times the circles may overlap more than others, but it should always be possible to find some common ground. Thinking about values issues in this way and identifying common ground and divergence can be useful in helping to analyse values issues and consider some of the other issues covered in this section.

In Summary

Our personal values are unique to us and are influenced by several factors. The professional value base for social care is expressed in shared formats such as the Code of Practice. Finding common ground can be complex, but should be possible.

2: UNDERSTANDING OPPRESSION

To understand the nature and backdrop of the professional value base, it is important to have a clear understanding of oppression. The value base of social care seeks to challenge oppression and ensure that workers practice in an anti-oppressive way.

<u>Definitions</u>

It is important to begin by looking at definitions of some of the key words in this area.

> *Prejudice*
  This is where an individual makes a judgement based on either inadequate or inaccurate information which leads to the development of irrational preferences. One of the main features of prejudice is rigidity or inflexibility of ideas. This means that new information may not have an impact on prejudicial views.

> *Discrimination*
  This does have a definition within the law, which stated briefly is treating somebody less favourably, for example, on the grounds of his or her gender, sexuality, race etc.

> *Oppression*
  The word oppression has its roots in Latin. It comes from the word opprimere which means to press on or press against. As such, it suggests people being pressed on and flattened. Looking at oppression in this way gives a very visual image of what it is like to be oppressed. Phillipson (1992) states that oppression suggests force, being flattened and squashed out of shape.

> *Anti-oppressive Practice*
  An old, but still a very clear definition of anti-oppressive practice is outlined by the Inner London Probation Service (1993). They state that anti-oppressive practice:

  "exposes, challenges and seeks to replace forms of oppression which lead to discrimination, and marginalisation."

To understand and apply anti-oppressive practice, it is therefore vital to have an understanding of the main types of oppression, and the ways in which it is manifest.

Anti-oppressive practice is practice which seeks to support people in a way which does not "squash" individuals. It is about practice which promotes equality and celebrates diversity. The word oppression is very often used as an "umbrella term" and the phrase "anti-oppressive practice" is in common usage and essentially describes the value base of social care.

Who is Oppressed?

Most people will have been oppressed in some way, at some stage of their life. However, it is widely accepted that some groups of people are more likely to be oppressed than others - e.g: Black people, women, older people, gay people, people with disabilities, etc. Some of the main forms of oppression which have been identified in British society are outlined in the following box.

Adultism

Adultism is the belief that adults are superior to children and young people. Adultism "is discrimination against young people. It happens anytime children or youth are ignored, silenced, neglected or punished because they are not adults. Every young person experiences adultism from the day they are born until the day the world around them recognises them as an adult." (Freechild Project 2008). As such, it is something every person will experience in life, and is apparent in Western cultures, where the idea that children should be "seen and not heard" is still powerful. The fact that "smacking" children is still not outlawed in British law is often cited as an example of adultism.

Ageism

Ageism is the belief that older people are inferior to younger people. This belief grants the right to dominance by younger people in terms of access to opportunities and cultural messages about what is valuable.

Disabilism/Ablism

People with disabilities experience discrimination and oppression based on the belief that to not have a disability is superior.

Heterosexism

This is the belief that "the only valid 'normal' and 'natural' relationships are heterosexual ones. Heterosexism assumes that heterosexuality is the norm and in social care can operate where workers assume everyone is heterosexual (service users, relatives, colleagues etc). Heterosexism is different from homophobia, but discrimination against gay, lesbian or bisexual people on the basis of heterosexism is one way in which homophobia operates (John Moores University 2009).

Racism

The Macpherson Report into the death of Stephen Lawrence (1999) defines racism as follows:

"Racism in general terms consists of conduct or words or practices which disadvantage or advantage people because of their colour, culture, or ethnic origin." Central to this conduct is the prejudicial belief that some races are superior to others.

Sexism

Sexism is *"the belief that one sex/gender is inherently better than the other"* (About Equal Opportunities 2009). In British society, the word sexism is usually used to describe the dominance of men over women.

These categories are by no means exhaustive – other examples of groups who are particularly vulnerable to oppression include people who are homeless, people who use drugs, asylum seekers, people who have mental health problems, people with long term health conditions… the list goes on!

Doubly Disadvantaged?

When looking at who is oppressed, it is important to remember that oppression is a complex process. Many people will be oppressed because of more than one characteristic. For example, Black people with a learning disability will be subject to racism as well as discrimination based on their learning disabilities. This complex process is often known as double discrimination (oppression based on two characteristics) or triple jeopardy (oppression based on three characteristics).

Types of Oppression

It is commonly accepted that there are three main types of oppression.

Individual Oppression

This is where the actions and attitudes (sometimes unconscious) of individuals towards marginalised groups support and sustain a broader social pattern of discrimination.

For example, a man may believe that women should be responsible for all household chores and childcare. The way this man acts towards women will sustain the broader view of women in society.

Institutional Oppression

This is where institutions (for example, schools, employers, churches, residential services etc) in reflecting the structure of the society they serve, maintain a set of rules, procedures and practices which operate in such a way as to perpetuate discrimination against marginalised groups.

The Macpherson report (1999) defines institutional racism as:

"The collective failure of an organisation to provide an appropriate and professional service to people because of their colour, culture or ethnic origin. It can be seen or detected in processes, attitudes and behavior which amount to discrimination through unwitting prejudice, ignorance, thoughtlessness and racist stereotyping which disadvantage minority ethnic people."

Structural Oppression

This is where oppressive institutions work together with the effect that a structure or societal system of oppression is generated and sustained. For example, class division and restricted opportunity for children from poor backgrounds have become entrenched. Education disproportionately benefits the middle class (for various reasons). The middle class then feel their wealth is justified since "all had equal chance at school." The middle class can pay for their children to have ballet lessons and learn to ski, which enhances their children's skills. Privilege leads to opportunities which enhance learning, skills and confidence, which in turn leaves a young person better prepared for adulthood.

Another clear example is that residential care services all have an accepted weekly costing that social services are willing to pay. Above this cost, senior managers will need to agree the funding. The accepted weekly cost of older people's residential care is the lowest of all. The accepted weekly cost of residential care for adults with a learning disability and adults with mental health problems is higher. The accepted weekly cost of children's residential care is higher still. This illustrates one structural inequality.

It is important to note that individual, institutional and structural oppression are very closely linked. After all, institutions are made up of a number of individuals. Therefore, individual beliefs and actions will have a profound impact upon organisations, institutions and society as a whole. The key to the difference, however, is that where the oppression is carried out by one or two people this is individual oppression. Where the root of the oppression is in an organisation this is institutional oppression. When oppression is endemic across a number of organisations this combination becomes structural oppression.

<u>Covert and Overt Oppression</u>

Any form of oppression can be described as either overt or covert:

Overt is obvious oppression and relatively easy to identify - e.g.: *Some local youths shout racial abuse at an Asian women.* Overt oppression can be more straightforward to challenge.

Covert is hidden (covered) oppression and can be more difficult to identify and to challenge - e.g.: *A company claims to have an equal opportunities policy but unofficially they won't offer jobs to young Muslim men.*

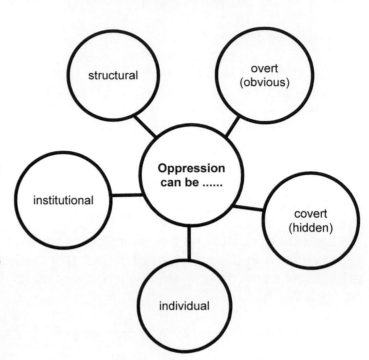

Professional Viewpoint

Competent workers need to be able to recognise how social care services can be part of the oppressive structure of society. Staff within services may conscientiously seek to apply the value base and to uphold the rights of people they work with. However, the total experience from the service user's perspective is to compound their sense of disadvantage. People working in social care need to be able to acknowledge the oppression that service users face and recognise that people may experience services in this way. It is important that people working in the sector take a professional viewpoint and that they do not see any comments made about the oppressive nature of services as a personal criticism.

How Services May Oppress Service Users

A report by the Commission for Social Care Inspection 'Time to Care?' (CSCI 2006) highlighted how older people living at home want an ordinary life, which includes going out, contributing to society and enjoying a sense of security. Domiciliary care services, however, focus on providing a 15 or 30 minute call to provide personal care to the older person in their home (and that's all). Often call times are set, so that the care worker could call as early as 6.00pm to assist someone into bed. The service user may be in bed until 8.00am when the morning care worker calls.

'Time to Care?' (CSCI 2006) raised concerns that some older people found their care workers felt they could not stay the whole allocated time since travel time was not included in their timetable. Therefore, even 30 minute calls were only 20 minute calls for some service users. Additionally, some older people expressed concerns about the number of care workers they saw and one older person related that she felt she had to train new staff!

The difficulties with residential services are well known. In adult services, there is a pressure to keep costs down which means maximising the number of service users whilst keeping staffing to the minimum possible. Older people's care homes can be large, too large.

Multi purpose day centres for adults are known for gathering together a whole range of people with different needs. Activities are often large group activities.

Research indicates that even small services (like for adults with learning disabilities or for adults with mental health problems) can have institutional practices and the experiences of service users can be very variable (Healthcare Commission / CSCI 2006).

The whole social services assessment process is blighted by structural constraints. The worker may assess a person's needs but they are under pressure to just focus on personal care needs. The local authority's eligibility criteria will determine if a person qualifies for a service, with various local authorities raising the level at which services are considered necessary.

This brief critique, outlining some of the ways in which services can oppress people, is not designed to criticise staff or indeed organisations. It is designed to highlight the way that services work within systems, structures and constraints which can lead to service users feeling oppressed. This is not the purpose of the service and systems, but it is often the result. Competent social care workers will be able to identify and analyse issues such as these within their own setting. It is only in having this kind of critical awareness that care staff can seek to ensure their practice is safe and that they work in an "anti-oppressive" way with service users.

 In Summary

Oppression operates at several inter-related levels. It affects many individuals and arguably all users of social care provision, and can be sustained by oppressive practices within organisations.

3: UNDERSTANDING POWER

Power is a big issue in social care work and it is vital to have an awareness of power to understand the value base of social care. In any relationship between two or more people power is an issue, and professional relationships can mean that the power differentials are heightened.

Sources of Power

In 1993 Raven listed five types of power. Some of these apply to social care workers, and some will apply to managers or other professionals.

> Legitimate Power. This is power that exists due to the way in which an organisation is structured or the way that society is ordered (e.g.: a social worker has the power to decide if a person is eligible for a service).

> Expert Power. This is where a person is seen as having a bank of knowledge or expertise.

> Reward Power. This is power gained through the ability to give rewards. In social care this is most likely to occur if a person is isolated and support staff are the main contact points for the service user. The service user will only get any sense of reward (social contact) from these individuals.

> Referent power. This is power created by the admiration and respect a person can have for another. A good example of this is a person's respect for their GP (although the GP's power is also derived from legitimate and expert power).

> Coercive power. This is power based on the ability to apply punishment or sanctions. The service user could be conscious of this power even if it has not been actively applied by social care workers.

The Inner London Probation Service (1993) identify power sources which are similar to those identified by Raven:

> Professional power. This is the power which is derived from being a "worker" in a situation rather than being on the receiving end of services.

> Expert power. This overlaps to some extent with professional power but is based much more on access to specialised knowledge and skills.

> Resource power/coercive power. This power base is seen as two sides of the same coin and involves the power to withhold or give resources, the power to provide resources appropriately. The power to challenge and confront oppression could also be included here.

It is important to recognise that in addition to these five sources of power there is societal power. Some people experience oppression at the hands of others. Oppressors are powerful and oppressed people are less powerful. So, for example, an older person who experiences ageism will feel less powerful than a younger person.

Whenever one individual provides care for another, there is an immediate power relationship. In terms of how services work, the power relationship is influenced by the following factors:

Power held by the service user:

➢ The service is meant to be for the benefit of the service user

➢ The service user has the right to complain if they are not satisfied with the service provided

➢ The service user may have other people to turn to for support (e.g.: family member)

➢ Personal qualities of the service user (e.g.: articulate, confident, educated etc.)

However, the service user's perception of their own power may be undermined by:

➢ One or more negative experiences that have markedly reduced their confidence

➢ A profound sense of vulnerability due to the fact that they are dependent on the social care worker, which inhibits making complaints

➢ A lack of knowledge of their rights

➢ Isolation

➢ Previous attempts at claiming power over their own life which have failed (this is known as "learned helplessness")

➢ The person may have their ability to express themselves impaired by mental health issues, a learning disability or difficulties in communication etc.

The social care worker will be powerful by comparison to the service user. Possible reasons for this could include:

➢ Possible age, gender or race of the social care worker compared to the service user (e.g.: a 30 year old white woman supporting a black woman in her 70s)

➢ The worker has a role or a job to do. This is heightened if the worker presents as busy or with lots to do

➢ The service user needs care support, not the worker and the worker knows lots about the service user etc

➢ The worker is one of a team and has the power to influence the viewpoint of team colleagues through recording or team discussion

A social care worker's perception of the limits of their power may be influenced by:

➢ The worker's professional values which prompt them to show respect for the service user, recognise that service users are experts about their own situation etc

➢ The knowledge that service users could complain about them

➢ Awareness of the presence of colleagues and of regular supervision from their line manager

Most professional workers have significant power compared to a service user. When a worker gives a service user choices, they are applying their power through the manner of the worker's presentation and by deciding which choices they are going to make available. Service users may pick up from workers what answer they feel the worker is wanting the service user to give and so comply with this.

We need to maximise service user autonomy and so all workers need to be conscious about what power they have and how they are using their power. Are workers using their power to enhance the service user's independent decision making skills or to guide the service user to an option that is easy for the staff and the service to respond to?

Powerlessness

Some service users can maintain some power over their own life, possibly because they are articulate or have active family support or make full use of direct payments etc.

Many more service users experience a significant sense of powerlessness. The service user is likely to have been through significant changes in their life, most of which were unwanted. They may have acquired a disability or mental health problem or may have been subjected to abuse. Having contact with services can be difficult for some people to adjust to. If the service user has had to move into a care home then this can be a profound change. Often the decisions the service user is still able to make are relatively minor. The service user has little real say over key decisions. The service user didn't plan or want to develop mental health problems or to acquire a disability. This can result in the service user having a profound sense of powerlessness. The attitude of workers, the way the service is organised and the ethos can all influence whether this sense of powerlessness is heightened or reduced. Many service users feel powerless and their lack of confidence (due to the knocks of life) is likely to result in a sense that they are unable to change their life in the way they would like to. If the service user develops the view that they cannot change anything because they are powerless this is termed 'learned helplessness'.

Recognising and "Owning" Power

Social care staff often lack knowledge and understanding of the power they have, perhaps because in terms of systems and structures in services they may feel powerless themselves. If asked to identify a situation where they felt powerful and a situation where they felt powerless, care workers can almost always more readily identify with feeling powerless than feeling powerful. This might be because empowerment is a key principle in social care practice so staff feel that having power is a bad thing. However, inquiries into failures in social care practice almost always identify that where staff do not recognise and "own" their power, they are more likely to abuse their power (perhaps unwittingly). It is therefore vital that staff recognise the significant power they have, so that they can use this responsibly and respectfully.

The Inner London Probation Service (1993) identify how the denial of power is generally much more common than the owning of it. The more power that social care workers have, the less they seem ready or able to own that power. Ironically, often the people who are the most able to articulate exactly where power lies and the impact of the power are those who are powerless.

The first steps towards empowerment can only be achieved by identifying and understanding who holds power, what the power consists of and how the power is used. This is never easy, but is one of the main reasons that social care staff must understand power and powerlessness.

In Summary

Anyone who provides professional care for others has power. Power can have various sources and can have positive and negative effects on people. It is vital that social care workers recognise the power they hold and seek to exercise this power responsibly.

4: THE MECHANISMS OF OPPRESSION

Having discussed what oppression consists of, where it can be found and the links with power, the final part of understanding the nature of oppression focuses upon the mechanisms of oppression. That is the various means by which people can be oppressed.

There are many mechanisms of oppression, such as:

➢ Language

➢ Media

➢ Stereotyping

➢ Trivialising (e.g.: jokes)

➢ Labelling

➢ Education

➢ Employment/unemployment

Social care workers will already be familiar with many of these as mechanisms of oppression. In this book we have decided to cover three of the main mechanisms of oppression in detail – language, stereotyping and labelling before considering other ways in which oppression may operate in the social care environment.

It is too easy to subscribe to mechanisms of oppression, often on an unconscious basis, and thus oppress people as a result. Enhanced understanding of the mechanisms of oppression can help avoid oppressive practice and thus promote service users' equality, diversity and dignity.

Language

The subject of discriminatory or oppressive language is a complex one. Sometimes, issues around language that aims not to discriminate are described as "political correctness" or a "play on words" and dismissed. However, language is a living tool that grows and changes to reflect broader shifts in society. For example, the language that we use can affect the way we regard and interact with other people. Words and phrases project certain images. We must ensure that these images do not reinforce offensive or discriminatory attitudes.

The following poems illustrate the importance of the use of language:

Tomorrow I am Going to Re-Write the English Language

I will discard all those striving ambulist
Metaphors
Of power and success
And construct new images to describe my
strength.
My new, different strength.

Then I won't have to feel dependent
Because I can't Stand On My Own Two Feet
And I will refuse to feel a failure
Because I didn't Stay One Step Ahead.
I won't feel inadequate
When I don't Stand up for Myself
Or illogical because I cannot
Just Take It One Step At a Time.

I will make them understand that it is a very
male way
To describe the world
All this Walking Tall
And Making Great Strides

Yes Tomorrow I am going to re-write the
English Language.
Creating the world in my own image.
Mine will be gentler, more womanly way
To describe my progress.
I will wheel, cover and encircle.

Lois Keith, Cited in J Morris (1989)

Who is Coloured?

When I was born
I was black,
When I grew up
I was black.
When I get hot
I am black,
When I get cold
I am black.
When I get sick
I am black,
When I die
I am black.
When you are born
you are pink,
When you grow up
you are white.
When you get hot
you go red,
When you get cold
you go blue.
When you get sick
you go purple,
When you die
you go green.
BUT YET YOU HAVE THE
CHEEK
TO CALL ME COLOURED!

Donna Davis
(Source unknown)

Anti-Oppressive Language

Issues around the use of language have become much more prominent in recent years. As we have seen, language can exclude and offend people (sometimes accidentally). The language that we use reflects our own value base, and therefore must receive careful attention in order to demonstrate an active commitment to anti-oppressive practice.

Exclusion

Some of the language which we might use can make people feel like they are excluded. For example, it is now commonly accepted that referring to a position as "chairman" may lead women to feel excluded. "Chairperson" or simply "chair" is therefore used instead. Using phrases which can exclude groups of people is potentially oppressive (e.g.: "every man for himself", "young person's game" etc.)

Depersonalisation

Language often depersonalises people – people can be viewed more as a label or as simply one of a group of people. For example, using language such as 'the disabled' or "the elderly" means peoples individuality is lost and they could be seen simply as a member of a group. "Ic" is often added to a medical diagnosis and then used to describe someone. This is incredibly depersonalising – for example, "they are a diabetic", "the schizophrenics". It is much better to refer to a person as having a diagnosis of diabetes rather than as a diabetic.

Dehumanisation

Dehumanisation is the process of people not being seen as a valued human being or the worth of a person being reduced so that they are seen as not quite human (sub-human). Whilst it might sound extreme, dehumanisation through language is actually very common in social care. The language used around personal care is a good example. People generally "eat" their meals but as soon as someone comes into contact with social care services they will be referred to as "feeding" themselves or as needing "feeding". In other situations we only use the word feeding to refer to animals or babies. I've been into care services which have a "feeding rota" up in the kitchen or dining area. It makes it sound like a zoo.

Another example is "toileting". I don't know about you, I go to the toilet, I don't toilet myself. The combined effect of the use of this kind of language is that the language used to describe actions we all do changes when people are in need of care. The central message received by people is that they are now 'less than human'.

It's not uncommon to hear other de-humanising language in social care settings. I remember once being asked to 'load the wheelchairs in the bus'. I looked all around the service and couldn't see any wheelchairs, so I asked the manager where I could find them. She looked at me as though I was asking a complicated algebra question – what she had meant was that she would like me to assist the service users who used wheelchairs to get on the bus. Apparently people within that service who used wheelchairs were generally referred to as "the wheelchairs"!

When we use dehumanising language, it becomes easier to abuse people and violate their rights. It is vital therefore that social care staff do not use language that dehumanises people. We should think through the language that we use about ourselves and use this when referring to people who need care and support.

For example:

➢ feeding should be replaced with assisting to eat

➢ toileting should be replaced with assisting to use the toilet etc

Stereotyping

Stereotyping is the process of ascribing set characteristics (often negative) towards all, or most members of certain groups of people. Stereotyping becomes particularly dangerous when people begin to act towards individuals based on the stereotypical characteristics ascribed to the group of people to which the individual belongs. For example, a common stereotypical comment about Asian people is that they *"look after their own"*. This may lead to no services being provided for people from the Asian population, even though they may be needed.

Some of the "milder" stereotypes of people who need support are often portrayed comically within the media: for example, think of Vicky Pollard or Lou and Andy (Little Britain, BBC). Whilst this may be entertaining, there are more dangerous aspects to stereotyping. For example, society's stereotypes of adults with mental health problems are often very negative.

Neil Thompson (1998) has described stereotyping as having various characteristics. He says that stereotypes:

➢ are resistant to change even in the face of evidence which conflicts with the stereotype

➢ are largely negative

➢ become so established that they are accepted as reality without serious question.

Thompson points out that stereotypes are transmitted both by individuals and by culture. They confirm, validate and entrench societal inequalities, because the stereotype is applied to a whole group or section of society.

A number of writers including Wolfensberger (e.g.: 1988) have identified that various common themes emerge in the stereotyping process and that people subjected to stereotypes are given a social role or category. Some of these common themes are outlined here as there is much to learn about oppression and how it operates from exploring these common themes.

The Person as Subhuman-Animal or Vegetable (Wolfensberger) or Dehumanisation (Thompson)

Whilst this may appear extreme, it is an incredibly common process. Chattel slavery was justified on the basis that Black people were subhuman. Black people, people with learning disabilities and people with mental health problems have all had animal images closely associated with them. The use of aversive punishments, e.g. hitting, electric shock, denial of food etc, is probably rooted in this. People who enter very deep comas can be labelled as in a "persistent vegetative state" and some of these people have then had all medication and food withdrawn.

Thompson focused on the way language is the means by which dehumanisation occurs. People who are discriminated against are at risk of being entirely described by a label e.g.: 'alcoholic' etc.

The Person as a Menace (Wolfensberger)

Many people who are devalued within society are considered a threat or as a potential criminal. Additionally, as a group, people can be seen as a social threat to the well-being of society. For example, people with mental health problems are often portrayed as dangerous in the media.

The Person as an Object of Dread (Wolfensberger)

This is related to the two previous characteristics. The person is seen as a dreadful entity or event. Associated with this is the medieval concept of the person as a "changeling". This can be seen in the way people with mental health problems could be described and in the way parents, who have been informed that their new born child has a learning disability, are described as grieving for the child they never had.

The Person as an Object of Pity or Burden of Charity (Wolfensberger) or Welfarism (Thompson)

The person may be viewed as being subject to misfortune for which they bear no responsibility, for which they therefore require special attention or services. The pitied person will be seen as blameless for the situation they find themselves in and perhaps therefore unaccountable for their actions.

Where there is no compassion, only a sense of duty, the person will be seen as a burden of charity. Whilst the person may be entitled to basic necessities, they are not entitled to anything considered luxuries, frills or extras. The recipient of such charity is expected to be grateful and, as far as possible, to work for their "keep".

Thompson (1998) uses the term welfarism. This refers to the situation where certain groups are seen as in need of state welfare support through health or social care services. Thompson makes the following points about welfarism.

> ➢ It is stereotypical; all individuals within a group are assumed to rely on state welfare despite evidence to the contrary

> ➢ It is demeaning and patronising

> ➢ It creates dependency and erodes rights

> It reinforces discriminatory viewpoints e.g.: people are seen as a social burden and drain on the economy

The Person as a Sick or a Diseased Organism (Wolfensberger) or Medicalisation (Thompson)

The person is labelled as sick or a patient: they receive a diagnosis, and are given treatment or therapy by doctors, nurses, paramedics or therapists, which is intended to lead to a cure. The person may be entitled to the privileges, as well as subject to the demands, that are characteristics of the sick role generally. Privileges include exemption from normal social responsibilities, and recognition that the condition is not the individual's "fault". The demands are that the individual must want to get well or at least "better", and must seek suitable and appropriate remedy for their condition.

Many people in receipt of services are involved in activities which are classified as therapy, e.g.: art therapy, drama therapy, art therapy etc. However, if the person was not stereotyped, these activities would probably just be described as a hobby – art, amateur dramatics etc.

Thompson (1998) goes on to develop and outline the additional effects on a person who is characterised as intrinsically "ill". These consequences include:

> Invalid status. A person who is sick is treated as an invalid – they are no longer a valid person. The person loses some degree of status whilst ill.

> Welfarism. The act of labelling as ill attracts welfare responses with a focus on care and not rights.

> Medical discourse and power. People who are viewed as ill are then placed in the domain of health professionals. Doctors and health professionals exercise significant power within a context that characterises them as the experts.

The Person as an Object of Ridicule (Wolfensberger) or Trivialisation (Thompson)

The person is not taken seriously and is the butt of jokes at their expense. Historically, Black people have been depicted by the media as servants or light entertainers. People with learning disabilities have been characterised as the "village idiot".

Thompson recognises the point that Wolfensberger originally made. Additionally, Thompson argues that the process of trivialisation is used to undermine anti-oppressive practice. The example given by Thompson (1998) is where discussions about sexism are hijacked by discussions focusing on whether a man should hold open a door for a woman. Reference is also made to the way the term 'politically correct' has been coined (and continues to be used negatively in today's media) to dismiss issues of language and anti-oppressive practice.

The Person as an Eternal Child (Wolfensberger) or Infantilisation (Thompson)

People with a learning disability are particularly at risk of being viewed as a child, although people with physical disabilities and older people can also be. When a person is viewed as a child their opportunities are likely to be limited. There is no expectation that the person can accept adult responsibilities and rights.

Thompson's use of the term infantilisation closely follows the meaning of Wolfensberger's eternal child. Thompson (1998) highlights the way language conveys this. For example, older people when they enter care or health settings 'lose' their name and staff use pet names (duck, love) as adults do with children. This can also be conveyed by the use of specific tones which people use in talking to the service user as they would speak to a small child.

The Person as a Holy Innocent (Wolfensberger)

The person is accorded religious characteristics. S/he may be perceived as incapable of consciously or voluntarily committing evil or malicious acts. Whilst this is probably the most benign social role perception, the danger is that people so viewed will be also considered as "other worldly" and not interested in ordinary human activity.

Invisibilisation (Thompson)

This refers to the process by which various groups of people are not represented in language or the media. Language has historically been male dominated and has used male terms for roles that could easily be gender free e.g.: Chairman.

Media images are noted for focusing on the dominant groups in society and by doing so ignoring other groups (making them invisible). Examples of this include the way older people, people with disabilities and people who are poor are significantly under represented in the media.

Marginalisation (Thompson)

Certain groups of people are pushed to the margins of society, they are excluded from the decision making process and the operation of power in general.

Examples of marginalisation include the way people with disabilities have been educated in "special schools" and the way speakers of minority languages can find that their first language is pushed to the fringe.

Labelling

Labelling is closely linked with stereotyping, as people can be labelled based upon the stereotype. Once someone has been "labelled", it can be very hard to move away from that label, and others see the "label" before they see the individual!

Labelling is the process by which a negative blanket term is applied to a person. The effect on other people, when they view that person, is to have a prejudiced and negative view which adversely influences their behaviour towards that person. The effect on the person, both of the label and of other people's actions towards them results in the person feeling judged and this undermines their confidence. The person who is labelled may then act in ways that are a distortion of their true identity but, to the observer, result in confirming the validity of the label.

We all have labels given to us. A few people are fortunate enough to have the label of "celebrity" or "aristocrat". Many of us have the label of worker or professional or student, partner, parent etc. Most of these labels are seen positively.

Whether we like it or not, labelling is part of life, everyone is labelled in some way. The issue is really about whether the labels attached to people are positive or negative.

Labels are closely related to power differentials in relationships. If a worker is labelled 'support worker' and the people they work with are labelled 'service users', this will add power dynamics into the relationship.

There are some labels that are negative and are not claimed by a person but are put on them by others. In social care, one of the problems is that most service users are given labels by professionals. In origin the intention by professionals is not to give someone a negative label, but to recognise that a person has identifiable specific needs. Unfortunately, many of the labels that professionals apply to service users are not neutral because they are used negatively within society.

Social care services and health services continue to use labels because it is the principle means they use to identify who should receive certain services.

Therefore there are benefits and disadvantages of having labels:

Benefits of Labelling

1. Having a recognised label can explain a characteristic of a person. If a child is struggling with reading and writing at school they may be at risk of being "labelled" lazy or slow etc. If the child is then assessed and found to have dyslexia, this can be a relief (in part) for the child and parents in that it explains why the child is having difficulties.

2. Having a specific label should enable the person to receive specialist services that are able to meet the person's needs.

3. Some professionals find it beneficial to label an individual. For example, a professional is working with a group of children or service users and one of them is presenting them with needs that demand more of their time and attention. By having the child or service user labelled it can result in the professional being given additional staff support, or the service user may be moved to a more appropriate group of individuals who have similar needs.

4. On a similar vein, organisations can benefit from labelling individuals if it results in being able to claim additional funds.

5. Most statutory services for adults can only offer support to a person if they have a disability, mental health problem, are frail or infirm due to their age or have other support needs (e.g.: an addiction to drugs or alcohol). Therefore, there is a requirement to give a person one of these labels if they are to "reach threshold criteria" and receive services.

Disadvantages of Labelling

1. The labels used by professionals are not neutral. They are nearly all viewed in society as negative. Some of the labels have a very significant stigma associated with them. The strength of this stigma should not be overlooked by those of us who are not given one of these labels.

2. The label given by health and social care professionals to service users is often related to perceived 'deficits' of the person. The labelling process is an indirect way of saying the person is incompetent (in one respect or another).

3. The label may have originally had some meaning and purpose. However, it can quickly become misused and the person who has the label applied to them quickly becomes covered by it as if covered by a blanket. The label becomes the person's identity and almost their name. For example – "schizophrenic", "alcoholic", "epileptic" etc. When an "ic" is attached to the end of a label, it is a sign that the person's individuality and identity has been lost under this label. Even without the 'ic', people can have their identity lost e.g.: "She's a hair puller!" Statements such as "he has special needs place a judgement on a person.

4. As noted by Wolfensberger, the label becomes a "self fulfilling prophecy". If a person is given a negative label then health and social care staff are likely to be influenced by this and their behaviour could be different. If a person is given the label of 'aggressive' then staff may stand at more of a distance, be cooler in their whole approach and maybe have a colleague present. This could result in the service user recognising that a label has been applied to them and resenting the label. The service user is angry about the label, but this gets viewed by staff as confirming the claim that the service user is aggressive.

5. Service users have <u>no</u> control over their label. It is passed to new staff by experienced staff. At one time or another, many of us have done something that could result in us being given a negative label. We manage to bury or lose the negative label. In Britain, by the age of 30, about 30% of men have a criminal record. Most men don't introduce themselves to someone new by saying "Hi, I'm Dominic, I've got a conviction for reckless driving. Do you want a lift home?" Most of us bury or lose our negative label by changing friends, moving etc and by not telling our new friends about our past. In services the label gets passed on and sometimes it is one of the first things a new staff member learns about a service user. Sometimes this label is inaccurate or exaggerated or it relates to an event that happened years ago. There are lots of ways to describe a person, but too often the negative labels are passed on to the new staff very early in their working life.

6. Often service users can be given negative labels which have a profound effect on their lives and opportunities. For example, adults with dyslexia often relate how they were labelled as "stupid" at school and were not given the support they needed. This has had a very profound effect on the self esteem of many people with dyslexia.

7. Adults may carry a mental health label such as "schizophrenia" or a label like "challenging behaviour". Expectations of recovery or improvement may be low (or non existent) which can result in a care plan that is 'standard' and does not aid personal development.

Labels can be very damaging to service users. The Disability Rights Movement states that labels belong on jars and not people! Some of the dangers of labelling are demonstrated in the following poem written by people with learning disabilities:

Copyright © Kirwin Maclean Associates Ltd

Sticks and Stones

Sticks and stones may break my
bones
But names can hurt and harm you
inside
They touch a tender spot
They make you feel horrible
Names stick in your heart
Once called a name
It stays in your mind all the time
When you are called a name enough
You get to think it is right

You can't get away from it
A name lingers
It starts with a doctor
A specialist
A head-shrinker
A social worker
Teachers
Headmasters…
It spreads like measles
Name calling is like an epidemic

The Rushland Poets (1997)

Other Ways Oppression may operate in Social Care Services

Service Décor

Many services have realised the impact that service décor has on how services are viewed and have tried to maintain a good physical environment. There are still some exceptions. Examples include some day centres which have uncarpeted corridors and a communal wall with loads of coat hooks. By comparison, most offices are carpeted throughout and office workers keep their coats either in their own room or close to them.

Names of Services

As the saying goes "There's a lot in a name." The names given to services very often have 'images' attached. For example, many older people's homes are called things like "Cherry Trees" or "Green Meadows". It sounds as though people are being put out to pasture! Swimming Clubs for people with disabilities are often called names like "Dolphins" or "Penguins". This gives a childlike impression as opposed to "Burtonwood Swimming Club". Many national organisations have changed their names or the names of individual service provision because of the importance of social imagery.

Social imagery should not be under-estimated. It can be belittled and minimised by reference to the term "political correctness". However, generally people using this term are not devalued people who are affected by social imagery and oppressive systems.

 In Summary

Oppression can be sustained via language, stereotyping, labelling or via subtle aspects of how services are constructed and delivered. It is important that social care staff have a clear understanding of this so that they can seek to ensure they practice in an anti-oppressive way.

5: PUTTING IT ALL TOGETHER: RECOGNISING COMMON EXPERIENCES

It is worth exploring some of the common experiences oppressed people can face:

EXPERIENCES	EXAMPLES
Rejection Kept at a distance from others. Placed with people in similar situations.	Segregated services keep people away from the general population and in groups of people with similar needs.
Diminished Experiences Less experience of different people, different places, different activities.	Devalued people may not be able to mix with the general population, activities may be limited etc. This is particularly so if people are in segregated services.
Low Expectations People have limited expectations of what devalued people can achieve.	A classic example is when people often ask a question to someone who is with a person in a wheelchair, rather than the person themselves "Does he take sugar?"
Loss People who are devalued often experience significant loss in their lives.	As a result of the negative experiences people will experience a loss of power, control, choice, rights, dignity etc.
Being seen as one of many Many people are not viewed as an individual, but as a label, or a condition or a problem.	Many people who are in receipt of services are viewed as a group. For example, going out in a group, the needs of the group over-riding individual needs etc. The general population may view people as a label etc.
Artificial Relationships A loss of real friends and contacts may lead to people's social networks being limited to paid staff and volunteers.	Many people living in residential services, or people who attend day services, are expected to rely upon other service users and staff to make up their social network.
Poverty People who are devalued are often reliant on benefits or trapped in poverty.	The weekly allowance of people living in residential care would not keep most people in the general population, even if all their daily living expenses (bills, food etc) were paid for.
Labels People are often ascribed negative labels.	In the general population, people are referred to by negative labels or terms – e.g.: "mad" "handicapped". Within services people may be labelled as "manipulative, attention seeking, etc"

Working in an anti-oppressive way is essentially about breaking what is sometimes referred to as the "cycle of oppression" and altering many of these experiences.

The mechanisms of oppression are all inter-connected and contribute to the experiences of devalued groups. Social care staff need to recognise and understand the main mechanisms of oppression and should seek to challenge them where possible.

In Summary

Values provide an essential foundation to social care practice. The fact that we refer to the 'value base' is no mistake – what we are talking about is the basis of all good practice. Social care professionals must have a clear understanding of the issues covered in this section in order to practice effectively.

The core value base for social care is shared with that of other professions, including health, education, social work, police housing, community work etc. What is distinct to social care work is the fact that the service user is usually in receipt of specific support from the worker in order to enable them to maintain their dignity. The very fact that the service user is receiving "care", in whatever form, is the reason why Biestek's seven key values are so crucial to effective practice.

A number of basic principles build on the value base (as covered in the following section). It is in following these core principles that a social care worker can bring their knowledge of the issues covered in this section to life.

SECTION B: THE PRINCIPLES OF SOCIAL CARE PRACTICE

Whilst the value base of social care provides the foundation of good professional practice, it is actually through following the principles of good care practice that social care workers express these values.

Whilst this section covers what we describe as the basic principles, many investigations into failures in health and social care services regularly identify that these basic principles are not followed by practitioners.

6: UNDERSTANDING RIGHTS

Where do Rights Come From?

The source of the rights we enjoy in the United Kingdom is the British Constitution. This is not a single document as is the case with some other countries, but it is actually a combination of formal written laws and unwritten conventions built up over many centuries and adapted to meet changing circumstances. It is composed of:

➢ Customs and conventions which are recognised as governing the rights which people enjoy.

➢ Statute law – that is, laws agreed by Parliament.

➢ Case law – law developed in the courts by judges whose job it is to interpret laws agreed by Parliament.

➢ European law – laws which have been developed for the European Community as a whole which affect us as a member state.

Individuals can take cases to court to enforce their rights and the constitution is both a source of rights and a source of protection of those rights. The fact that it is not a single document can be seen as both a strength and a weakness depending upon your perspective. Its strength is that because it is drawn from so many diverse and changing sources it can always be adapted to meet new circumstances. Critics of our constitution, however, argue that because it is difficult to tie down, it has been difficult to uphold the rights of vulnerable people and minority groups.

Rights and the Law

The Human Rights Act 1998 came into effect in October 2000. It is probably the most well known legislation in terms of rights in the United Kingdom.

Other pieces of legislation also positively state a limited number of rights which are relevant to social care. For example:

➢ The NHS and Community Care Act 1990 gives people with social care needs the right to an assessment and the right to complain.

➢ An adult who is eligible for social care services has the right to a direct payment. This right has evolved through various legislation including the Community Care (Direct Payments) Act 1996 and the Health and Social Care Act 2001.

➢ Informal carers have the right to an assessment of their own needs. Again, this is a right which has been extended since the Carers (Recognition and Services) Act 1995, through the Carers and Disabled Children Act 2000 and the Carers (Equal Opportunities) Act 2004.

THE HUMAN RIGHTS ACT 1998

The Human Rights Act came into effect across the United Kingdom from October 2000 and was an important change. It is an example of how European Law can affect our constitution as it embedded the provisions of the European Convention on Human Rights into our legal system. Until this point our legal system lacked an explicit statement of the rights to which we are entitled unlike the US constitution which includes a Bill of Rights. This is not to say that rights were not defined in the legal system, but rather that they were either implied or were reflected in numerous areas of law.

Schedule 1 contains sixteen articles which list various rights. These include:

➢ Article 2: the right to life

➢ Article 3: the right to be protected from torture, inhuman or degrading treatment or punishment

➢ Article 5: the right to liberty and security of person

➢ Article 8: the right to respect for privacy

➢ Article 9: the right to freedom of thought, conscience and religious belief

➢ Article 10: the right to freedom of expression

➢ Article 11: the right to freedom of association with others

➢ Article 12: the right to marry, form relationships and have a family

➢ Article 14: the right not to suffer discrimination on grounds such as sex, race, religion, political affiliation or other reason

Rights and Responsibilities

Closely tied to rights are responsibilities that the person enjoying those rights has an obligation to observe. Various rights and responsibilities are listed in brief on the following table. The table is not comprehensive but gives an idea of some of the responsibilities that follow from exercising rights.

Right	Responsibility
To life	To respect right of others to life
Freedom of movement	In exercising it not to infringe rights of anyone else
Freedom of speech	To be prepared to hear what others say in response; not to say anything that incites racism or violence
Freedom of association	To seek to be with those who also want to be with you
Make decisions that affect own life	To acknowledge and face any reasonable and likely consequences of your decision
Practice religious beliefs	Not to infringe same right of anyone else in exercising this right
Pursue cultural and other interests	Not to infringe same right of anyone else in exercising this right
To vote (subject to age)	To make decisions based on knowledge of political options
To have sex (subject to age)	To ensure it is a mutual decision and to be aware of possible consequences e.g.: sexually transmitted diseases
To get married (subject to age)	To be aware of the nature of commitment and intent on upholding your promise
To own property	Stewardship of such property
To be treated with dignity and respect	To treat others in the same way
To be treated fairly and equally	To treat others fairly and equally
To due process of law and legal representation if arrested	To co-operate in police investigation
To be protected from unnecessary risk of harm, neglect, abuse etc	Not to subject others to harm, abuse, etc and not to place oneself in situations where there is unnecessary risk of harm or abuse
To medical treatment based on clinical need	To provide relevant information to medical staff
To maximise personal development; spiritual; emotional, intellectual, physical	To pursue opportunities for personal development
To take risks	To accept the consequences that could reasonably be expected to follow
To privacy	Not to infringe same right of anyone else

Tensions within Rights and Responsibilities

There can easily be potential conflicts when considering rights and responsibilities, which can take one of several forms:

Tension between a person's own rights and responsibilities

It may be that there are times where a person's rights conflicts with their responsibilities. For example, an adult may have the right to smoke, but they also have the responsibility not to endanger others. In situations where a person smokes irresponsibly there is a danger of fire e.g.: a person smoking in bed and falling asleep as they smoke.

<u>Tension between different people's rights and responsibilities</u>

In any shared living or recreational environment tensions between people will arise. For example, one person's right to pursue their own interest can conflict with another person's right to do something different in the same place at the same time. A basic example of this could be an argument between people about what television channel to watch.

When Rights Cannot be Upheld

At times in social care, the duty of care can be in conflict with upholding service users' rights. This may be because of some of the tensions between rights and responsibilities covered above. Workers need to be very clear about the question "When should rights be over-ridden?" This is a difficult but vital question. The key answer is risk and relates to situations in which exercising a particular right may place someone in danger. Essentially, this applies in two main ways:

> *Danger to others*
> No one has the right to violate or infringe the rights of someone else. If a person is acting in a way that intrudes on someone else's rights (e.g.: hitting someone else), then action needs to be taken.

> *Danger to Self*
> Certain actions can place people at risk. Examples may include self-harm or significant self neglect.

It is vital that if someone's rights are restricted (because of a danger to themselves or others), the reasons for this should be explained to them clearly. Where people are unclear about boundaries and rights they may be left confused and frustrated.

The following poem written by Chrissie Elms Bennett based on her experiences as a young person in residential care illustrate this very clearly.

Clearly, from this poem, Chrissie Elms Bennett feels that her rights were violated. There may have been reasons for this but it appears that these were not made clear, which left Chrissie with many questions and a feeling of powerlessness. It is vital that we remember that a fundamental right is to have things explained clearly and honestly.

Why do they speak to me this way?
What happened to my right to have my say?
Why do they speak to me this way?
What happened to my right to protection?
Why do they reject and push me away?
What happened to my opinion and viewpoints?
Why do they assess me this way?
What happened to my freedom I must say?
Why do they label me this way?
What happened to my right to the things I do?
Why do they take everything from me this way?
What happened to my possessions? Feelings?
Emotions?
Why do they act this way?
What happened to my rights?
They took them away.
What I need is more power.
Please let us stand together,
Because I don't want to fight you.

Chrissie Elms Bennett,
Cited in Dalrymple and Burke(1995)

Upholding People's Rights in Practice

Social care workers need a range of key skills and knowledge in order to uphold peoples' rights. These are summarised in the table below:

Knowledge of	Skills in
• Legal rights • Agency policies and procedures • Charters of rights • Complaints procedures • Key principles such as advocacy and empowerment	• Listening to people • Supporting people to make choices and express themselves • Negotiating (e.g.: around tensions which may arise) • Advocating on behalf of people • Active support

Promoting a rights based culture

Social care workers and managers need to work to cultivate a service culture where:

➤ All staff understand and have a commitment to service users' rights

➤ Service user requests are responded to

➤ Staff commitments and responsibilities are met

➤ Tasks which are essential for service users' basic needs are carried out without service users having to make repeated requests

➤ Staff ensure that service users are aware of their rights

➤ Staff acknowledge and respond to comments and complaints without being defensive

➤ Staff challenge one another

➤ Positive values are promoted in the service at all times: discrimination and prejudice is challenged

➤ Service users are aware of their responsibilities towards others

 In Summary

Many people who are in receipt of care services have, until recently, had many of their rights infringed or denied, or were never supported sufficiently to exercise their rights. Even now, many of the rights we take for granted may be only partially or half heartedly upheld for people receiving a care service.

7: DIGNITY

The concept of dignity is central to all person centred care for vulnerable people. There is a growing focus upon dignity as a key principle in social care because of wide public and professional anger following horrific incidents and public exposures around poor care practice (see chapter 51 for more information on learning the lessons from such situations). Promoting people's dignity is not only linked to good practice in social care, but it is also about recognising service users' legal rights to protection from abuse and poor care provision which fails to recognise their individuality.

Cass, Robbins and Richardson (2009: 6) define dignity as follows:

"Dignity consists of many overlapping aspects, involving respect, privacy, autonomy and self-worth. The provisional meaning of dignity … is based on a standard dictionary definition: a state, quality or manner worthy of esteem or respect; and (by extension) self-respect. Dignity in care, therefore, means the kind of care, in any setting, which supports and promotes, and does not undermine, a person's self respect regardless of any difference. While 'dignity' may be difficult to define, what is clear is that people know when they have not been treated with dignity and respect."

The Government launched a "Dignity in Care" campaign in 2006. This focuses on the need for all services in health and social care to improve the care provision which exists for vulnerable adults by eradicating practices which are disrespectful and / or abusive. The aim of the campaign is to promote service users' rights to standards of care which meet their needs while respecting their dignity. The concept of "zero tolerance" to abusive and poor practices is at the heart of the challenge to all of us as potential users of care services in the future (if not now).

The Department of Health state that the campaign aims to:

➢ ***Raise awareness*** *of dignity in care;*

➢ ***Inspire*** *local people to take action;*

➢ ***Share*** *good practice and give impetus to positive innovation;*

➢ ***Transform*** *services by supporting people and organisations in providing dignified services;*

➢ ***Reward*** *and recognise those people who make a difference and go that extra mile.*
(Department of Health 2009)

Promoting service users' rights to dignity is more than "treating others as you would like to be treated". This is because the term itself forces us to recognise that for vulnerable adults who need the support of others in order to ensure their basic needs are met, there are implications around feeling "undignified" in the very fact of needing this assistance. Sometimes this is because of changes in personal circumstances or health which mean that care is provided in the first place, or that it is provided by people outside of the immediate family. It could be because of very personal feelings around the types of intimacy which may be involved in the provision of care support. Sometimes too, those working in social care must remember that people who need support are not valued within society as individuals who have a contribution to make, whose opinions are valid, and whose rights are equal to those who do not need this care.

Wolfensberger and Social Role Valorisation

Wolfensberger (1983) described the processes by which society can create situations whereby those who need care are less valued than others. Issues around labelling in relation to this are explored on pages 32 – 35. Don't be put off by the jargon. Think back to your childhood and try to identify the first time you came into contact with someone who had either a physical disability or a learning disability. It may be that you have *always* known a person with a disability (for example a family member) so in this case think back to your earliest memories of them. Alternatively, you may remember isolated examples such as seeing a person using a wheelchair when you were out etc. Whatever the situation was, think about how you felt and what you did at the time. Remember this is about when you were a child, no one is going to judge or assess you on the feelings you had then or on what you did. You must be as honest as possible to understand the basic concept of social role valorisation fully.

What you might find, as you reflect back, is that one of the feelings you had was curiosity. Children are often curious about people with disabilities. As a result of this curiosity they ask questions, of the person themselves, their parents, a teacher etc. If you have contact with children yourself you may have heard questions such as *"Why does that man walk like that?"*, *"Why does she look like that?"* etc. The problem comes when adults don't give reasonable answers to these questions. Children might be told *"Shush – stop looking. I told you not to stare"* or *"He's very poorly"* or *"She's no different to you or me"*. Of course these answers are the start of some of the other feelings you might have identified. If you were told as a child that someone was "poorly" – you might feel sorry for them (pity); on the other hand if you were rushed away and told not to look you might have begun to feel afraid.

This is basically the process of socialisation. Our early experiences often form our values and feelings and very often these are negative. If we are honest, we will have a mixture of feelings towards the people we work with and these may change over time, or in terms of context. These current feelings may not always be respectful and positive and some of them may be influenced by our earlier experiences.

Both individuals and society in general carry negative feelings towards people who need care services. These are usually unconscious and can be formed throughout our socialisation. Since human services are staffed by individuals and form part of society, these feelings can be expressed through service delivery. Social care staff need to be honest about unconscious thoughts and processes within services, so that they can be directly addressed.

Society values some qualities (e.g.: young adult, attractive, wealthy etc) as positive and views some qualities as negative (ageing, physical disability, learning disability etc). In relation to the qualities society views negatively, it feels it cannot be honest and explicitly negative. So society's negative view goes into the societal "unconscious". Society masks its dislike of people who are different by creating services that are meant to "care" for the people who are viewed negatively. But these "care services" have an unspoken (and primary) goal of keeping people viewed as different and deviant away from mainstream (valued) society.

The explicit goal of care services (to help service users) is only their secondary goal. Since society considers the people in the services to be unimportant the services are poorly resourced. Hence the quality of care is at risk of being poor. Therefore

Wolfensberger's insight was that traditional care services are part of the oppressive structure that service users face. Services need to be honest about their origins and the need for services to change and improve before they can adequately support service users to become valued members of society who are afforded the same dignity as other members of society.

Dignity in Care

With the above in mind, it is possible to see that services and structures can sometimes be part of the way in which vulnerable people are oppressed, and can lead service users to feel that their dignity has been compromised. Anyone working in health and social care is likely to have heard statements around time which is allocated to service users' care being made which are not person centred ("I've only got 5 minutes to do Mr C's meds"). This is not a criticism of staff delivering care or those determining resources within an increasingly challenging environment. However, the principles of dignity, person centred care and the service user's rights to choose their own care offer a challenge to us all as members of the public as well as professionals working in the field of social care.

The Department of Health give some challenging examples *"from people when they felt their dignity was not respected:*

➢ *feeling neglected or ignored whilst receiving care*

➢ *being made to feel worthless or a nuisance*

➢ *being treated more as an object than a person*

➢ *feeling their privacy was not being respected during intimate care, e.g.: being forced to use a commode in hospital rather than being provided with a wheelchair and supported to use the bathroom*

➢ *a disrespectful attitude from staff or being addressed in ways they find disrespectful, e.g.: by first names*

➢ *being provided with bibs intended for babies rather than a napkin whilst being helped to eat*

➢ *having to eat with their fingers rather than being helped to eat with a knife and fork*

➢ *generally being rushed and not listened to"*

(Department of Health 2009)

Other examples could be:

➢ A change in a workers' tone of voice when speaking to some service users which can be perceived by others as infantilising (treating the adult as a child)

➢ Care being "delivered" in people's homes which is little more than the meal and the medicines with little conversation or personal contact

➢ Care being provided which misses out on the principles of active support by doing tasks for somebody which they can do for themselves

➢ Food being provided cheaply which fails to meet service users' nutritional or cultural needs

➢ Workers not challenging stigma or discrimination on service users' behalf

The alternative is for workers and services to consider in more depth how they can work towards promoting people's dignity. Again, the Department of Health state that:
"High quality care services that respect people's dignity should:

1.   *Have a zero tolerance of all forms of abuse*

2.   *Support people with the same respect you would want for yourself or a member of your family*

3.   *Treat each person as an individual by offering a personalised service*

4.   *Enable people to maintain the maximum possible level of independence, choice and control*

5.   *Listen and support people to express their needs and want*

6.   *Respect people's right to privacy*

7.   *Ensure people feel able to complain without fear of retribution*

8.   *Engage with family members and carers as care partners*

9.   *Assist people to maintain confidence and a positive self-esteem*

10.   *Act to alleviate people's loneliness and isolation."*

(Department of Health 2009)

Dignity Champions

Champions have been developed from all levels within a wide range of services to challenge provision around the concept of dignity in care, to promote whistle blowing around poor practice, to listen to users of services, and to promote good practice. The role of Dignity Champions is to push for services to consider the 10 key principles outlined above, and to promote the concept of dignity in other fields, as well as those within health and social care. A champion could be a staff member or service manager, or they could be a relative of a service user, or a local councillor. Workers undertaking qualifications in social care could make valuable links with local champions to learn about good practice, or they could take on a champion's role within a service or broader care setting to gain evidence for their award.

 ## In Summary

Service users have the fundamental right to be treated in a dignified way. However, people in receipt of care services often report feeling that their human dignity was compromised. In recognition that this basic principle is so often missed, the Government has set up the Dignity in Care campaign.

8: INDIVIDUALITY

A fundamental aspect of the dignity campaign and a key principle of social care practice is individuality.

The different people that social care staff work with may, in some ways, have much in common. However, they will also be unique in many ways. As human beings we all share a common humanity and in <u>some</u> ways we are all the same (for example, biologically). In this way we all share a common humanity. In some ways, some people are the same – for example, we may share common characteristics with others (whether we are a man or a woman, for example). Finally, in other ways we are all different and therefore unique. The following figure first presented by Thompson (1994), demonstrates this well:

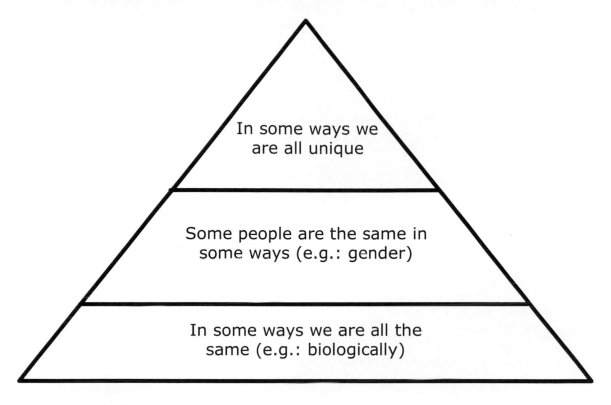

What Makes Each of Us Unique?

To begin to look at this area, consideration needs to be given to what makes each of us an individual, different to the people around us.

Many things make each of us unique – from the way we look; our upbringing; our life 'story'; family; our name; whether we prefer tea to coffee; how we like these drinks……. the list is exhaustive. Essentially what makes each of us unique is our identity.

Identity can be defined as:

"the state of having unique identifying characteristics held by no other person…….the individual characteristics by which a person…….is recognised".

(The Collins English Dictionary)

Identity is often seen as being influenced by two main areas – self image, and self esteem. Self image is essentially about how we *see* ourselves and self esteem is about how we *value* ourselves.

The development of a healthy and strong sense of self image and self-esteem is largely dependent on an individual having a positive sense of their own identity. However, this sense of personal identity can be undermined by a number of things, including poor care practices, aspects of oppression, the messages we receive from others etc.

Identity is important in social care since it is a person's right to have their identity and beliefs respected. In addition, all people in contact with social services are immediately at risk of having negative images and labels associated with them. This can lead to poor self image and a fragile identity.

One of the main ways to promote self esteem, dignity and a general feeling of well being is to support service users in a way which takes account of their individuality and shows the service user that they are valued as a unique individual.

In order to look at valuing diversity in social care practice it is helpful to begin with a consideration of the ways in which diversity is denied/ignored within services.

➢ People are seen as "problems" or cases

➢ People are labelled, removing their individuality eg. "epileptic, diabetic" etc

➢ People are subjected to institutionalised practice which ignores individuality

➢ Lack of privacy for individual care

➢ Lack of time

➢ Group care can compromise individuality

➢ Decisions are made by others without full and informed discussion with the individual

Some of the main methods used to promote individuality in service delivery are covered in the remainder of this chapter.

Narrative and Biographical Approaches

One of the main ways in which care staff can promote individuality in their work is to make use of what could be referred to as a biographical or narrative approach. These approaches are drawn from a range of sources, mostly from within the counselling profession.

The biographical approach is about understanding the impact that a person's biography (or life story) has had on the individual. It is about recognising every person as a unique individual with a unique life story. Most staff working in social care have heard or seen the following poem which was found in the hospital locker of an older woman after her death:

LOOK CLOSER SEE ME

What do you see nurses
    What do you see?
A crabbit old woman
    Not very wise
Uncertain of habit
    With far-away eyes
Who dribbles her food
    And makes no reply
When you say in a loud voice
    "I do wish you'd try"
Who seems not to notice
    the things that you do
And forever is losing
    a stocking or shoe
Who unresisting or not
    Lets you do as you will
With bathing and feeding
    The long day to fill
Is that what you're thinking
    Is that what you see
Then open your eyes nurse
    You're not looking at me
I'll tell you who I am

As I sit here so still
    As I use at your bidding
As I eat at your will
    I'm a small child of ten
With father and mother
    Brothers and sisters who
Love one another
    young girl of sixteen
With wings on her feet
    Dreaming that soon now
A lover she'll meet
    A bride soon at twenty
My heart gives a leap
    Remembering the vows
That I promised to keep
    At twenty-five now
I have young of my own
    Who need me to build
A secure happy home

A Young woman of thirty
    My young now grow fast
Bound to each other
    With ties that should last
Now grown will soon be gone
    But my man stays beside me
To see I don't mourn
    At fifty once more
Babies play round my knee
    Again we know children
My loved one and me
    Dark days are upon me
My husband is dead
    I look to the future
I shudder with dread
    For my young are all busy
Rearing young of their own
    And I think of the years
And the love I have known
    I'm an old woman now
And nature is cruel
    Tis her jest to make
Old age look like a fool
    The body it crumbles
Grace and vigour depart
    There is now a stone
Where once was a heart
    But inside this old carcass
A young girl still dwells
    And now and again
My battered heart swells
    I remember the joys
I remember the pain
    And I'm loving and living
Life over again
I think of the years
    All too few-gone too fast
And accept the stark fact
    That nothing can last
So open your eyes nurses
    Open and see
Not a crabbit old woman
    Look closer – see ME

This poem makes clear the importance of seeing each person as a completely unique individual as opposed to one of many.

The biographical approach is essentially about understanding the impact that a person's life history has on them. Very often people in receipt of care services are seen purely in terms of their current needs and requirements. The impact of a person's history and experiences on their needs, their choices, their behaviour etc is often ignored. Ignoring the biographical approach and focusing simply on presenting needs at best is likely to lead to the provision of mechanistic care and indeed it may increase the difficulties faced by individuals. To illustrate this, it is interesting to consider the example of an older man with dementia recently admitted to hospital. He began moving furniture around the ward which was causing problems particularly in terms of the health and safety of other patients. The staff team met to discuss this and various approaches were suggested, most of which focused on increasing his medication. A social care worker who knew about the man's background talked about how he had been a furniture removals manager for most of his working life and was able to identify that this was probably the reason for the behaviour. As a result of this insight a plan was developed which included discussing this with the man and encouraging him to become involved in other related activities in the ward. Through using a biographical approach, this social care worker was able to support an individualised care plan as opposed to an increase in medication for this man.

The narrative approach is very similar to the biographical approach. It is essentially where a social care worker gives the service user the opportunity to describe their own life in their own words. This enables the service user to describe their own identity in the form they wish to. When a person goes through a period of change, they often need time to absorb what some of the consequences are for them. Some people require the time to talk around a subject or personal experience in order to absorb it. The narrative approach can be helpful to enable the person to adjust to their new situation.

Life Story Work

Life story work began in services for looked after children but it is now used quite widely in adult services – mostly in learning disability services.

In life story work with adults with a learning disability, the aim is to generate a book or a personal record (sometimes in the form of a memory box or a DVD) of that person's life. It becomes their property. Where a person has experienced many changes, life story work can result in them understanding more about their life.

Life story work activities can include visiting former placements (e.g.: the site of an old long stay hospital) and photographing this. This can generate further discussion which can be recorded. Active visits like this may not be suitable for all adults. The life story work undertaken, like the individual it reflects, should be unique.

Reminiscence Work

Reminiscence work is usually associated with older people although its parallels with life story work are very close.

Reminiscence work is often done in groups. There are often props or prompts which can consist of photographs or videos from the past, music, clothing or household articles (also from the past). The intention is to support the person talk about their past, both in terms of employment and personal life (right back to childhood).

Where reminiscence work is carried out in groups, the group needs to be carefully selected to ensure that there will be common factors to their experiences.

Reminiscence approaches can be very usefully employed on a one to one basis – perhaps simply by a social care worker asking a person to talk about their memories and showing a genuine interest in the person's reminiscences.

Reminiscence work helps confirm a person's identity and reinforces their individuality. It has been seen as a practical application of theories of human growth and development, giving the person the opportunity to review their life, address unresolved questions etc.

In reminiscence work, there is usually no individual book kept (which is one difference from life story work). However, staff could support a service user to generate one if the service user wanted one.

Person Centred Approaches

Person centred approaches are originally derived from counselling and the work of Carl Rogers. Person centred planning is widely used in learning disability services where it is seen as a challenge to service centred approaches. Essentially being person centred is about focusing on individuals and supporting people in individualised and unique ways. In dementia services, this approach is often referred to as person centred care.

According to the Joseph Rowntree Foundation, person centred approaches involve:

> *taking service users needs and views into account*

> *Working effectively with family members*

> *Providing good quality care and support*

> *Supporting relationships between carer and service user*

> *Promoting independence*

> *Offering flexibility and reliability to service users*

> *Effective communication*

(Innes, Macpherson and McCabe 2006)

Person centred approaches are at the heart of Government policy and guidelines and the term "person centred" is often used glibly. However, truly person centred approaches call for a range of knowledge and skills and employing many of the techniques covered in this chapter and the remainder of this section.

One to One Days

Some residential services design their rota systems to ensure that time is allocated for residents to have regular time for "one to one" sessions with a staff member. This time may be used to assist the individual to develop their interests outside of a group of service users. It is also often utilised to assist people to do their personal shopping etc.

Keyworker Systems

Many services have devised systems where each service user is allocated a keyworker – sometimes referred to as a linkworker. This can help to ensure that each service user is treated as an individual and that diversity amongst service user groups is clearly recognised and responded to. Problems with this system occur when staff members have many service users allocated in "keyworker groups" – once again moving away from working with individuals.

In Summary

Recognising and responding to individuality is a key principle in social care practice. Recognising everyone as a unique individual rather than simply as a recipient of care services is vital to ensure good quality care provision.

9: CULTURAL SENSITIVITY

Cultural sensitivity is in many ways an extension of the concept of individuality. Services and care practice should be tailored to people's individual needs, and this means meeting any specific cultural needs which people may have.

However, social care services are very often "Eurocentric" in their outlook and their provision. This basically means that they focus on White European culture and provide care and support which reflects this. This means that the needs of many service users (and potential service users) are ignored and that people have to "fit into" inappropriate service provision. Research by the Joseph Rowntree Foundation identifies that people from minority ethnic groups experience a range of barriers to receiving person centred care. These barriers include a lack of accessible information, services which lack cultural understanding and language and communication difficulties (Innes, Macpherson and McCabe 2006).

To understand cultural sensitivity, it is worth looking at a range of definitions.

Essentially we would say that:

- ➢ *Culture* is an aspect of identity, which we all have. Culture is based on a number of things shared with others, such as language, shared history, beliefs, attitudes, celebrations, musical taste, dress, diet and many others. Culture is basically about a shared understanding with others of the same culture. Cultures are neither inferior or superior they are just *different*. Cultures are constantly evolving.

- ➢ *Multi-cultural* - British society is constantly changing and becoming more multi-cultural. That is, British society is made up of people from a wide range of different cultural backgrounds.

- ➢ *Cultural sensitivity* is basically about service delivery being inclusive rather than excluding people. Services which are culturally sensitive will recognise the need to address each person's unique cultural background and the complex way in which this may affect their individual needs.

- ➢ *Diversity* is essentially about difference. Difference should be valued and celebrated. What a boring place the world would be if we were all the same!

Within care settings there will be a rich mixture of people from a variety of backgrounds and cultures.

It is important, however, not to make assumptions based on individual people's culture. Culture does not mean uniformity and we still need to treat people as individuals. For example, we could say that "English Culture" involves:

> Eating fish and chips / Sunday roast

> Attending Church of England services

> Monogamous relationships

> Wearing business suits etc.

This would lead us to believe that all English people wear business suits, are in life long monogamous relationships; attend church every Sunday and eat fish and chips in the week and roast dinners on Sunday. Clearly this is not the case.

It should be obvious by this stage, that making assumptions is dangerous. Making assumptions about what people might eat or wear based on a very basic understanding of cultural norms can be misleading. Our belief is that we should never make assumptions about people. After all if you take the word ASSUME and look at it carefully it does the following:

ASSUME makes an ASS out of U and ME

The experience of service users from different backgrounds may differ radically from the cultural background of any member of staff. Cultural beliefs and practices will vary between generations and within a racial group. Certain cultural beliefs will be shared with others from the same background and certain things will not. The final collection therefore is completely unique to that individual.

Finding out about a person's cultural and religious beliefs is an essential first step in working in a person centred and an anti-oppressive way. It is central to the other principles covered in this section such as dignity and individuality. Whilst individual workers have a duty to work in an anti-oppressive way it is also the responsibility of the employing agency to promote such practice, and ensure that it operates along the lines of equal opportunities.

Good Practice Guidelines in Valuing Cultural Diversity

Social care professionals should:

> Celebrate difference – difference must be viewed as a strength and not a weakness. Difference should be celebrated and not denied or viewed as a problem.

> Ask people about their cultural background and beliefs. They should never assume that based on some knowledge which they may have generated from experience or reading that they understand a person's cultural background.

> Use the information they have access to in order to help them to reflect on difference and think what to ask people about their culture.

> Review their knowledge and regularly talk to others in their team about cultural diversity.

Meeting the Needs of a Multi-Cultural Society

In order to appreciate the different cultures to which people associate and to form effective working relationships with service users and carers, it is important to understand the diversity there is within daily life.

Within all cultures and religious groups there is wide variation in practice and it is important to realise that degrees of strictness and observance are individually defined. Culture is not monolithic, and it will be dangerous to provide services based on stereotypical concepts of, for example, a Jew, a Hindu, or a Muslim. Some people born into a religious community may not consider themselves to be members of that community. For others their religion, traditions and rituals may be very important but they may not observe, say, strict dietary requirements. Therefore, it is important to allow individuals to define their own culture and religion.

The way in which a person views themselves, and their identity, will be affected by their culture and their religion. As explained above, this can vary between different groups and personal preference. The environment within which we all live affects how we live our lives. People from different cultures encounter one another in various ways. Historically we have travelled for leisure, commerce and military reasons. Additionally, one of the greatest modes for intercultural contact is emigration and asylum. The identities of individuals and communities will vary as they come into contact with their host culture. People may adopt the host culture, adapt their cultural practices and beliefs, or totally reject the host culture. This is a way of surviving within their environment and their evolving culture may be passed on through the generations and become tradition. This is also known as social variations across cultures.

Different cultures and people from across the world speak a variety of languages. Many people for whom English is not their primary language speak English as a second language, although this will vary. Language is also about body language and this will also vary. For example, people from some cultures will shake hands on meeting someone, others will kiss each cheek of the person they meet, and some may see touching between different sexes as being inappropriate. The same degree of variety can be seen within facial expressions, eye contact, and signals such as nodding, shrugging shoulders and hand movements.

Naming systems vary across cultures and a person's name is personal to them and can in some cultures define their cultural and religious identity. For example, Singh (men) and Kaur (women) are names given at a ceremony in the Sikh culture. There are many different naming systems and offence can be caused by inappropriate use.

Diet is important to many cultures and for some the preparation, storage and serving of food are fundamental to their dietary requirements. The way in which food is eaten varies within cultures where some use their fingers, others knives and forks and some chopsticks. Food and drink play different roles in different cultures, some cultures involve fasting at different times and some foods and drink may be forbidden or regarded as "unclean" in certain cultures.

Customs also vary and this is evident in the different rituals around death. Some cultures are opposed to post mortems as they believe in after life, or re birth, some prefer cremation and others prefer to be buried. The reading from different holy books or prayer books is also common within cultures. In some cultures decisions are made by the family and community not by individuals and for others there may be an identified person.

Providing Culturally Sensitive Care Services

In order to provide culturally sensitive services, social care professionals need to:

➢ Ask people what they wish to be called

➢ Avoid forms or questions that request information such as "Christian" name

➢ Observe individual dietary needs

➢ Ensure they have knowledge of local provisions for halal, kosher foods etc.

➢ Use separate cooking utensils for vegetarian, halal, kosher and other foods and store food separately

➢ Respect the individual choices people make and allow them to define their own preferred ways of living

➢ Treat each person as an individual and not see people by a stereotypical view of their assumed culture or religion

➢ Never assume they know and always ask the person themselves

 In Summary

Services are very often Eurocentric and expect people to fit into service delivery. However, the United Kingdom has a long history of multi-culturalism. People interpret their cultural roots differently and services must provide individualised care which is culturally sensitive.

10: EMPOWERMENT

As explored in chapter 3, most social care workers have significant power compared to a service user. When workers offer choices to service users, the manner of their presentation and their choice of the options they select represents the application of the worker's power. Service users may pick up from workers what answer they feel the worker is wanting and so comply with this.

All social care practitioners need to maximise service user's autonomy, and so all workers need to be conscious about how they are using their power. Are workers using their power to enhance the service user's independent decision making skills or to guide the service user to an option that is easy for the staff and the service to respond to?

Using the power effectively, rather than abusing or misusing it, is what is important. A good start is to examine how empowering practice can be role modelled in social care work generally.

Empowerment in Care Practice

Empowerment is about a service user having choice and control in their own life. However, empowerment theory recognises that this is easier said than done and so it outlines what needs to be in place in order for the service user to be able to take control.

Empowerment has become a very significant concept within the last twenty years or so. Arguably, this is because there has been an increasing level of honesty and realism in respect of services.

A new realism arose in the late 1980s that many services provided to people were not good enough. The very services that should be upholding and valuing people were not doing this. Care and health services were actually often contributing to service users' sense of powerlessness. Decisions were made by organisations or by professionals that directly affected individual service users, both in field and residential settings.

Empowerment theory makes clear that it is not enough for professionals to just say "Okay, we'll let the service user decide, it's over to you, take it away!"

Empowerment theory (and practice) recognises the need to address each of the following areas (and others) to give the service user a true chance of making decisions about their own life.

Helping Service Users to Develop Resources

One of the starting points of empowerment is to acknowledge that the service user is the expert about their own life and what they want to achieve. From here services need to support the person to develop a range of resources. These include:

➢ Information: This should include information that is broader than simply what services are available. Information may need to be provided about the person's past, or their condition (if they have a condition). All the information should be available to the person in an accessible manner.

➢ Networks of support: Who is there to provide emotional and moral support? Who can the service user express their frustrations to, knowing that the listener will still help them renew their resolve and determination?

➢ Skill development: In a status and class conscious world, it's not always what we say but how we say it that counts. The service user may need to learn various social or technology skills (e.g.: using e-mail); or they may need to consider how to shape their argument and list points so that the person they are addressing is aware of why they need to listen to the service user.

➢ Confidence: Service users need to have confidence to express themselves. Confidence building can be a difficult and slow task. Ways to enhance confidence can include: joining with others who have had similar experiences and have successfully changed their life positively; individuals choosing an aspect of their life they want to change so there is a good chance of this being achieved; allowing a person to have a supporter present when they raise an issue of concern etc.

➢ Having a voice: When a service user expresses something about their own life, services should listen. In the past, services were so poor at listening that the advocacy movement developed. Therefore having a voice may involve having an advocate.

➢ Problem solving / solution focused approach: The service user will need to recognise that practical difficulties could arise in seeking to change their own life in the way they would like to. To achieve their goal, they will need to adopt a solution finding attitude. For every problem there is a solution. Helping people to focus on solutions rather than problems is a key aspect of empowerment.

➢ Resolve: Individuals need to recognise that services and groups of professionals can have an inertia and inflexibility that is surprising considering the fact that services are meant to help service users and professionals are, on the whole, keen to listen to service users. A service user who wants to change the way a service does something so it meets her or his own needs will need a great deal of personal resolve. This is a personal quality but it can be supported by a social network or the provision of information etc.

➢ Resources: Most of life's achievers already have practical, financial and other resources. If a service user is to achieve their goals they will also need resources in some form. The idea is that services will provide the resources. When a service user has care needs but wants to continue their present lifestyle, established services can struggle to provide the flexibility needed. The introduction of direct payments and individualised care budgets has attempted to address this in providing service users with a pot of money that they can use flexibly to meet their needs. The money could be used for access to employment, housing support etc. Direct payments, arguably, represent one of the most practical tools for empowerment currently provided.

Risk and Empowerment

One important aspect of empowerment is that it acknowledges the dignity of risk. In the past, opportunities for adult service users were restricted because of anxiety about risks to the service user. If anything there is still a split between adult and children's services. Children services struggle to reduce risks, adult services could allow more risks (clearly this is a generalisation, take it for what it is worth).

Very often, risk assessments are used to prevent service users from engaging in activities which pose a risk. However, the whole idea of risk assessment is to support the development of a risk management plan which can support a service user to engage in the activity whilst minimising risks.

There are many examples where adult services have got better at managing risk. Often the risk management plan is decided through multi-agency meetings, involving direct care staff, professionals from outside the service and the service user. Such an approach can enable the service user to live the way they want to even though there is significant risk. This is an important aspect of empowerment.

Hopefulness

Many of the people we support have had their confidence so extensively undermined and have experienced so much discrimination and stigma that the road to empowerment is long and slow. This means that all individuals who work with people need to develop an attitude of hopefulness. Service users may make a commitment to do one or more things but then not follow through or relapse – this does not mean that they will never be able to achieve their goals. Workers need to avoid becoming cynical and dismissive about the service user when the service user next expresses a desire to change some aspect of their life.

To avoid situations where staff members' hopefulness appears superficial, then it may be more helpful to describe the professional quality as realistic optimism. The service user could well find any planned change demanding, but change is possible.

User Involvement

Organisational structures that facilitate service user and carer involvement are vital in terms of empowerment. Social care services need to 'build-in' service user and carer involvement into their structure and decision making process. Services need to evaluate whether they are doing a good job and a key aspect of this is what the service users think. Therefore services need to regularly find out from service users how they experience the service.

All services need a comments and complaints procedure and this is one aspect of gaining some sense of service users' views, but on its own it is not enough.

Services need to have regular, planned involvement of service users. This can take various forms including:

➢ Managers having regular meetings with a self advocacy group or service user group

➢ If there is a management board then service users and carers should sit on this board

➢ If there are plans to develop or alter a service, then service users and / or carers should sit on the sub committee or planning group

➢ The involvement of service users and carers in the training of new and existing staff.

These are just some examples. Some social care services give the impression of being more developed than other services. Arguably, children's services involve service users (or former service users) in decision making better than adult services. Some services for adults with mental health problems and some services for adults with physical disabilities have also demonstrated how service users can be involved. Progress in services for older people and adults with a learning disability has generally been more patchy.

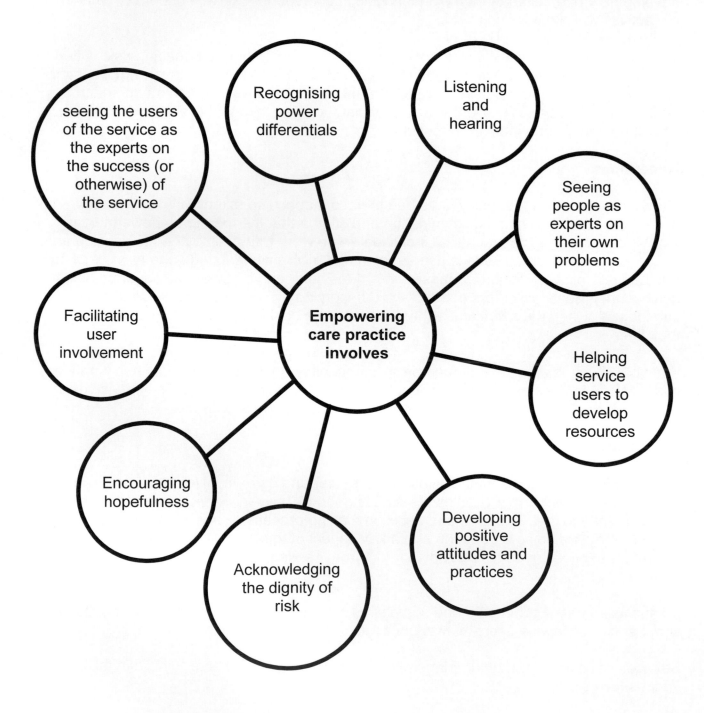

In Summary

Empowerment is a vital principle in effective social care practice. However, it is very often misunderstood. For example, we have heard statements like "I let my service users be empowered!" – how much further away from an empowering approach can you get? In many ways, empowerment is much more complex than many people recognise, perhaps because of the complexity of power and powerlessness. It is vital that all social care practitioners understand empowerment and seek to apply this in their practice at all times.

11: ADVOCACY

As an approach advocacy is very closely related to empowerment – since service users having "a voice" and service user involvement is such a key aspect of empowerment. Here though, it is worth considering some of the basics about advocacy in social care services.

The word "advocacy" quite literally means "speaking for or on behalf of". Mencap, a leading voluntary organisation for people with a learning disability defines advocacy as

"taking action to help people:

> *say what they want*

> *secure their rights*

> *represent their interests*

> *get services they need*

> *represent their views and wishes"*
>   (Mencap 2008)

There are several different kinds of advocacy:

Self Advocacy

Self advocacy is about people speaking up for themselves. A commitment to self advocacy entails enabling and empowering people to act on their own behalf.

There is no doubt that this is a powerful way of helping people achieve independence, although it might not be feasible for all service users. Generally speaking, assertiveness training is needed as this can help people to raise their confidence and sense of self-worth and teach them the skills necessary to make other people listen to them.

Often self advocacy sessions are set up by service user led groups, with a focused slant taken on assertiveness.

Many services now have links with self advocacy groups. However, if managers and staff teams limit their understanding of self advocacy to these groups, they misunderstand the aim of the whole advocacy movement. People should be listened to on a day to day basis as they express their views and make decisions about their own life and the services they receive.

It is the failure of workers and services to listen to people that has resulted in the rise of the organised self advocacy movement.

Peer Advocacy

In peer advocacy the advocate shares a similar perspective to the individual. For example, a person with learning disabilities may support another person with learning disabilities to get their views across. Peer advocacy is often arranged through advocacy groups.

Representative (or Citizen) Advocacy

Individuals who use health and social care services may have difficulty in putting across their point of view. This can be because they have communication difficulties, because they lack confidence, because ill health or disability make it difficult for them to put their opinions across or because they lack the capacity to be able to make decisions for themselves. Although social care staff are expected to support people to express their views, it can be difficult or impossible for workers to do this if the person wishes to raise concerns about the service they are receiving. One option which may be appropriate in these circumstances is to use the services of an independent advocate to represent the individual.

The role of an advocate is one which takes skill to exercise and is different to that of a support worker. Advocates can help in situations where:

➢ it is difficult for others to understand the person's means of communicating

➢ the person is not happy with the service they are receiving and wishes to complain

➢ where supporters such as family, friends, paid carers or health and social care professionals disagree about how to support the person or with the individual's point of view

➢ when a significant change has taken place in relation to the individual. This may be in relation to the person's health or social well-being or a major life change.

An advocate will initially work with the person to understand the way they communicate and to find out what is important to them so that they can represent them in a variety of situations. They will usually go to a meeting alongside the person they are supporting and must always be clear about representing the person's point of view even if the advocate believes that this may not be in the person's interests. The aim of the advocate is to empower the person by making sure that their views and interests are heard. The advocate will try to obtain permission from the person to represent their views and to contact others who may be able to help. Effectively, an independent advocate is simply a 'mouthpiece' for the service user. They ensure that the person's views and wishes are heard by others.

Non-instructed Advocacy

This is where the person is unable to put their views across, perhaps because of profound disability and they lack the capacity to make decisions. Just as with the various forms of instructed advocacy, the advocate will work hard to form a strong relationship with the person, to learn about their preferences and to do their best to represent their interests.

Independent Mental Capacity Advocates

Sometimes referred to as IMCAs this is a specific role which came about as a result of the Mental Capacity Act 2005. This Act established a role for Independent Mental Capacity Advocates to work with individuals who:

➢ have no social support network

➢ have to make significant decisions

➢ lack capacity

Where an NHS body is going to provide serious medical treatment or provide accommodation for such an individual, they must appoint an IMCA to speak for the person. If a local authority is to provide accommodation for more than 8 weeks or arrange a change in accommodation, then they must appoint an IMCA where relevant for the individual.

Independent Mental Capacity Advocates are expected to:

➢ support the person who lacks capacity to be as involved as fully as possible in decision making

➢ gather relevant information

➢ identify what the person's wishes and feelings would most likely be

➢ identify alternative forms of action

➢ where medical treatment is proposed, obtain a further medical opinion if felt necessary.

IMCAs are not decision makers but represent the individual's views in decision making processes. They are also given the option to challenge any relevant decisions.

Staff Advocacy

Social workers, social care staff and other professionals often talk about advocating on behalf of service users. They may well do so on some occasions. However, it is often difficult, if not inappropriate, for staff to advocate on behalf of service users as this often involves challenging the organisation which employs the worker.

In Summary

Advocacy is an important principle in social care provision. Social care staff do advocate for service users at times. However, since they have a role in supporting the service user and they are employed by a service, there will always be a potential conflict of interest and so many service users will need an independent advocate.

12: PARTICIPATION, COMMENTS AND COMPLAINTS

To promote many of the principles covered in this section such as empowerment, dignity cultural sensitivity and empowerment, service users need to be meaningfully involved in the life of the service and its development.

Service users should be involved in the different levels of service provision such as:

➢ their own care and care plan

➢ the provision of the service generally

➢ service developments

➢ future service provision

➢ wider discussions about community care

Many services and service providers are beginning to recognise the need to encourage service user participation and have responded to this in various ways through actions such as:

➢ involving service users in management groups and service planning groups

➢ involving service users in staff interviews, induction and training

➢ setting up service user consultation groups etc.

Whether or not these processes are in place, service users should be encouraged to make comments and complaints about service provision.

Complaints Procedures

An effective complaints procedure is essential for service users, but it can also be helpful for social care workers in that it can:

➢ bring attention to lack of resources

➢ emphasise the need for a high quality service provision

➢ identify areas of poor practice

➢ support staff to develop their practice

➢ clarify misunderstandings

It is therefore important that social care professionals do not view complaints procedures negatively or as a threat. A good quality complaints procedure is a positive attribute to a service. It will encourage recipients of the service to participate more in the service and have more control over the care they receive.

However, service users often experience problems in making use of complaints procedures.

Happless Care, Complaints Procedure

As part of our commitment to improving all our Care Services, any person wishing to make a complaint may do so, following the procedure outlined below:

1. Please make your complaint using form C7.0000.bd.XIX
2. If your complaint is make on behalf of a relative, then please use form C7,0090.SS.XXXX (part A) only. Part C and D should only be completed if your relative incurred any financial loss in relation to the complaint, but no personal injury. If personal injury was incurred, please complete parts D, supplemented by form C3.0010…S. (ignoring part B).
3. Forms are available from floor 40, Bleak Tower, Middle of Nowhere. Please collect by hand.
4. Please collect the appropriate form prior to the incident in question.
5. Please return the form promptly, making sure all fifty questions are answered in full, with supporting evidence from your GP and other referee.
6. Please complete your full name and address, and include a photograph of yourself and/or your loved one. This is to ensure that members of staff can be absolutely clear about who is making a nuisance of themselves.
7. Please obtain a receipt of postage, though a Microchip trace may be the only means of ensuring the complaint will not get completely and entirely lost.
8. If you do not have any response within 12 months of making your complaint, please complete form ZZ.23,000,SSI
9. Forms are available in a variety of languages, though it is doubtful if these can be found anywhere at all.

"HAPPY TO HELP"

(Basnett and Maclean 2000)

Some of the difficulties experienced in putting a complaints policy into effect can be caused by the following:

Lack of Accessibility

A complaints system may exist in the form of a paper document in the Policy Manual, for example, but it can only be a living document if those who may need to use it are aware of it and understand how they can use it. So social care services should:

➤ Refer to the complaints policy in any brochures or explanatory information which they give people when they begin receiving the service.

➤ Ensure that relatives and other people who are important in the lives of the people who use the service are aware of the policy, together with who they might need to raise a complaint with and how to do so.

➢ Ensure that the policy is available in different formats depending upon the needs of the people who use the service, for example, on an audio tape or in larger font for people with impaired vision.

Negative Power Balance

➢ Although individual members of staff may not feel as if they are especially powerful individuals in their own right, they will be perceived by the people who they provide a service to as being more powerful than they are. For this reason, service users may find it more difficult to raise concerns if they have them.

➢ Individuals may feel that they do not have much control over their own lives. This could be because they may require assistance in many aspects of their lives, and they are dependent upon members of the staff team to enable them to access the community.

➢ Service users and their family members may be afraid to raise a complaint in case they lose the service. They may feel no one will listen or they may find it difficult to act assertively.

Therefore social care professionals need to:

➢ Recognise power differentials and work with them effectively

➢ Ensure that service users are empowered by the service

➢ Promote a positive culture of support which welcomes comments and complaints about the service provided

Individuals having had Negative Experiences in the Past

➢ Past experiences of "care" (perhaps in long stay institutions where people may have had even less control and many elements of daily life were directed by nurses, doctors and others) may mean that individuals have low expectations of service provision.

➢ Memories of institutional care and behaviour patterns learned in this environment are often very difficult to shift, even many decades later, and we may see this in behaviours such as a reluctance to raise complaints, expectations etc.

The Need to Combat Defensiveness on the Part of Staff

One of the most difficult elements of a healthy complaints policy to establish is a positive culture towards complaints.

One difficulty can be that there is a fear that a complaint will inevitably lead to disciplinary action being taken and could lead to a person losing their job. In some organisations where the culture is quite punitive, people may have grounds for thinking in this way.

This feeling can also come about because employees habitually regard a complaint as reflecting solely upon their own work. It is preferable that everyone in a service shares the understanding that complaints need to be dealt with as a reflection on the service as a whole, rather than any specific worker's failing.

Experiences of Complaints Procedures

Research by Finnegan and Clarke in 2005 identified that:

➤ 76% of staff agreed or strongly agreed with the statement that "very few service users use the formal complaints procedure".

➤ 82% agreed with the statement that service users "do not understand the process."

➤ 76% agreed with the statement "they do not understand their rights."

Comments from the staff about the lack of use of complaints procedures included the following:

"Service users just don't like complaining. I can see why they wouldn't because I don't think I would feel at ease doing that if I was them. I'd be worried about being seen as a troublemaker I suppose, and you might be worried about how you might get treated afterwards."

"My worry is that they complain less and less because nothing is ever done…"

"The service users really do not feel that they can complain against someone who has power over their lives. It stays within the house and is not properly recorded or followed up."

"I know that every time there is an incident or complaint, everything should be written down but that is never the case."

(Finnegan and Clarke 2005)

 In Summary

An effective and accessible complaints procedure is a key aspect of empowerment. Social care staff must work to ensure that service users are able to participate fully in services and that their comments and complaints are taken seriously.

13: ACTIVE SUPPORT

It can be difficult to get the balance right between upholding people's rights and ensuring they are protected from abuse and harm. Services trying to get this balance right can sometimes "over" support people to the point that they can stifle them – ultimately preventing their legal rights.

Active support is about providing the right amount of support to individuals which recognises their rights whilst providing opportunities for growth and skill development. It can be difficult for services to work on a model of active support.

Get the balance right

Active support was first established as a model of care for people in learning disability services. It was designed as a model of support to challenge what has become known as the "gift model" of care provision.

> The gift model is where care is provided *for* or *to* people e.g.: tasks are done for or to people

> The active support model involved working *with* people to enable them to take part in all the activities of daily life.

Active support has four key components:

> Service users are offered opportunities to take part in everyday activities and all care tasks.

> Staff pay particular attention to working as a team and co-ordinating their approaches.

> Staff focus on helping service users take part in minute by minute activities and opportunities ("every moment has potential"). They find parts of even very complex tasks that all people can do and undertake other parts of the task themselves.

> Staff monitor carefully the degree to which service users are taking part in everyday activities using simple record keeping procedures. Regular staff meetings allow for plans to be modified in the light of experience and learning.

In recent literature, the model is referred to as "person centred active support".

The Tizard Centre says of active support:

"The inclusion of the phrase "person centred" along with active support, denotes that this approach involves more than just providing opportunities and direct assistance for activities – the ultimate aim is to support people to live the lives they want to live, doing the things they want to do, following their agenda and respecting their decisions."

(Tizard Centre 2008)

Service users may need support to ensure that they are protected from abuse and harm, but this support must actively promote their right to make their own decisions and choices and to be fully involved in their own care. Services need to ensure that people are enabled and supported to take risks which are as safe as possible in order to promote their learning, life skills and competence in effective decision making. Research (for example, Mansell et al 2002, and Stancliff, Jones and Mansell 2008) demonstrates that active support is essential for the well being of service users of all ages. Key messages from research show that:

➢ Service users' activities and independence both increase significantly where staff adopt active support approaches.

➢ The self esteem of service users is significantly improved where active support is implemented.

➢ Staff job satisfaction is significantly enhanced where a service's main model of care is active support.

➢ Although active support has been demonstrated to be a powerful model, it has not yet had a significant impact in the delivery of most services. Typical staff performance in community services is still characterised by low levels of staff and client interaction and little direct facilitation of service user participation.

Wider Contexts

The idea of active support is widely supported within Europe and European policy makers are currently considering how active support can become the basis of all practice in social care. In a recent Briefing Paper, the Social Platform state:

"The disability movement challenged the term "care" replacing it with the "right to support. For many disabled activists, the very concept of 'care' embodies an oppressive history in which the practices of paid (particularly professional) and unpaid carers have maintained disabled and older people in a position of unwanted dependency, at worst, abused, segregated and stripped of their dignity, at best, patronised and protected from exercising any agency over their lives. Instead care needs are reinterpreted as having choice and control as the strategies for the empowerment of disabled people."

(Social Platform 2010: 1)

With this issue high on the European political agenda, it is likely that active support will become more influential as a model in social care services in the future.

 In Summary

Active support is an important principle in social care practice. However, many services do not fully embrace this model of support. Social care practitioners need to understand how to employ the principles of active support in their work.

14: PARTNERSHIP WORKING

Being able to work effectively in partnership with a wide range of other agencies and professionals is an essential skill for everyone in the social care field. Understanding the issues around partnership work and being able to work with others from a wide range of other backgrounds is therefore seen as essential in all qualifications in health and social care.

Partnership working with service users and carers is a key aspect of effective social care, and engaging effectively with people is explored in more detail in section C on communication. Some of these skills are central to good practice around interprofessional working too, although some of the challenges in working with people from other settings, services, professional backgrounds and agencies go beyond interpersonal communication skills.

The agenda around skilling up all professionals to work together is at the heart of all governmental policy in social care work. The idea of a range of professionals forming a "team around the person" is one which is key to providing person-centred services to vulnerable people which truly meet their individual needs, as Douglas (2008: 9) states:

"Whilst many of us will receive the help we need from a single professional such as a GP, the persistent and enduring problems which form the average social care caseload will only be helped through a multi-agency or interdisciplinary approach."

The National Service Framework for Older People (2001: 24-25) also outlines clear expectations around integrated working between health services and social care agencies, who are expected to work towards single assessment and joint commissioning:

"Person-centred care needs to be supported by services that are organised to meet needs. The NHS and councils should deploy the 1999 Health Act flexibilities to:

➤ *establish joint commissioning arrangements for older people's services, including consideration of a lead commissioner and the use of pooled budgets*

➤ *ensure an integrated approach to service provision, such that they are person centred, regardless of professional or organisational boundaries."*

In addition, the Code of Practice for Social Care Workers states an expectation that social care staff must be competent in:

"Recognising and respecting the roles and expertise of workers from other agencies and working in partnership with them" (2002: 6.7).

Benefits of Working in Partnership with Other Agencies

There are a range of benefits to working in partnership, which might include:

➤ *Being able to "tap into" resources which other agencies hold*
Not only does this lead to better outcomes for service users, but it means that people can access specialist help from the right people at the right time. The idea of the single

---

assessment process is about reducing the need for people to have to keep repeating their "story" to different professionals.

➢ *Being able to be clear about services' roles and responsibilities*
Effective interprofessional working necessitates all workers being clear about the roles and responsibilities of other professionals (i.e.: "horizontal knowledge" see page 6). This means that workers need to be clear about the boundaries of their own role, so that this can be communicated to service users and other agencies. It also means that people working in social care need to be clear on the roles of others (Occupational Therapists, District Nurses, Community Psychiatric Nurses, Social Workers, etc.), so that when the team is formed around the person everyone knows:

- Who is doing what?
- When?
- Where?
- Why?
- What each professional can and cannot offer

Being clear in this way means that service users can also feel confident in understanding why so many people may be involved in their lives. It also means that service users can potentially be supported to understand what may be expected of them in terms of supporting themselves in line with the principles of active support.

➢ *Being able to put into place effective and safe practices around confidentiality and information sharing*
Where multiple agencies and workers are involved in the person's care, it is vital that good practice around confidentiality is organised and agreed (see chapter 15). This is essential as working together usually means that certain information needs to be shared so that effective care and support can be offered. At the same time, it is a service user's legal and moral right to know which information is shared and what the purpose is for this sharing of knowledge about them.

➢ *Growing in confidence in professional knowledge and expertise*
Working with others enables social care staff to feel confident around their own area of specialism (or their "vertical knowledge" as covered on page 6).

➢ *Reciprocity and Interdependence*
Douglas (2008) argues that the term "partnership" invokes the idea of relationships and to work in partnership in social care means that each worker needs to:

- Recognise that they <u>cannot</u> do the job as well alone (so they are interdependent along with other professionals to get the "job" of care and support done)

- Get something out of working together with other professionals, so that the benefits are agreed to be reciprocal for everyone involved. This could be because people in the relationship enjoy working together, or because of a shared agreement that better outcomes for the service user are much more likely by the very nature of professionals working together and sharing knowledge and expertise.

The Challenges of Partnership Working

Although working with other agencies and professionals can be one of the most enjoyable aspects of social care for many workers, most people will have experienced challenges and tensions in partnership working. These might include:

➤ *Organisational culture*
All organisations have their own ethos, values, status and culture (Glasby and Dickinson 2008). The concept of organisational culture applies to agencies, professional roles and to individual teams. This can mean that tensions arise where professional cultures are expected to work together as there may be several factors which create stress, such as:

- Lack of a mutual understanding around the roles and boundaries of other professional roles

- Stereotyping of other agencies and professionals (e.g.: Social Workers just want to close cases, District Nurses don't take enough time with the person etc)

- Issues around leadership – managers need to be committed to the ideals of partnership working and communicate this consistently, as well as challenging stereotyping of other agencies

- Factors within teams or services creating stress at certain times which lead professionals to "shut down" and work in an insular way (e.g.: when facing change, redundancy or high workloads)

➤ *Relative values of different professions and status issues*
Tension can arise in decision making as certain professionals have more status granted them within society than others. This can be made apparent by differences around length of training, pay, attitudinal behaviours, and by actions which accord some individuals more status. The obvious example of this is around GPs – how many of us have found it hard to question decisions and actions taken by the GP because they hold expert, resource and societal power? Similarly, this can apply for social care workers on a professional level as it can feel hard to challenge other agencies' views about a service user's needs. This is why social care workers need a good standard and depth of vertical knowledge about their role and why workers need to demonstrate their ability to explain their reasoning and judgements to other agencies.

➤ *Learning how to challenge others*
All relationships involve differences of opinion at some point. However, social care workers need particular sensitivity when challenging other agencies' views, decisions and actions. It is a difficult task to challenge other workers' decisions without it seeming like a reflection on their professional judgement. Being able to do this is a core skill in all professional practice in all fields. Sometimes, personalities may clash, or another worker may simply not be in the right frame of mind to hear a challenge which is made. Therefore, social care workers must be able to plan, weigh up and action the best way of making challenges in order to achieve the desired outcomes for an individual service user.

➤ *Protectiveness of jobs*
Sometimes working in partnership can be difficult because other professionals might perceive unintended threats to their own jobs and status. One of the key skills in partnership working involves the ability to consider the other person's standpoint, their pressures and their anxieties, in the same way as with service users. Workers too can

feel threatened by other people coming into the picture and offering support which they may feel it is part of their job to deliver. The ability to share this openly can be a core skill for those working in social care, particularly when a relationship is new or already feels strained. Openness can achieve great change though as other professionals may respond well to someone taking the time to find out what the barriers are to partnerships from their point of view. In this way shared solutions can be created so that closer partnership working can be achieved, although this can be an ongoing struggle in trying to form shared visions with some individuals.

➤ *Ethical issues*
Sometimes there may be moral or ethical considerations which need to be looked at. This again might involve managers from two services taking a clear view together as to the way forward. An example of where this may be necessary could be around disagreements over information which can be shared. It is important for social care workers in this instance to ask managers for advice on the possible legal ramifications around partnership working and confidentiality (see chapter 15).

In Summary

Most people that social care workers support will have contact with a range of other professionals. It is important that all professionals work together to provide an effective team of support around the service user. Social care staff need to develop their knowledge in a range of ways in order to work effectively in partnership with service users, family members and others involved in the service user's life.

15: CONFIDENTIALITY AND INFORMATION SHARING

As far back as 1961, Biestek defined confidentiality as:

"The preservation of secret information concerning the client which is disclosed in the professional relationship. Confidentiality is based upon a basic right of the client; it is an ethical obligation.... the client's right, however, is not absolute. Moreover, the client's secret is often shared with other professional persons within the agency and in other agencies; the obligation then binds all equally."

(Biestek 1961 quoted in Thompson 1994)

All services should have clear policies and boundaries around confidentiality. Confidentiality enables people who receive care services to have a sense of trust in professionals and a sense of control over their life and the service they receive.

In the recent past, confidentiality has, arguably, not been treated seriously enough, so that some service users have had information shared without their permission, and others have not had information shared which should have been passed on in order to keep them safe. This has dovetailed with some social care workers feeling a lack of clarity about what information needs to be passed on and to whom, and what information does not need passing on.

Codes of Practice and Legal Issues

The NHS Code of Practice on confidentiality (Department of Health 2003) applies to workers in health and social care. This states that:

"A duty of confidence arises when one person discloses information to another (e.g. patient to clinicians) in circumstances where it is reasonable to expect that the information will be held in confidence. It is a legal obligation that is derived from case law, rather than an Act of Parliament, built up over many years and often open to different interpretations. It is also a requirement established within professional codes of conduct."

(Department of Health 2003: 29)

The Code of Practice for Social Care Workers (GSCC 2002) also refers to:

"Respecting and maintaining the dignity and privacy of service users (1.4)" and

"Respecting confidential information and clearly explaining agency policies about confidentiality to service users and carers (2.3)"

 In addition, service users have legal rights under the Data Protection Act 1998 to be able to see records which are kept about them, and under the Human Rights Act people have a right to have their privacy respected (Article 8).

WHAT THE LAW SAYS: DATA PROTECTION AND ACCESS TO RECORDS

The Data Protection Act 1998 concerns the recording of personal and sensitive information. It also covers confidentiality and access to records.

The Act sets out eight principles for the recording and use of information.

These principles are that information and the recording of information must be:

1. used fairly and lawfully

2. use only for a particular and lawful reason

3. adequate, relevant and not excessive

4. accurate and up to date

5. kept for no longer than is necessary

6. used in line with the rights of individuals

7. kept securely

8. information must not be transferred between countries which do not have adequate protection for individual's personal information

The Act also gives people the right to access all information held about them. This applies to paper based records, such as care notes and incident/accident forms as well as information held on computer.

Confidentiality within Social Care Settings

Clearly, social care staff should not "gossip" about people in the setting where care is being provided. It can be difficult to challenge colleagues if this is occurring, but workers have responsibilities to "whistle blow" (see pages 160) if service users' dignity, confidentiality and rights are being compromised in this way.

Workers also need to consider where in the service certain conversations take place as discussions about individuals' needs should not be held in public places where others can overhear sensitive information.

It is important that workers only know information that is relevant to supporting the people they work with. Workers do not have a right to know everything about a person. It is also vital that staff are clear that the information which they receive is given to them because they are staff members, and that such information must remain confidential within the care team responsible for each individual person.

In casework, it is important that information is shared in order that everyone is working in a consistent way to meet people's needs. However, when information is shared within an agency or even between agencies, the information remains confidential. The fact that it has been shared does not mean it can be shared further – the obligation to maintain confidentiality is shared just as much as the information itself.

Information Sharing: Government Guidelines

There are some circumstances where information has to be shared, particularly around safeguarding (see section D). This is not least because several inquiries have detailed that service users have been put at risk when information is not shared which ought to be. Ideally, service users should consent to information being shared with others unless it would put them at greater risk to do so.

Social care workers need to be clear on the purposes of information sharing so that justification can be provided if necessary as to why information has been disclosed to others.

As part of the *Every Child Matters: Change for Children* initiative, the Government published a Practitioners Guide to Information Sharing in 2004. With a number of inquiries and investigations identifying social care staff uncertainty about the sharing of information the Government revised their Guidance and extended it to cover professionals working with adult service users in 2008. The focus of "Information Sharing: Guidance for Practitioners and Managers" is on sharing information legally and appropriately. The Guidance comes with a range of associated materials designed to support good practice in information sharing between professionals.

The Guidance contains the following seven "Golden Rules" for information sharing:

1. **Remember that the Data Protection Act is not a barrier to sharing information** but provides a framework to ensure that personal information about living persons is shared appropriately.

2. **Be open and honest** with the person (and/or their family where appropriate) from the outset about why, what, how and with whom information will, or could be shared, and seek their agreement, unless it is unsafe or inappropriate to do so.

3. **Seek advice** if you are in any doubt, without disclosing the identity of the person where possible.

4. **Share with consent where appropriate** and, where possible, respect the wishes of those who do not consent to share confidential information. You may still share information without consent if, in your judgement, that lack of consent can be overridden in the public interest. You will need to base your judgement on the facts of the case.

5. **Consider safety and well-being:** Base your information sharing decisions on considerations of the safety and well-being of the person and others who may be affected by their actions.

6. **Necessary, proportionate, relevant, accurate, timely and secure:** Ensure that the information you share is necessary for the purpose for which you are sharing it, is shared only with those people who need to have it, is accurate and up-to-date, is shared in a timely fashion, and is shared securely.

7. **Keep a record** of your decision and the reasons for it – whether it is to share information or not. If you decide to share, then record what you have shared, with whom and for what purpose.

The Guidance also contains a framework for decision making in relation to information sharing. It clearly identifies that practitioners and managers should make decisions about information sharing by working through the following seven key questions:

1. Is there a clear and legitimate purpose for you or your agency to share the information?

2. Does the information enable a living person to be identified?

3. Is the information confidential?

4. If the information is confidential, do you have consent to share?

5. If consent is refused, or there are good reasons not to seek consent to share confidential information, is there a sufficient public interest to share the information?

6. If the decision is to share, are you sharing information appropriately and securely?

7. Have you properly recorded your information sharing decision?

The full Guidance is very useful and contains a range of case studies and guidance. It can be downloaded from: www.dcsf.gov.uk/everychildmatters/resources-and-practice/IG00340/

Carers and Confidentiality

Relatives and others who act as a service user's carer may also need to know certain information in order to be able to provide effective care for the person. This can be a sensitive issue for many families and many workers in health and social care can struggle with the need to inform carers whist not breaching the service user's rights to confidentiality.

The Royal College of Psychiatrists and Princess Royal Trust for Carers give some helpful advice around liaising with carers and the potential risks in not doing so, whilst also outlining the concerns many professionals have around breaking the service user's confidentiality by sharing information with their carer. They suggest that good practice occurs where:

"Even when the patient continues to withhold consent, carers are given sufficient knowledge to enable them to provide effective care. They are also given the opportunity to discuss any difficulties they are experiencing in their caring role and help to try and resolve these." (2004:6)

Workers have legal duties around confidentiality to the service user and should seek their consent where possible to share information with carers. Some workers may also feel anxious about what they can and cannot discuss with relatives. Where the service user does not give consent for their carer to know certain issues, the worker should record the person's decision and the discussion around this. Regular reviews of this consent are essential to continuing to provide a high quality of service.

In Summary

Confidentiality is a fundamental right of service users. However, this does not mean that information should not be shared where people have a need to know. The Government has produced clear Guidance for practitioners on information sharing and social care workers need to understand this so that they can apply the principles of confidentiality and information sharing in their practice.

16: ETHICAL PRACTICE

Ethical issues have been widely discussed in social work and health arenas for a number of years and interest in ethical issues is rising in the field of social care. It is therefore important that social care practitioners develop their understanding of ethics and ethical practice.

Ethics

Maclean and Caffrey (2009) identified that if asked what the word ethics means, the general public are likely to identify ethics as:

➤ involving feelings / intuition about right and wrong

➤ linked to religious beliefs

➤ doing what the law says

➤ acceptable standards of behaviour within a society

However, these are largely misinterpretations of ethics, certainly within a professional arena. For example:

➤ Feelings and intuition are personal. It's not acceptable as a professional to justify actions on purely personal feelings. This would lead to different workers acting very differently in the same situation, justified solely by their personal feelings. This does not constitute a profession.
➤ Ethical actions are not the sole preserve of religious people. People with no specific religious beliefs can certainly act in an ethical manner.
➤ Legislation can at times be unethical. For example, in South Africa legislation created and supported Apartheid for a number of years. Apartheid was clearly unethical.
➤ Societies can at times have standards which are unethical – for example, Nazi Germany was a society based on unethical standards.

Philosophers suggest that the word ethics does indeed refer to standards of behaviour, but that to act in an ethical manner:

➤ Actions must be based on consistent and well founded standards of what is right and wrong. These standards transcend individual societies and are often presented in terms of basic human rights and responsibilities.
➤ Individuals need to strive to ensure that their moral conduct is well founded. Ethical practice requires study and reflection. It won't just happen.

Ethical Dilemmas

Ethical dilemmas are said to occur when workers have to choose between two contradictory ethical directives or when every possible alternative in a situation would result in an undesirable outcome for an individual. Ethical dilemmas can also involve conflict between stakeholders who have an investment in the issue being considered. Such conflicts might arise between service users, families, staff members, government regulations, Codes of Conduct etc (Loewenberg and Dolgoff 1996; Clemens and Hayes 1997).

You will find references to ethical dilemmas throughout this book. However, we felt that this area was worth specific mention in this section, partly since ethical dilemmas often occur because of conflicts in areas covered in this section and in section A.

Here, it is worth considering a framework which can be used to address ethical dilemmas. The following framework can be useful in this respect:

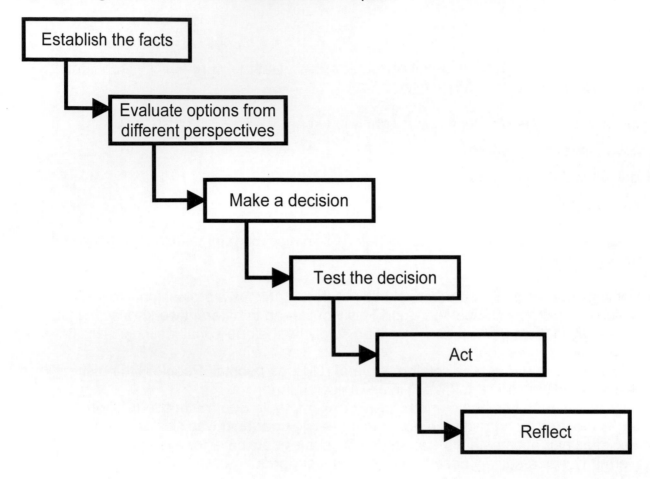

Establish the facts

In establishing the facts, it is important to think about:

- What is the dilemma?
- What is known?
- What is not known?
- Who has a stake in the outcome?
- What are the options?
- What would those affected say about the options?

Evaluate options from different perspectives

In every situation there will be a range of different options for action. The various options need to be considered from different angles and perspectives. This will involve thinking about:

> Which option will do most good or least harm?

> Will rights be respected?

> Which option is fairest to all stakeholders?

> Which option helps all to participate as fully as possible?

Make a decision

After reflecting on the above, social care workers should be able to make a decision. However, it is important that decisions relating to ethical dilemmas are not made in isolation. Decisions should be made and tested in wide consultation.

Test the decision

In wide discussion with other professionals the decision should be tested. Is this the same decision that others would reach in the same situation?

Act

When the decision is acted upon, it is important that flexible plans are in place to address all the possibilities which might arise.

Reflect

Once the plan has been actioned, it is important that the social care worker and others involved in making the decision reflect on it and evaluate the impact of the decision.

Ethics Committees

Many organisations use ethics committees as part of the process of testing out decision making as described above. Ethics committees started out in terms of looking out research and are still most often used when a panel of experts decides as to whether a piece of research which has been proposed has any ethical issues which need to be addressed for the research to go ahead. The NHS National Patient Safety Agency website (www.npsa.nhs.uk) contains information about the National Research Ethics service. This describes the role of research ethics committees, which they see as critical in promoting the rights, dignity and well being of those taking part in research and people whose care may be affected by that research in the future.

Ethics committees or ethics panels are now growing in use and their remit is beginning to widen so that some organisations hold ethics panels on a regular basis where workers can take situations which pose ethical dilemmas to the panel for an open discussion. Often these panels use a process such as the one suggested in this chapter to act as a framework for decision making.

 In Summary

Ethics are difficult to define, but are clearly linked to rights, dignity and principled practice in social care. Ethical dilemmas are common in a field of work which centres on upholding people's rights and individuality. Solving these dilemmas involves a process which usually includes testing the decision against what others in the field would see as ethical practice in similar circumstances.

SECTION C: COMMUNICATION

Communication is a core skill in social care practice. It is often taken for granted but is never straightforward. As a two way process communication is never about one individual but is about relationships, environments and an understanding of individual needs. In pages 6 and 7 we explored the relationship between knowledge and skills, and communication is perhaps the best example of the links between these. To develop good communication skills, a social care worker needs to have knowledge in a range of areas. This section will explore this key knowledge.

17: COMMUNICATION: THE BASICS

What is Communication?

This sounds like a very basic question which surely everyone would know the answer to. However, there are many definitions of communication and most academics agree that communication is difficult to define. That said, most writers agree that communication is a two way process which involves the transmission of information.

One useful definition of communication is offered by the Royal College of Speech and Language Therapy:

"The transmission and reception of meaning between one individual and another, or between an individual and a group - where "Meaning" is taken to include social and affective intentions and reactions, as well as propositional content. The mode or medium of the exchange (speech, non-verbal signals, symbols, signs, electronic code etc) does not alter this definition of the central essence of communication."

(RCSLT 2006)

One aspect which we feel is missing from the various definitions of communication is that the root of the word communication is the same as the root of the words common, community and communion – all of these words are about sharing. For us, sharing is the key aspect of communication, whether this is about sharing information, sharing experiences, sharing power or sharing humanity. As such, all communication in social care must reflect the shared value base explored in section A.

Moss (2007) describes the way in which communication in social care work must demonstrate the core values of the profession. He argues that:

"The helping relationship …….. that communication skills are there to facilitate, needs a measure of humility, human warmth and genuineness that reflects the common humanity that we all share, and a willingness to respect and enhance the determination that other people display in tackling the problems and difficulties which beset them."

(Moss 2007: 5)

Communication and Relationships

Communication and relationships are very closely linked. The way in which we communicate with others will be affected by the relationship we have with them. In much the same way the quality of communication will have an effect on relationships. For example, when people in a personal relationship don't communicate effectively their relationship will suffer ("he/she doesn't understand me!") The links between communication and relationships should never be under-estimated by social care professionals.

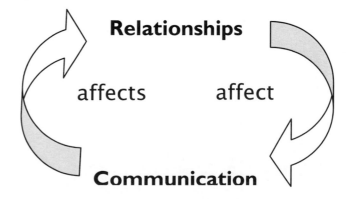

Behaviour and Communication

In much the same way as relationships and communication are closely linked, behaviour and communication are closely linked.

Where there are many barriers to communication and a person is not being understood by those around them because of these barriers, a person's behaviour may become more defined and extreme in an attempt to communicate more effectively. This can lead to behaviour which staff and services find challenging.

Issues of communication and behaviour which is challenging are very closely linked in two main ways:

➢ It is likely that the behaviour in itself is a result of the individual trying to communicate something

➢ Improved communication by staff and within the service is the most effective way of addressing behaviour which challenges

Recognising that communication and behaviour which is challenging are closely linked is vital to effective social care practice. More information on this is covered in chapter 21.

Why do we communicate?

There are four functions to communication that is four reasons people communicate. These are:

<u>Instrumental</u>

➢ to ask for something

➢ to refuse something

➢ to choose something

➢ to tell a person our needs

<u>Informative</u>

➢ to obtain information

➢ to convey information

➢ to describe something

<u>Expressive</u>

➢ to express thoughts or feelings

<u>Social</u>

➢ to attract attention

➢ to build relationships

➢ to maintain relationships

How do we communicate?

Everyone uses a wide variety of communication methods, for example:

➤ talking

➤ writing

➤ by telephone

➤ electronically – for example, texting, emailing

➤ facial expression

➤ gestures

➤ drawing

➤ signing

➤ augmentative communication etc.

Essentially, all the different forms of communication can be categorised into three areas:

➤ verbal communication

➤ non verbal communication

➤ written communication

This chapter will explore aspects of verbal and non verbal communication and some of these themes and issues will be explored in more detail in the following chapters. Written communication is covered in chapter 24.

Verbal Communication

When thinking about verbal communication, people tend to focus on the words they use. Obviously it is important to use words which treat with respect and to choose words which people understand. However, it is an interesting paradox that the words we use are less important than other aspects of communication in conveying or understanding our needs. Only a small proportion (7%) of communication is conveyed in the form of words with 55% being conveyed in the form of body language and 38% from the tone, volume and pitch of the voice. (Mehrabian and Ferris 1967).

In using verbal communication, social care staff need to think about the following areas:

Speed

The speed at which someone talks is very significant. It might indicate someone's emotional state – for example, fast speech is associated with anger or excitement whilst slow speech can be associated with tiredness or a low mood. The speed at which someone speaks can be interpreted in a range of ways – for example, slow speech can be interpreted as showing a lack of interest.

Tone

People are often not aware of the tone of their own voice. However, it is important for social care staff to develop this awareness as tone of voice has such a significant impact on communication.

Volume

How loud or softly we speak has a very significant impact on communication. For example, loud speech can indicate anger or aggression and yet many social care staff raise the volume of their voice when talking to service users. This is something which we will explore in later chapters.

Register

The 'register' of speech refers to how formal or informal it is. You will know that people will change the formality of their speech depending on the situation they are in.

Non Verbal Communication

Non-verbal communication (also referred to as body language) refers to the messages given out by body actions and movements rather than words. Body language is an important part of the communication process. As the saying goes, "actions speak louder than words". Usually verbal and non-verbal communications are in agreement (eg. someone saying "I am happy" and smiling) but at times they may contradict each other (eg. someone saying "I am happy" whilst they look positively sad!).

There are some key do's and don'ts in terms of body language. However, it is important not to become too pre-occupied with body language – a badly judged eye movement is unlikely to cause lasting emotional damage! When considering body language (and communication as a whole) try to remember the three R's rule. Communication should always be:

➢ Respectful

➢ Receptive

➢ Relaxed

The following table gives some guidelines on this.

Respectful, Relaxed, Receptive ✔	Disrespectful, Tense, Not Receptive ✖
Hands, resting, still	Hands, fidgeting and clenched
Face relaxed	Brow creased, mouth drawn
Shoulders relaxed	Shoulders raised and tense
Posture, upright, able to breathe easily	Strained or hunched
Breathing slow and deep	Breathing rapid and shallow
General position comfortable and easy to retain when either sitting or standing	Requires lots of fidgeting and movement to remain comfortable
Mouth visible!	Mouth covered up or chewing finger nails
Feet and legs, still and comfortable	Feet and legs, fidgeting or tapping
Appear interested in what is being said	Doodle, sigh, look away, look at the watch etc.

The table can also act as an indicator of how the other person is feeling. Sensitive observation provides insight into how the exchange is progressing. This is an important point, because communication depends upon responding to the verbal and non verbal messages provided by others within the exchange. Therefore, if a person's body language becomes tense, the situation may be causing anxiety. Appropriate measures to address this may include:

➢ Slow down

➢ Offer re-assurance

➢ Ask if the person has any questions or concerns

The Use of Touch in Communication

Touch is a very powerful form of non verbal communication. Think about the way that you might experience touch yourself – when someone you know well touches you, you might feel comforted and safe, but when someone you don't know touches you, you might feel vulnerable and threatened.

When used appropriately, touch can be a very positive form of communication in that it can:

➢ Provide comfort and re-assurance when someone is distressed making them feel safe and secure

➢ Show respect

➢ Calm someone who is agitated

However, when used indiscriminately touch can:

➢ Invade privacy, making people feel vulnerable

➢ Embarrass people

➢ Undermine trust

➢ Be harassment

So, this is a sensitive area. The best approach is to keep touch to a minimum, because it can easily be experienced as threatening, inappropriate or uncomfortable especially for a service user who may already be feeling vulnerable. If a social care worker needs to touch someone as part of the care process, they should explain what they are doing and always ask permission. Failure to ask permission and obtain consent is an intrusion on that person and an abuse of power.

Total Communication

Social care workers are likely to experience a wide variety of communication methods. It is important always to question and be clear about an individual's own preferred methods of communicating and never to assume. For example, some service users can find pictures to be a really helpful tool to help them to communicate, but someone else with similar needs might not respond at all to the same method.

Whatever method of communication workers use, the style and content must vary in relation to the person or people who are being communicated with, whether they be service users, team colleagues or other staff members, other professionals or other organisations.

Most people use gestures and facial expressions together with the tone and pitch of their voice to give added emphasis to what they are trying to say. On one level, this can add to the effect of what is being said, making a story more entertaining and memorable. However, for some people, the use of these techniques is essential if others are to understand them. A term often used for non verbal communication of this type is Augmentative and Alternate Communication (AAC).

You will have noticed that in a noisy bar, club or other social setting, your need to rely on augmentative communication methods increases and you find yourself making greater use of gestures and facial expressions. It is not a great step to imagine the importance of these communication methods for people who have little or no speech. These non verbal signals or communication cues, as they are also known, are used in a variety of ways by people – sometimes in ways which are unique to that person. This individuality requires workers to make time to get to know the person they are supporting and use many, if not all, of the sources of information available to them. In order to find out what the person means by a particular communication cue. However, sometimes people may have no alternative but to use simple trial and error to attempt to find this out.

'…the most essential aspect of any attempt at communication is that it is presented in the way that is most likely to be understood… we need to explore alternatives and those alternatives are wide-ranging. We need to look at the whole repertoire of a person's body and facial language, how they move, and the sounds they make. Even if the language consists of incidental grunts, or clicks which are non-intentional, these may relate to activities which the person enjoys.'

(Caldwell, 2000)

Some of the communication methods people may use include:

Method of Augmentative or Alternate Communication	Features of this method
Makaton	Makaton was devised by a speech therapist (Margaret Walker) in the 1970's. It is a language system based on BSL (British Sign Language) where key words are signed in word order alongside speech. This means that information is given in a very visual way. Makaton has been shown to be not only an effective form of signed communication, but also an effective method in encouraging the development of speech. The Makaton Charity's website (www.makaton.org) contains useful information about the benefits of Makaton in reducing people's frustration in enabling them to be understood as well as in increasing the likelihood of a person being able to communicate around any safeguarding concerns (the Makaton Chairty 2008).
Touch	Perhaps using a tap on the arm to obtain your attention or guiding you to indicate what the person requires. In this way, a person might guide you to a room where they want to be or show you something of interest.

Method of Augmentative or Alternate Communication	Features of this method
Objects of reference	Using an object or a picture to indicate what the person wants can be a key means of communication for many people. The person could pick up a cup to indicate that he or she would like a hot drink or could use a picture or symbol to indicate this. A particular object or picture may have a specific meaning for that individual which may not be immediately apparent, which is where observations, together with feedback from others, will be especially helpful. Objects of reference can be used to prepare someone for their day's routines – for example showing someone a swimming costume when they are about to go swimming. For people with a visual impairment objects of reference with a definite texture which can be held and felt can be useful. Objects that the person is familiar with should be used over a period of time so that the individual comes to associate the object with the message being conveyed.
Behaviour and movement	This can be used by many people as a communication method. Behaviour which may be labelled as challenging or difficult may in fact be much more about a person communicating some aspect of their needs.
Sounds	If people have relatively few or no words, they may use other sounds to indicate what they want. The meaning of some sounds may well be obvious, such as laughter or shouts of joy or pleasure. As with the use of objects of reference and touch, the association made with some sounds will be specific to that individual.
Smell	Where other senses are impaired, the sense of smell may take on added significance and some people may, for example, sniff different types of foods and toiletries to make their choice.
Drawing	Some people may prefer you to make a drawing to indicate what choices are available or what may be taking place. Symbols are often used in communicating with people to help understanding.
Writing	Some people may prefer to write rather than speak. This may be the case if someone's speech is temporarily impaired due to illness or it may help them to clarify what they mean.
Technological aids to communication	Technology has enabled an increasing number of electronic and digital aids to communication to become available which help people who have difficulty speaking. Many of these devices enable messages to be recorded and stored and played at the touch of a button. The devices range in sophistication and price. Examples include the "Go Talk" series of devices with different sizes and numbers of keys; "Lightwriter" which is a portable keyboard with a screen which is available in the QWERTY layout; and the "Talking Photo Album" which allows ten second messages to be recorded alongside photos, symbols and photocopies. Information, advice and guidance on choosing the most suitable devices is available from Speech and Language therapists to whom a referral can be made within the NHS.

Method of Augmentative or Alternate Communication	Features of this method
Hearing aids	Hearing aids make sounds louder and can make a big difference to the quality of life of people with hearing loss. Hearing aids can be in either analogue or digital format. Digital aids are now increasingly available and can be tailored to meet the person's own hearing needs and to suit different environments including those where there is more background noise.

In Summary

Communication is something we all do, all of the time. Perhaps this is why it is often taken for granted. Communication is however very complex and social care practitioners need to have a wide range of knowledge in order to communicate effectively.

18: SPECIFIC COMMUNICATION SKILLS

There are a number of specific communication skills which are important in social care settings. These largely relate to verbal communication, although it is important to remember that non verbal communication is important as it will impact on these areas of communication. In this chapter we have chosen to look at three specific communication skills which are essential in social care – listening, reflecting and asking questions.

LISTENING

Most social care workers can talk very fluently, but they may not be able to listen so "fluently". However, it is important to remember that listening is always more important than talking:

"We have two ears and one mouth so that we can listen twice as much as we speak."

(Epictelous)

Active Listening

Active listening involves demonstrating to the "speaker" that you are listening. It is not enough to have heard what someone has said – you need to show the person that you have heard them:

"Perhaps the most important point to emphasise is that listening is an active process. It involves not only hearing what is being said, but also indicating to the other person that we have heard it. This provides reassurance for the speaker and encourages him or her to speak freely and openly."

(Thompson 1996)

Active listening involves a range of issues covered in the rest of this section. For example, skilful reflecting can clearly demonstrate effective listening. Effective non verbal communication can demonstrate that you are listening. For example, if a person maintains good eye contact and nods their head etc, this indicates active listening.

The importance of effective listening is highlighted in the following poem written by a person with learning disabilities:

"To work with me,
You have to listen to me
And you can't just listen with your ears.
Because it will go to your head to fast.
You have to listen with your whole body.

If you listen slow,

Some of what I say
Will enter your heart."

(Written by a Canadian Student with learning disabilities – Source Unknown)

What should I be listening to?

On the face of it this seems a strange question: "I should be listening to what the person says". However, as we have covered, communication is about far more than words so we need to *listen* to far more than words. To listen effectively we need to listen to what a person is saying AND:

> *How the person is speaking*
> You can tell a great deal from the way someone speaks. For example, if someone is speaking quickly they may be excited or anxious and if someone is using a monotonous tone they may be feeling low. It is important of course not to make assumptions. Always check out your views, e.g.: by saying "it sounds as though you are happy/sad etc about that?" By making the statement a question it is likely that the person will let you know how they feel.

> *A person's body language*
> Observe the whole person, but be aware that body language is culturally specific. In some cultures avoiding eye contact can be seen as ignorant whilst in others making eye contact can be seen as offensive. However, it is probably safe to assume that if someone is smiling they are happy etc.

> *A person's behaviour*
> Some behaviours such as crying and aggression can communicate a great deal. However you need to listen to the "whole person" to be clear exactly what the behaviour is communicating. For example people can cry tears of either joy or sadness. Chapter 21 gives more information on the links between communication and behaviour.

Being a "good listener"

This quality is valued both by those providing and those using social care services. It is of key importance in helping people feel valued and ensuring that their preferences and choices are recognised. Listening well and attentively is undoubtedly an important aspect of communication in social care. Although some people are naturally good and attentive listeners, along with other aspects of communication, this is a skill which can always be further developed.

Giving the other person the space and opportunity to talk is of great importance. Some people with learning disabilities, dementia or mental health problems may find it takes them a while to process information and frame their thoughts. People may have reduced energy levels due to illness or for other reasons. Giving an immediate response can be difficult and people may find it stressful to feel under pressure to reply. For this reason, workers should try to put aside their own need to move quickly and allow sufficient time for people to communicate, if possible in an environment where they will not be interrupted and can have some privacy. Workers should listen attentively to anything the person says, but avoid feeling the need to fill silences, as it may be sufficient just to be there with the person. Where possible, workers need to be led by the individual and to proceed at his or her pace. Remember that listening to what people say is not just about listening to words – as we have covered, people can "say" a lot even if they do not use words.

Techniques which help in active listening include:

> Allowing the other person to do the "talking"

➢ Demonstrating to the other person that you have been paying attention

➢ Giving the other person encouragement, perhaps by nodding or indicating in some other way that you have understood. Perhaps the most straightforward of all is for the worker to nod or indicate simply in words that they have understood and encourage the person to continue

➢ Acknowledging what the other person has said without appearing to judge them

➢ Using open rather than closed questions to encourage the person to develop what they are saying and say more about it, perhaps adding more supplementary questions to help them to develop what they are saying

➢ Reflecting back what the person has said using his or her own words. Used with care, this technique can reassure the other person that the worker has been paying attention to what they have been saying. It can also give the other person the opportunity to check whether what the worker has heard is really what they meant, for them to take stock and then develop their line of thought further.

REFLECTING

Reflecting and summarising are important to demonstrate that you are listening to someone, and to check out that you have heard correctly. When you repeat key words it tells the person speaking that you are hearing them correctly and that what they are saying is important.

Reflecting is a technique often used in counselling, and since care staff are not trained as counsellors it is important to use the skill with great care.

Reflecting basically involves repeating the important things that are being said back to the speaker. This can encourage the speaker to say more. However, the listener shouldn't interrupt the speaker but simply reflect things back to encourage the speaker to say more.

Two "conversations" follow. One where reflecting is over used and is therefore not helpful and one where reflecting is used effectively to encourage the speaker to say more.

Badly Used Reflection

Well Used Reflection

Although reflecting back what has been heard can be very useful when the technique is used well there is a danger that it can seem a bit stilted and artificial. Social care workers need to think through how they use reflection – this may be as straightforward as paraphrasing what the person has said.

ASKING QUESTIONS

Questions are a vital part of the process of communication. Whilst we all ask questions at different times, sometimes to be effective as social care practitioners, people need to learn how to ask questions.

Questions can be useful to gather information, to help understand situations to develop trust etc. However, incorrect use of questions can lead to a total breakdown in effective communication.

Types of Questions

There are three main types of questions:

Question Type	Example
OPEN	"What's your favourite drink?"
CLOSED	"Is tea your favourite drink?"
LEADING	"Tea is your favourite drink isn't it?"

Open Questions

Open questions ask the speaker to think about their answer and give more information.

Open questions demonstrate an interest in a person because the questioner has effectively said "tell me more. I'm interested".

Open questions encourage people to think about the answer they are giving and the answer often gives a range of information to the questioner, allowing the conversation to develop further.

Open questions use the following:

➢ Why?

➢ Where?

➢ When?

➢ How?

➢ What?

➢ Which?

➢ Who?

Closed Questions

Closed questions allow for limited responses (usually a 'yes' or 'no' answer).

Closed questions are not that helpful in gaining further information since the response is limited. However, they can be useful to gain specific basic information where the speaker regularly goes off the subject. They can also be used to end a conversation.

Asking closed questions can be frustrating for both the person asking and answering a question, as it can be a much more straightforward to ask a simple open question. For example, in this scenario, lots of closed questions didn't get the desired result (i.e. an answer) whereas one open question did.

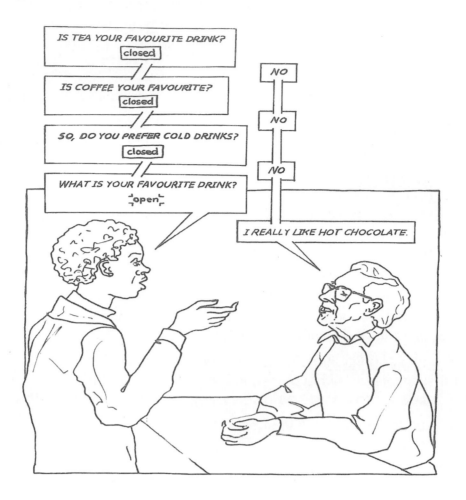

Leading Questions

This type of question gives the person being asked a clear indication about the expected answer. This can be about the words that are used in the question or by the tone of voice in which the question is asked.

On the whole leading questions should be avoided. However:

"Sometimes it is useful to use leading questions. If a person lacks confidence a leading question may give a clue as to the expected answer and so encourage a response. This may then by the start of a useful communication. By hinting at the expected answer, the questioner can give the respondents the confidence to answer."

(Reddington and Waltham 1995)

Solution Focussed Questionning

Solution focussed work is becoming very popular in social care. It is drawn from the field of counselling and Brief Solution Focussed Therapy which is attributed to the work of Steve de Shazer (1985) and his colleagues at the Brief Family Therapy Centre in the United States. Solution focussed approaches are based on focusing on goals and outcomes (solutions) rather than problems. As such, it has been found to be very helpful in current social care practice.

One of the skills within BSFT is the use of supportive questions aimed at enabling the service user to recognise their own strengths and abilities. Various types of questions are used, including:

> Goal setting questions. This is about allowing the focus at the start of a contact to be about why the service user has presented to the service in their own opinion, what they hope to achieve through their contact with the service, and how they would know that this goal had been achieved.

> The Miracle Question. This supports the service user to identify how the future will be different when the problem is no longer present. The practitioner should shape the miracle question to be relevant to the person they are with. One aspect that is often focused on is how the service user would know or sense that the miracle (the problem they had in the past has now gone) had occurred. This is sometimes referred to as "magical thinking" questioning.

> Scaling questions. The service user is asked to score the present on a scale of 1 to 10. The practitioner could then ask what would it take to move one point up the scale. This can also be used for identifying immediate goals.

> Exception finding questions. The practitioner supports the service user to identify the successful strategies they have used in the past. The intention is to give the service user the confidence to apply their own strategies to improve their situation.

> Coping questions. These seek to support the service user to recognise the general strengths and resources they have. This approach aims to assist the service user move from an internalised problem focussed narrative to recognition of their capabilities.

BSFT has become an increasingly popular tool in social care and social work practice. The underlying principle of this approach is that people can get preoccupied with their problems and are not able to see past them with any confidence. Workers use this approach to support service users to see beyond the difficulties and reframe the individual's way of looking at them. This in turn promotes a change in the way the problems are viewed and the solutions are utilised.

In Summary

There are a range of specific skills which social care practitioners need to develop. This chapter has focussed on the use of questions to illicit information and on listening. Listening is probably one of the most important communication skills in social care practice. It is, however, often taken for granted. Social care practitioners should be able to demonstrate how they employ specific communication skills.

19: PROMOTING EFFECTIVE COMMUNICATION: UNDERSTANDING THE BARRIERS

To promote effective communication, it is important to understand the potential barriers to communication. Essentially, all of the barriers to effective communication come down to two areas – problems relating to the message being given or problems relating to the message being received.

Problems with the Message being Given

Problems with the message being given can include:

> It may be difficult to understand because of jargon

> It might contain too much information

> It might be contradictory

> It might be distorted by perhaps being passed through too many people

> Verbal and non verbal messages may not agree

> The message might be given inappropriately e.g.: aggressively

> There might be cultural barriers

Problems with the Message being Received

These can be varied, but basically all will fall into the following categories:

> Environmental barriers

> "Clinical" barriers

> Emotional barriers

> Attitudinal barriers

> Cultural differences

> Bureaucratic barriers

Environmental Issues

The environment we are in can affect communication both in terms of being able to pass on a message or being able to receive a message. For example:

> In noisy surroundings, people may not be able to hear what is being said, or even be able to formulate a message to pass on ("It's so noisy I can't even think!")

> In environments which are not private, people may not raise certain issues which they see as very personal

> If people are not comfortable, are too hot or too cold etc. This can affect the quality of

communication taking place.

➤ The formality of the environment needs to be matched to the communication method. For example, a person may feel inhibited in communicating informally in a very formal environment.

There are a range of environmental barriers to communication and these will vary widely in terms of the environment in which social care workers operate.

Many social care staff have little, if any influence over the environment in which they communicate. For example, where a worker goes into a service user's own home. Others, however, can have control over environmental factors. For example, a worker in a day service can have an influence over the environment – where to position chairs etc.

The best way to arrange the environment to facilitate effective communication will depend on the needs of individual service users and are specific to each work environment. Where environments cannot be adapted, it is worth putting some thoughts into how barriers can be overcome.

"Clinical" Barriers

According to the Royal College for Speech and Language therapy, there are a range of clinical barriers to effective communication:

➤ Genetic or medical conditions

➤ Trauma

➤ Mental health problems

➤ Learning difficulties or disabilities

➤ Speech (clarity, stammering, etc)

➤ Voice (lack of voice, hyper-nasality etc)

➤ Fluency (processing the delivery and receipt of language)

➤ Language

➤ Psychologically based communication disorders

➤ Social skills

➤ Problem solving skills

➤ Literacy issues or dyslexia

When considering specific clinical issues and the barriers that can be created, it is vital that staff do not pathologise people (i.e.: blame the individual for the problem).

Working in a holistic way, recognising the individual needs of service users means that any specific "barriers" should be addressed – but always remember that it is not the service user that is the barrier. Any difficulties faced in terms of communication can be as much about the staff member having a limited understanding and having a very rigid approach to communication.

Emotional Barriers

A range of emotions can have an impact on communication. For example:

> Embarrassment: If someone is embarrassed about an issue they may avoid discussing it

> Stress/Distress: It can be hard to communicate if you are feeling stressed or distressed. The impact of stress on communication is particularly significant

> Anxiety: If people are particularly anxious they may find communication difficult. Having to communicate certain issues can create anxiety in itself

> Shock/Anger: People can be shocked or angry about what they are hearing. This may result in a person not listening effectively

> Fear

> Powerlessness: Sometimes people may feel that they have no control over their environment, choices or opportunities, so they may feel that communications can offer no new information or insight

> Lack of confidence

> Lack of self esteem

Attitudinal Barriers

Where people have negative attitudes towards the person/people they are communicating with, it is likely that the quality of communication will suffer. For example, the following attitudes will create barriers to good communication:

> Prejudice

> Lack of respect

> Arrogance

The barriers created by attitudes are often referred to by staff in terms of service users (eg: "He's got a real attitude problem in terms of authority figures." etc). However, it is important to recognise that attitudinal barriers often lie with staff.

Addressing barriers created by attitudes can involve a range of approaches.

Social care workers need to take a whole system view of communication. What is the communication ethos, atmosphere or culture of the service? How do individual staff members reinforce that ethos or cut across it by their own style?

The L'Arche organisation has always promoted the importance of support staff being present with service users. Sitting with a service user is not seen as 'skiving'. It is one of the crucial aspects of the role of support staff.

In so many services, support staff busy themselves or gather in the "office" or sleep in room or by the emergency exit door where they have their cigarettes. In these situations, it's not unusual for service users to bang on the office door, "hang around" outside the office or wherever the staff gather.

Cultural Differences

Where there are cultural differences between people communication can be adversely affected. For example:

➢ Assumptions may be made, which can effectively prevent open communication

➢ There may be differences in language, the use of words, accent, dialect etc.

➢ Non verbal communication can be culturally specific

➢ Interpreters may need to be used which will clearly have an effect on communication

Don't forget that "culture" covers a range of areas and could include generational differences etc.

Bureaucratic Barriers

One of the things staff and service users generally agree on is that there is too much "red tape" involved in social and health care. Access to services often involves navigating a range of red tape which can be confusing and can clearly have a significant negative impact on engagement and communication.

Great improvements have been made by changing things at the point of engagment: e.g.: "One Stop Shops" with several local services under one roof working together, which have less imposing reception areas or application processes, and of course plenty of information available in a variety of languages and formats.

When anyone contacts an organisation, they don't like to hear "The person you need to speak to is on long term sick." Services could consider what systems they have for reducing the alienation that family members can have when contacting the service.

An example specific to written communication is the use of easy to read type fonts, printed on pastel shades of paper. This is very helpful for some people with dyslexia. There are many people with mild dyslexia who do not know they have it so these methods can have a wide appeal for both service users and staff.

Promoting Effective Communication

Probably one of the most effective ways of enabling people to communicate effectively is to understand the potential barriers to communication and to seek to minimise these.

It is important for workers to be aware of the best way to communicate with individual users of social care services and to pay careful attention such matters as the environment in which they are talking to the person. Even if the person normally communicates well using words, workers should bear in mind when and where they are speaking. The person may be reserved by nature or as is the case with many older people, may not want to "be any trouble". Some people, often those who have lived in long stay institutions, may be eager to please staff members and may communicate what they think staff want to hear rather than what they really think.

Some key things to consider for communication to be effective include:

➢ Is the person comfortable and relaxed enough to be able to respond well?

> Are there any distractions? Someone with a hearing loss may well find it difficult to distinguish what you are saying against background noise

> If someone has a hearing loss, ensure that you are sitting opposite each other and that the light is good enough for you to be able to see each other's faces, particularly if the other person lip reads. If the person has a hearing aid, ask them to ensure that it is switched on and operating correctly

> Can you speak in a place where you are unlikely to be disturbed?

> Is the timing right for that person? If an individual has had a serious illness, or is on certain kinds of medication, he or she may be more alert at certain times of the day and may be more inclined to speak at those times

> If the person has a hearing or speech disability, can he or she use or understand sign language and are you able to use this?

> Does the person respond well to pictures or symbols which you can use to communicate with them?

> Ensure that the person knows that what the purpose is for the communication – is it for an assessment of their needs, to discuss a specific issue, or is it of a more general or informal nature?

> Use open questions which encourage people to respond more fully

> Check out that the person is happy to continue and is not distressed

And avoid:

> Closed questions which are likely to draw a yes or no response

> Rushing the person. Don't move swiftly on to the next question, but allow time for the person to digest the question and give a considered response

> If you are finding it difficult to understand the person, ask him or her to repeat themselves rather than pretend that you have understood

Changing Needs and Differing Perspectives

It is important for workers not to become complacent once they have established effective communication with a service user and it is quite possible that a person's communication needs will change over time. For example, when working with a service user who has developed a particular communication system such as a Picture Exchange Communication System (PECS), at different times the service user may add new pictures as their communication skills develop. Alternatively, a worker could be supporting a person with dementia whose ability to communicate verbally declines over time. The worker and the whole care team therefore need to be able to adjust and develop their approach.

Whose communication "problem" is it?

We have probably all heard service users described as "unable to communicate". Given the complexity of communication, how is this so? Communication is two way. If staff are failing to understand what a person is communicating, the problem is with the staff, not the service user. It should be more like "The staff working with this service user can't communicate".

Where there are difficulties in communication, these are often put down to the service user in question. In fact, the problem can be about staff difficulties with communication. This is well demonstrated by the following quote which although old, is still very relevant today. This is written from the perspective of a service user.

"It is an unfortunate fact that one of the areas in which you greatly lack skill is in dealing with us. Your disability is great when you come into contact with us, and that fact increases our disability. When one of us meets one of you, especially if it is for the first time, we are quite likely to lack many of the skills for successful communication. We may not be able to think of anything appropriate to say, or put it into the right words, or to control our facial expression. But you also will show a great lack of skill. You will be embarrassed, you won't be able to think of anything appropriate to say, you will tend to talk in an inappropriate tone of voice, you will tend to have a wide grin on your face and ask questions without really being interested in the answer. The disability is thus a mutual one. Both of us have difficulty in communicating with, and forming relationships with the other. The trouble is that you have lots of opportunity to go off and find other people with whom you can communicate better and form relationships more easily. We don't. You can deny your disability. We can't – we live it all the time".

(Williams 1978)

In Summary

An essential aspect of promoting effective communication is in understanding the barriers to communication. Often where there are communication difficulties this is put down to service users being unable to communicate. However, communication is a two way process and the difficulties are much more likely to lie with professionals who are unable to view communication in its totality.

20: COMMUNICATING WITH PEOPLE WHO HAVE SPECIFIC NEEDS

Facilitating effective communication is all about the groundwork of identifying the most effective way to communicate with any individual.

When a social care worker meets a new service user, some documentation about this person should be shared – this might be assessment documentation or a care plan. This paperwork should provide information about how the person communicates. Occasionally, there may even be an assessment report by a communication therapist (sometimes referred to as speech and language therapist). However, such reports are likely to be written for only a minority of service users.

Apart from the assessment documentation and the care plan, the main sources of information about how to communicate with a new service user are likely to be:

➢ The service user themselves

➢ Family members of the service user

➢ Staff who have already worked with the service user

Using all of the sources of evidence, a social care worker should be able to develop an effective communication strategy.

Developing communication profiles

In many ways social care work requires good investigation skills. This is no more so than in terms of communication. Workers need to explore the best way to communicate with any individual. You should work with your colleagues to identify a communication profile for each service user and to devise an effective strategy. Using the contents of this section may help you to think about methods of effective communication.

PERSONAL COMMUNICATION PASSPORTS

Developed in the 1990s by Sally Millar, a specialist speech and language therapist at the Communication Aids for Language and Learning (CALL) Centre, Personal Communication Passports are a person centred and practical way of supporting people who cannot easily speak for themselves. Passports aim to:

➢ Present the person positively as an individual, not as a set of 'problems' or disabilities

➢ Provide a place for the person's own views and preferences to be recorded and drawn to the attention of others

➢ Describe the person's most effective means of communication

➢ Draw together information from past and present, and from different contexts, to help staff and conversation partners understand the person and have successful interactions

➢ Reflect a "flavour" of the person's unique character

Some organisations have developed and adapted this approach and refer to the system as individual communication profiles or something similar.

A person's communication needs are a key element of their care and support needs, and the person's preferred communication and any specific communication needs should be recorded in their care plan. As with any aspect of care planning, the process should begin with an initial or baseline assessment. Planning should then take place to find the best way to support the person's needs and help them to develop or maintain their skills if possible. The plan should be implemented and monitored to see what changes may be taking place. Periodically the person's communication needs should be reviewed, as with any other aspect of their support needs, and they should be re-assessed as necessary. A review may need to consider advice from relatives of the person or from a specialist, such as a communication therapist.

Even if all this information is carefully recorded, it would be of no use unless staff who are supporting individuals are aware of it and have any necessary training to put it into practice. Information about the person's communication needs should be clearly and simply recorded and the record should be easily accessible by those workers who need to access it. It needs to be accessible in two respects:

➤ The information needs to be recorded in an uncomplicated format which is easy for the worker to grasp, perhaps on a profile card, rather than having to wade through pages of care notes.

➤ A copy of the record itself should be with the worker rather than put away on a shelf in the manager's office. This is particularly important where staff are working alone, away from their base, as is the case with domiciliary care services.

COMMUNICATING WITH PEOPLE FROM A DIFFERENT CULTURAL BACKGROUND

Communication techniques should be flexible in order to respect different cultural needs. The following guide provides key suggestions in communicating with people who are from a different cultural background to your own:

➤ There is no "standard" form of address (e.g.: Mr or use of first name). It is individual choice how different people would like to be referred to. The best way is to ask people what they would prefer to be called.

➤ The term "Christian name" should not be used, as people may not be Christians. Use "first name" or "forename" instead.

➤ The use of tactile introductions, such as shaking hands, may be unacceptable in some cultures.

➤ Confirm with the individual that they are comfortable with your way of communication.

➤ Respect differences. You need to understand that diversity may affect a whole host of things including accent, dialect, slang and non verbal communication. Find out as much as you can about the person's background and the effects this may have on communication.

Communicating with People whose First Language isn't English

Where a person is not fluent in English workers will need to adapt their communication. The following pointers may be helpful:

➤ Speak clearly but not too loudly.

➤ Pace your communication well. If the worker speaks too quickly people may not understand, but if they speak too slowly this can be patronising and it can be difficult to understand the whole sentence.

➤ Use clear language. Where someone is from a different cultural background to your own they may not be familiar with culturally specific sayings (e.g. "I've got a frog in my throat, it's raining cats and dogs" etc).

➤ Use pictures and symbols.

➤ Pronounce names correctly.

➤ Check and rephrase as you go along.

➤ Provide written information in the person's first language to back up other communication.

➤ Get a trained interpreter to help if possible.

Using Interpreters

People who do not speak English as a first language may need the support of an interpreter. In certain circumstances, family or friends can act as interpreters. However, there are important disadvantages to this which include:

➤ Individuals receiving care may not want members of their family or community to know personal details and information

➤ Interpreting is a task that requires great skills in remaining objective and translating information in a completely neutral manner. Professional interpreters receive specific training in these issues

➤ In rare circumstances, family or friends may be actually perpetrating abuse against the person receiving care

When you work with interpreters communication is clearly affected because instead of being a two way process communication becomes a three way process. So perhaps the most important thing for the worker to consider when working with an interpreter is to ensure that they still create a relationship with the service user. Workers will also need to think about their relationship with the interpreter. They will need to be clear with the interpreter about roles and to negotiate expectations around working together to facilitate effective communication with the service user.

Many people believe that their communication skills will not be used when working with an interpreter, because communication will be managed by the interpreter. However, professional skills will be more vital than ever. For example:

➤ Workers will need to maintain good eye contact with both the service user and the interpreter. Listening skills will be very important. Workers will need to listen to what the interpreter is saying, as well as attending to the non verbal communication of the interpreter and the service user. Using an interpreter adds another layer to listening.

➤ Workers will still need to use all of their verbal communication skills so that the interpreter understands what is needed.

Attitudes

Workers need to be very aware of their attitudes when working with people whose first language isn't English.

➤ ASSUMING – people assume all sorts of things which clearly affect communication. For example, you may have assumed that in discussing people whose first language is not English we are talking about people whose first language is a foreign language. What about deaf people who use British Sign Language? English is not their first language.

➤ "DUMPING" RESPONSIBILITY – in some care services where one member of staff speaks the same language as a service user then it is sometimes thought to be best for that staff member to work with the service user. This implies that other staff members don't need to think about their communication.

COMMUNICATING WITH PEOPLE WITH LEARNING DISABILITIES

Everyone who has a learning disability is different and has different needs and desires and as such the barriers that people face in communicating are very varied. Such barriers *may* include, one or more of the following factors:

➤ Inaccurate and dangerous assumptions about understanding

➤ Lack of speech

➤ Lack of anything of interest to communicate about

➤ Sensory impairment

➤ Mental health problems

➤ Inappropriate environment

➤ Staff lack of understanding

➤ Being supported as one of a group, rather than an individual

➤ Staff not making time to listen

The British Association of Learning Disabilities (2009 online) suggest that up to 90% of people with learning disabilities have issues with communication, and 60% of people find symbolic techniques helpful in aiding communication. They argue that people's unwillingness to learn the skills required to communicate with people who need different forms of communication is the primary cause of the frustration which many people with learning disabilities experience.

We will start by exploring how assumptions about understanding can act as a primary barrier to communication.

Exploring Understanding

As we have covered, communication is a two way process, which involves the sending of a message and the receiving of a message. It is important to be aware that a person with a learning disability may not understand what is said – because of the way the worker has said it!

Workers need to be conscious of the words and phrases they use. In essence it is important that the phrases we use are concrete and direct as possible. This should mean the phrases are simpler and more direct. An example could include instead of saying:

"We won't be going out"

say

"We will stay in today".

Time concepts can be difficult for a person with a learning disability. Staff need to be conscious to avoid references to times of the clock. However to talk about after lunch or this evening may be more comprehensible.

The more significant a person's learning disability is then the more likely it is that they may not understand all the words in a sentence. The words that are more concrete – nouns or proper nouns – may be recognised but not other words.

"Don't drink your tea – it's hot"

may be understood as

"Drink your tea".

Again the simpler and more direct the language the better. In the light of this, humour and especially sarcasm can be confusing. Staff should try to avoid the use of humour and sarcasm if they are wanting to convey something.

For some people with a severe learning disability, information overload can occur with just two or three sentences. If the person can only absorb one piece of information at a time then workers should recognise this and space out the presentation of information.

Where information is new or complex then visual representations of that information may be helpful.

For individuals with a learning disability who do have verbal skills it is important not to assume from a couple of words they say that they understand you. Some people with learning disabilities repeat the last thing a person has said to them. Also, if a staff member says to a service user "do you understand what I've said?" the service user could well say "Yes" even when they have not understood. Try to ask more open questions e.g. "Tell me what we have just agreed will happen?"

Recognising and Respecting Personal Communication

People often use personal systems of communication. We need to learn to recognise and value these systems of communication. For example, someone may convey the message that they want to use the toilet by rocking on their chair. Someone may communicate their happiness by clapping. Social care workers need to ensure that they clearly recognise and respond to the methods of communication which service users may use.

Taking Responsibility

Taking responsibility for improving communication is the first step in developing effective communication. Remembering the following points can also be helpful:

➢ Make sure that the person has a way of attracting attention to let another person know that she/he has something to say. Some people do not realise that they need to attract a person's attention. They may simply sit in a chair signing or speaking. When no one responds, they may either become frustrated, or decide that communication is a waste of time and give up

➢ Have supplementary communication equipment such as objects and pictures available

➢ Adjust what you say and do to make it clearer

➢ Use additional cues to make sure people can understand

➢ Be on the look out for opportunities for people to have enjoyable and successful interactions, and create them if necessary

➢ Improve communication between different care givers and different settings in order to provide a consistent approach

COMMUNICATING WITH PEOPLE WITH A HEARING IMPAIRMENT

The following guidelines may help promote effective communication with people who have a hearing impairment:

➢ Never assume a person only hears what they want to hear. There may be differences in hearing at different times and people may be able to hear some people better then others

➢ Show somebody with a hearing impairment what you would like them do, rather than telling them

➢ Use gestures, signs, pictures or photographs

➢ Make sure people can see you when you are talking to them and never cover your mouth, this will aid lip reading

➢ It is tempting to raise your voice when speaking to a person with a hearing impairment. However, remember not to shout as this can distort speech sounds (and if the person wears a hearing aid it can really hurt)

➢ If a person has a hearing aid ensure it is correctly used and maintained

➢ Avoid background noise like the TV or radio

➢ Ensure that people have access to any necessary equipment (e.g. minicom etc)

➢ Help a person make use of teletext subtitles to watch the TV

➢ Speak clearly, naturally and slowly and make sure that your non verbal communication is in line with what you are saying

➢ When you need to repeat something do so with patience, do not get exasperated

➢ It can be helpful to ask the person you are talking to, to tell you what they heard – it might be very different to what you said

➢ If the person uses BSL, get an interpreter

The Royal National Institute for Deaf People (RNID 2009 online) website also has useful factsheets about people's rights and tips for effective communication.

COMMUNICATING WITH PEOPLE WITH A VISUAL IMPAIRMENT

The following guidelines may help promote effective communication with people who have a visual impairment:

➢ Make sure people can hear you coming towards them and introduce yourself verbally. If the person has poor hearing they may be able to sense you by smell or touch

➢ Tell the person that you are leaving when you are going to depart

➢ Touch people in a way that is respectful, firm and gentle. Remember touching a person without warning from behind is very threatening

➢ Be careful that you do not block someone's light

➢ Always consult people when their environment changes

➢ Give as much information and explanation as possible, so the person knows what to expect

➢ Ensure people are not isolated from conversations and activities

➢ Describe objects and events to people to ensure they feel included

COMMUNICATING WITH PEOPLE WHO HAVE A MENTAL HEALTH PROBLEM

There are many issues to consider when communicating with people who have a mental health problem. Essentially, many barriers to effective communication can be created when working with people with mental health problems. Workers need to be aware of these barriers and develop strategies to deal with them to ensure effective communication.

Barrier	Strategies
Symptoms of Mental Health Problems Some of the symptoms of mental health problems can have a negative impact on communication. For example, if someone is experiencing auditory hallucinations (i.e. is hearing voices) they will find listening to another person difficult. If someone is depressed they may lack the energy and motivation to communicate etc.	*Recognise the barriers* The first step in promoting positive communication with people with mental health problems is to recognise the barriers that exist. Don't put difficulties with communication down to the individual, explore their surroundings, think about the impact of oppression etc.
Prejudice and Fear Many people are fearful of mental health problems. This may affect health and social care workers who may discriminate against service users with mental health problems. Where a service user senses prejudice and fear they are unlikely to communicate openly, and where the "listener" is fearful they are unlikely to listen effectively.	Ensure that you value people and that you work in an anti-oppressive way at all times.

Barrier	Strategies
Medication Much of the medication that is used to treat people with mental health problems has very negative side effects such as drowsiness, blurred vision etc. These side effects can create significant barriers to communication. For example, if someone is tired their ability to communicate is likely to be affected.	Think about the best time to convey information. Some people are more receptive to information at particular times of the day.
Lack of Understanding Many people with mental health problems face not only discrimination, but also a lack of understanding which can create a barrier to effective communication. For example, how would you feel if you were told to "pull yourself together"? It's likely that you would not communicate openly with that person again.	Consider the person's individual situation and take account of this in your communication.
Other Barriers All of the other barriers referred to in this section can also apply to people with mental health problems (e.g.: difficulties with the environment, cultural difference, assumptions etc).	Always listen to what people are "saying". Do not make judgements or assumptions

COMMUNICATING WITH PEOPLE WHO HAVE DEMENTIA

The principles of good communication and the value base of social care apply fully to working with a person who has dementia. People with dementia are not in "their second childhood", they are adults with a lifetime's experience enduring a disabling, little understood condition.

Due to the additional difficulties and discrimination faced by people with dementia, forming an effective relationship can present particular challenges. The Alzheimer's Society's web site contains useful information about language, clarity of speech, respect, and the importance of remembering other factors such as the effects of pain, discomfort, ill fitting dentures or difficulties with vision which the person may be unable to communicate (Alzheimer's Society 2009 online).

The following ideas may also serve as a practical guide to promoting positive communication:

➢ The effect of dementia on communication and level of functioning will vary from day to day or even hour to hour. Physical illness, stress, fatigue and environment can all have a significant impact. Therefore, a person may understand something on one occasion, but not on another.

➢ The effect of dementia is not consistent across all areas of functioning. Hence, a person may be unable to work out the sequence in which to dress themselves, but still be able to judge appropriate clothes to wear.

➢ The impact of dementia on short-term memory may be such that people may need continual reminders of what is happening, and why. For example: "I am undressing you to help you to use the toilet".

➢ Wearing name badges, labelling items, rooms etc. may all help in terms of communicating with a person with dementia, particularly in the early stages of their condition.

➢ The use of other aids to memory, such as pictures, smells, demonstrations can sometimes be of assistance. Reminiscence can also be a helpful tool in promoting communication.

It is important to remember that people who have dementia may have particular communication needs and more time may be required to build a relationship.

In Summary

A range of strategies can be employed to communicate with people with specific communication needs. However, building on an understanding of total communication, social care practitioners should recognise that every individual has unique communication needs.

Social care workers should avoid making assumptions about the specific needs of different individuals where there are barriers to communication. It is more appropriate to observe the individual, find out from them about how they prefer to communicate, and where possible to consult specialist resources or organisations for ideas and guidance.

21: UNDERSTANDING BEHAVIOUR AS COMMUNICATION

The most straightforward way of understanding any behaviour is, as has been said many times, to recognise the behaviour as a form of communication. Whilst the question "What is this person communicating?" sounds very straightforward it is very often missed. One of the major problems when a person has reached the stage of exhibiting behaviours which are challenging to services is how to find out what is being communicated. Sometimes finding the answer to the very straightforward question is extremely complicated and staff might almost feel like a detective with few clues to go on.

Whenever a social care worker encounters a behaviour which is challenging they need to ask themselves (and colleagues) many questions to try and 'detect' what the person is communicating. The following questions, though by no means exhaustive, may be a good starting point.

What is the Person Communicating?

Health Related Reasons

> Is s/he in pain e.g. dental pain?

> Has the person suffered an injury that hasn't yet been noticed e.g. a sprained ankle?

> Is the person suffering from stomach problems?

> Does she have P.M.S?

> Is the person tired due to disturbed sleep?

> Is s/he constipated?

> Does the person have sensory impairments e.g. a hearing impairment? tinnitus? a visual impairment?

Situational Reasons

> Is the person being asked to do something they don't like?

> Is s/he being overloaded with information/demands?

> Is s/he bored?

> Is the person uncomfortable in some way. For example, are they hot or cold? Is their clothing uncomfortable?

> Have there been changes that the person had little control over and/or little notice about?

> Has the person had to stop doing something they liked doing?

> Does the person engage in the behaviour with certain staff or when certain service users are around?

> Are there any triggers e.g.: when staff arrive to start working? Loud noises etc?

> Do staff attend to the person as a result of the behaviour?

> Do staff leave the person alone as a result of the behaviour?

> Is the person given confusing and conflicting information by staff and/or carers?

> Are they angry? If so, why are they angry?

General Reasons

➤ Is the person feeling insecure? Are there new staff around? How can the person be sure they can trust staff?

➤ Can the person communicate their needs in other ways?

➤ Could the person have been abused in the past?

➤ Is the person with others who display behaviours which challenge services and so:
  • Models their behaviour
  • Feels that to be noticed s/he needs to do something significant etc.

➤ Has the behaviour been established over many years? Any changes may be gradual. Can staff notice these improvements and acknowledge them to the person themselves?

➤ Does the person only have a sense of control over their life when they engage in the behaviour – in that it prevents staff action/plans?

The extent of this list of questions demonstrates how difficult it can be to detect what a person is trying to communicate through their behaviour. However, the main starting point is to recognise the behaviour as a method of communication and then start to try to identify exactly what the behaviour is communicating.

The Cycle of Behaviour

There is very often a clear cycle in behaviour which is considered challenging to services. To begin to understand this, we first of all need to consider the consequences of behaviour.

Possible consequences to the person who displays behaviour which is challenging

➤ This person may receive attention from staff immediately following or soon after the episode.

➤ Staff may talk about the person in disrespectful ways. The person may be informally labelled according to the behaviour they display.

➤ Some may lack confidence in working with the person such that only a few staff are able/willing to work with the person.

➤ Staff may be reluctant to go out with the person except as one of two staff. This may reduce the opportunities for activities the person can enjoy since it can be harder to allow time for two staff to go out with one person.

➤ Staff may say to the person directly "I hope we're not going to have any trouble from you today" or some such comment.

➤ Other service users may avoid the person or talk about them.

➤ The service may view the person principally in terms of their behaviour and lose any meaningful sense of their abilities and strengths. Service interventions can become focused simply on addressing the behaviour which challenges and therefore not meeting the service user's needs.

➤ The service and staff lose the sense of the person having the potential for personal development.

The combined effect could be that the person engages in fewer activities, especially activities away from the service. More time is spent in the service with the person involved in an increasingly limited range of activities which are repeated, possibly daily. The person may well have an increasingly restricted network of social contacts and staff who work with them. Imagine a situation where you lost your friends and your opportunities for activities were limited. How would you feel?

The negative consequences faced by people who challenge services can lead to anger and frustration, which in turn can lead to further behaviours which challenge. In this way, a negative cycle can be created:

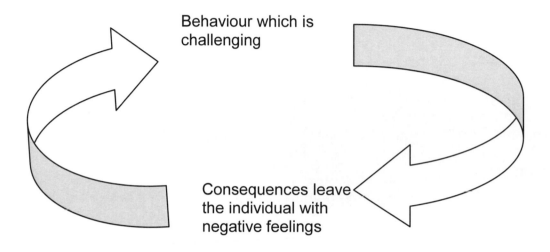

Behaviour which is challenging

Consequences leave the individual with negative feelings

Responding to individuals who display behaviour which challenges

In seeking to support individuals with challenging behaviours various professionals have argued that specific programmes should be adopted to reduce the incidence of the behaviour.

Programmes for addressing challenging behaviours include:

➢ Functional Analysis. This is based on seeing the behaviour largely as a form of communication and providing alternative socially acceptable ways of communicating.

➢ Behaviour Modification. This can take various forms and can include reinforcing positive behaviours that the person is known to engage in at times.

➢ Gentle Teaching. This seeks to generate a environment where the person is positively valued.

When each of these approaches has been delivered in a focused way then the results have been mixed. For some individuals there have been positive and significant improvements, for some marginal improvements and for others little or no effect at all.

This implies that for many people behaviours are an expression of a variety of causes and reasons. This means behaviours which challenge services are complex to address and staff have to recognise that support for an individual has to be seen in the long term, possibly over five years or more.

In seeking to support people who display behaviour which is challenging, it is important to work as part of a team to develop a consistent approach. The following guidance may help.

Aspects of a support plan for individuals with challenging behaviours

It is important to develop behavioural support plans that are proactive rather than reactive.

Plans are often reactive in that they focus on reacting to behaviour which challenges once it has occurred. Such plans will not encourage behavioural change.

Proactive behavioural support plans need to recognise that:

➢ People with behaviour which challenges have very complex needs
➢ It appears that many behaviours which challenge are a form of communication or demand avoidance

In working with people who exhibit behaviour which is challenging, staff should consider supporting the individual to engage in a range of activities. However, this is not to say that people should simply be "kept busy". Thought needs to be given to:

➢ Presentation of tasks

➢ communication style of staff (how the person is approached, what is said etc)

➢ Time tabling of activities

➢ Duration of activities

➢ Presentation of rewards and opportunities to pursue own interests

➢ Availability of methods of requesting breaks

➢ Number of people present

To draw up a comprehensive proactive behavioural support plan will require a multi-disciplinary approach.

One such plan for a person who has autistic characteristics may include increased emphasis on routine and structure to the day, discussions with the person would be far more concrete. For example, if the person was going out the staff member would say "We are going horse riding and then we are coming back here for lunch" etc.

Other support plans may include opportunities for the person to relax with one member of staff and to have the chance to do something they choose e.g. play own music, foot spa etc. Consideration may also need to be given to avoiding contact with other individuals the person does not like.

Services need to give people ways to indicate that they do not want to continue with an activity so that the person can be reassured and adequately supported or an alternative found.

Where behaviour support plans are developed it is vital that these are considered alongside of communication profiles. Where communication with an individual is improved, social care practitioners almost always report that the person's behaviour becomes less challenging to services.

In Summary

Perhaps the singularly most important aspect of understanding behaviour which challenges services is to recognise that the person is trying to communicate something through their behaviour.

Various approaches have been developed in responding to people who have behaviour which challenges. These approaches have been utilised with differing effects. All approaches used by social care staff should be agreed by the team as part of a person's care plan.

22: THEORIES TO INFORM COMMUNICATION

Theories around how communication works and where and why blocks to communication may occur are a helpful tool for social care staff in evaluating where communication is effective and how to address problems. In reviewing the requirements for a range of social care qualifications a few specific theories are referred to in relation to communication. Four of these are covered in this chapter. More detailed information on a wider range of theoretical approaches can be found in Maclean and Harrison (2009).

Transactional Analysis

Transactional analysis is a framework for understanding the communication between people (transactions). As such this theory can help explore communication and relationships. The idea was first developed by Harris (1970) and has since been further developed by various writers (eg: Berne 1978, Jacobs 1999 etc).

Transactional analysis (TA) is based on an understanding of ego states and personality development. The idea is that we all have certain elements to our personality:

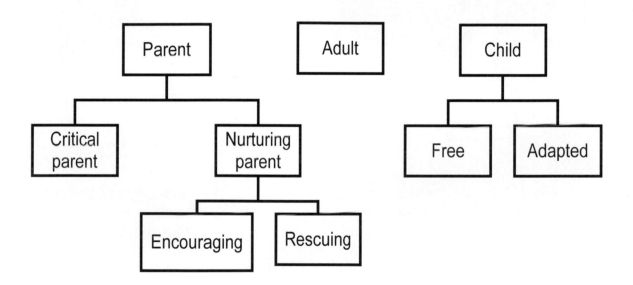

When we communicate with others, we may be "in" different states to the other person, which will impact on relationship development.

It is more straightforward to understand this using diagrammatic representation, as follows:

Appropriate Relationships

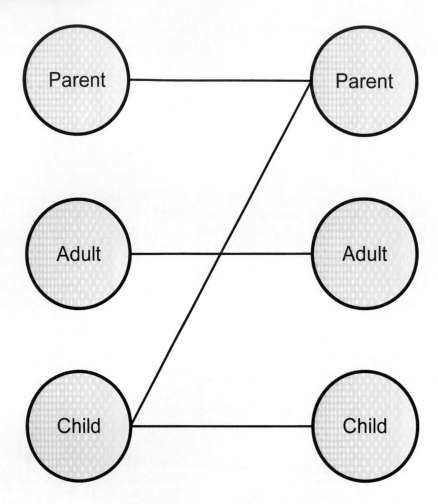

Generally, complimentary relationships are evenly balanced (represented by the straight lines). So that a parent to parent, adult to adult, child to child relationship is appropriate. A parent to child interaction is also appropriate and this may in fact appropriately denote the transactions between two adults. For example, where one person is acting in a sulky, childish manner, it might be appropriate for the other to respond in a parental way.

Problematic Relationships

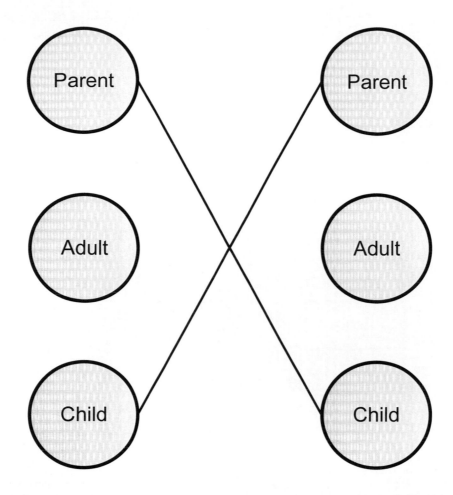

Sometimes people may experience difficulties in relating to others, which can be as a result of their childhood, their personality or the situation they find themselves in. For example, a service user may feel powerless because of the power invested in the social care worker and this may lead them to respond to the worker in a child to parent manner. The worker will want to engage with the service user on an adult to adult basis, so there are likely to be problems in the interactions and relationship.

Berne (1978) suggests that life experiences can "hook" our parent and our child which can then take over from our adult (which as adults is the preferred state). He suggests that professionals may be able to support service users to rehearse using their adult state in communications more often. In this way, practitioners may be able to support service users in developing their relationships.

Transactional analysis is a complex theory based within the psychodynamic tradition. What is presented here is a simplified explanation of the approach. However, having a basic understanding of TA can help social care staff to recognise why people respond to them in certain ways and why they may respond to others in different ways. It can also help to explain why relationships may become problematic and dysfunctional.

Karpman's Drama Triangle

The drama triangle is another "common sense" theory which can be really useful in supporting social care workers to understand and analyse situations where:

➢ They find it difficult to engage service users in discussing situations

➢ Families are locked into conflicts with each other or with services

➢ The person suddenly disengages from working with the service or the worker

This was developed out of Transactional Analysis and it links with developing the ability to understand "game playing" and enabling people to solve problems collaboratively as adults.

Karpman's drama triangle (1969 in Orriss 2004) suggests that people are often locked into cycles as shown:

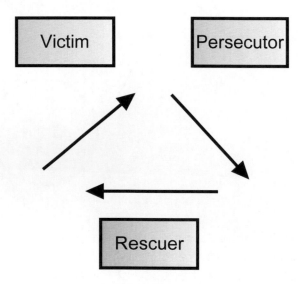

The model suggests that many vulnerable people have learned to perceive themselves as 'victims'. To be a victim requires somebody else to be the persecutor, whose behaviour towards the victim is what is creating the situation. The victim then seeks a rescuer who can come in and sort out the persecutor so that the victim is no longer subject to that oppression.

➢ Persecutor = Power

➢ Rescuer = Responsibility

➢ Victim = Vulnerability

The issue with this is that the victim does not have to do any changing themselves, and that often a rescuer is unable to enforce changes in the persecutor or their behaviour. When the rescuer fails to rescue the victim as is inevitable, the person sees the role as victim as being re-confirmed, and the rescuer then becomes the persecutor.

This is useful as a theory because many individuals often enter social care work wanting to "help people". However, unpicking the causes of people's difficulties and facilitating change in any individual requires the "helper" to have the ability to stand outside a situation, and to facilitate people's ability to make their own informed choices rather than to try to "rescue".

Trans-theoretical model of change

One model which is useful for many social care workers in understanding how communication may become "blocked" is Prochaska and Di Clemente's stages of change model (in Bundy 2004). The word "transtheoretical" is based on the idea that this is a model which is based on lots of different theories and ideas combined together. This is another "common sense" theory about understanding people's readiness to make changes in their own lives. It works from the premise that nobody changes things by force and change occurs best and most sustainably when it is something which people genuinely desire. It links closely to the need for social care workers to understand the boundaries of their role when they are encouraging and supporting people in making changes.

The model is most well known and most widely used in supporting people with substance misuse difficulties. However, its use in working with people experiencing any level of "change" is growing.

The model suggests that people go through a cycle in making significant changes as follows:

1. Pre-contemplation
   This is where a person is not ready to consider changing the behaviour. The idea that "ignorance is bliss" is key and the worker's skill here is about clarifying that the decision is the individuals, explaining the risks in not changing, and encouragement. A person in this stage will not respond to action, but this is more about them being able to explore the situation for themselves.

2. Contemplation
   A person who is in the contemplation stage may be perceived as ambivalent about making changes and reluctant to set a timescale for doing things differently. The worker's techniques here are similar to in stage 1, but may move towards looking at the costs and benefits both of the individual's current situation and of a scenario where things are different.

3. Preparation
   This is characterised by "testing the waters" and may be where a person might set themselves a target date for making changes. Here the worker would look at problem solving to support the person to remove the barriers they feel exist to making change occur, and identify resources which they could access to support them to move forwards. The idea of small steps is key and further encouragement that everyone has the skills to make changes if they want to.

4. Action
   As the name suggests, this is where the person begins to practice a new way of behaving. Again, here the worker would focus on the support which is available to the person and on encouraging the person to note their successes. Feelings of loss may be apparent for the person in moving away from their old way of living, so the idea that there are benefits to the new situation should continue to be encouraged.

5. Maintenance

This is the process of the individual continuing to act on their changed behaviour and to sustain this over time. Support from the worker would reduce at this stage in a planned way, and would focus on discussing and agreeing strategies to prevent relapses.

6. Relapse

Many people will relapse and return to the behaviour and here the worker would focus on reassessing the motivation of the person and the barriers they face, evaluating the reasons for relapse and promoting strategies for the person to continue with the change. Sometimes a relapse can be so significant that the person will feel that they are right back at stage 1 of the cycle, so different strategies may be needed for individuals in this situation.

(Prochaska & DiClemente 1983)

Prochaska and Di Clemente's model can be depicted as follows:

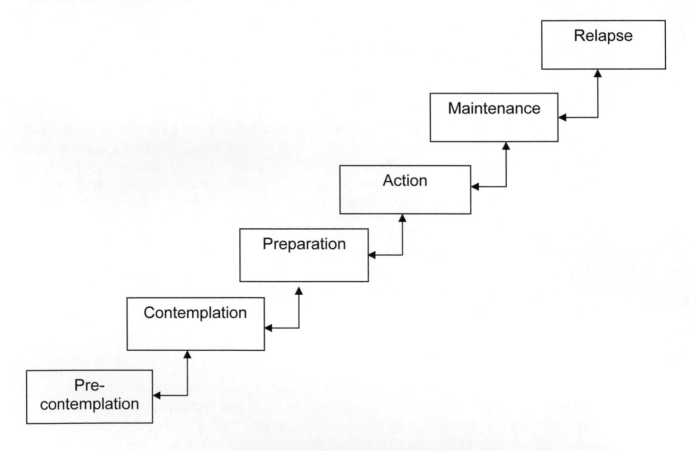

This model is probably familiar to most workers and if ever you have made a "New Year resolution" you've probably gone through this model to some extent! The model can certainly be useful in providing a framework for understanding how people's motivation and behaviour changes. If social care workers understand the perspectives which theories such as this can offer, then they are more likely to hear in service users' communication what stage of the process of change the person is probably at.

Conflict Resolution

Social care staff may often find themselves managing conflicts between service users or between service users, family members and colleagues. In such situations, communication is probably the key skill.

Conflict resolution has been characterised by the initial headline of "win/win". However, there is significantly more to it than just saying that phrase as a mantra.

There are a wide range of theories and models of conflict resolution. Most of these models recognise that there are a number of stages to conflict resolution. Different writers have generated different numbers of stages but essentially most of the models can be summarised as follows:

1. When you are in a situation of potential conflict with another person, you need to avoid entering into an adversarial and defensive approach. The initial task is to have an attitude where you want yourself and the person who is in dispute with you, to benefit from any shared decision (win/win).

   To do this, the starting point is to find out what the needs are of each party. Skills required include supportive questioning (to identify the other person's needs), effective listening and the ability to communicate your own needs. In communicating your own needs you should be assertive, use the "I" word without expectations of what the other person should do. Conflict resolution recognises that the person could be very angry with you. Options include:

   - Don't defend yourself at first, this will antagonise the situation

   - Deal with their emotions; explicitly acknowledge that you recognise how angry they are

   - Acknowledge their perspective. You do not need to agree with them but you do need to understand them

   This process should enable the person to calm down. From then on the process should follow the same stages.

   One of the key elements to conflict resolution is attitude:

   - there must be an openness to recognise the benefit of differences

   - a willingness to adapt or trade for mutual benefit

   - a view that the difficulty is to be addressed and not the person

   - disagreements or potential conflicts are not a problem. They are an opportunity to engage with the other person.

2. Once the needs of each individual have been expressed, the next stage is negotiation. As part of this, the focus must remain on the issue. Where possible, explicitly acknowledge common ground. If it appears to be a big problem, can it be broken down?

   If negotiations get heated:

   - Manage your own emotions

   - let some barbed comments go without responding to them

- have a break but agree when to resume

In seeking a solution:

- make a trial proposal
- suggest a trade "I will do this if you do that"
- make an agreement temporary or time limited

3. Mediation

If it is not possible to reach a win/win situation, it may be necessary to go for mediation.

A mediator requires various skills, including:

- being explicit that mutual benefit is the aim
- the mediator must have a clear sense that both parties are willing to address the problem
- enabling each party to express themselves and check the other party has understood them
- an ability to encourage suggestions (the mediator should avoid making their own suggestions)
- discourage personal comments or behaviours that could be provocative (name calling, ignoring, threats, belittlement etc.)

4. Resolution

Be clear about the agreement. It is easy for two people to leave a conflict situation with each of the people having a different understanding of what has been agreed.

The key aspect to conflict resolution is effective communication. The importance of effective communication in conflict resolution has been recognised in the majority of models of conflict resolution (Bercovitch and Jackson 2009). Likewise the importance of good conflict resolution skills is widely recognised as essential to effective communication.

In Summary

Theories about communication can give social care workers useful insight into people's motivations, needs and the barriers they face. When workers are able to apply theory to their practice, this can give the worker the tools they may need to move forwards and to communicate effectively in a situation which feels stuck.

23: COMMUNICATION IN ORGANISATIONS

Good communication within teams and with other parts of an organisation as a whole is just as important to providing high quality care and support as interpersonal communication. This communication can only happen reliably if it is underpinned by effective systems which ensure that information is passed on in a consistent manner.

At some stage in your career you may have had the experience of working in an environment where communication was poor. If so you will have experienced how unsettling it is not to know what is going on and to feel that you are missing out on vital information. If this is how the people who work for such an organisation feel it is also invariably also the case for those who receive services from it. Phrases like, "One hand doesn't know what the other is doing," express the frustration of dealing with an organisation where internal communication is poor.

Effective communication within an organisation has many advantages, in that it:

➢ enables feedback and information on the outcomes for individuals to be available to those who need to know and enables action to be taken as a result.

➢ enables team members to be able to make a contribution to important decisions which not only improves their motivation by helping them to feel involved but ensures that their experience and perspective can be taken into account.

➢ promotes a "seamless" service where each level of the organisation is kept aware of key information and this in turn provides a sound foundation from which to ensure that other organisations who need to know are also kept informed.

The need for formal communication systems is not recognised in all services, particularly those which are relatively small in scale.

However, the majority of social care services are subject to continual change and tensions. These may be changes to the health, ability or other circumstances of the people the service is being provided to, or changes within the team such as the recruitment of new staff. Tensions may arise from shortages of staff and other resources or the demands of providing the service within an ever-changing environment. Good communication systems do not have to be a symptom of excess bureaucracy but can give advantages by providing:

➢ Accountability. The service can be demonstrated to be effective to those who purchase and receive it, or where it is falling short, there may be greater opportunities to determine why this is the case and to rectify it.

➢ An audit trail. A further aspect of accountability. The formal communication systems of an organisation and documentation can provide a means to monitor the effectiveness of service delivery and to provide evidence of how key decisions were reached.

➢ A means of sharing information. Ensuring that there is a way for people whose shift patterns and work demands may mean that they do not often meet to share information and views.

➢ A means of recording key information for future reference.

Communication, or lack of it, is often blamed for all the troubles in an organisation, not always fairly. Managers need to learn to communicate with their staff for a wide range of functions, and certainly if they are not able to do so, problems will ensue. Greenbaum (1974) suggests four main objectives that managers have for organisational communication:

➢ *Regulation*: seeking to ensure that employee behaviour conforms with organisational objectives - for example, a meeting about a new policy and procedure statement

➢ *Innovation*: seeking to change aspects of organisational functioning in specific directions - for example, how to cut down on sickness absence

➢ *Integration*: maintaining the morale of the work force and developing a feeling of identity with the organisation and its members - for example, teambuilding exercises

➢ *Information*: giving the mainly factual information that people need for their everyday work - what has to be done, quality standards, customer complaints, etc. - for example, how to use a new piece of equipment

Methods will of course vary according to the objective. Given that communication can be oral or written, as well as non-verbal, Greenbaum suggests the following model:

Greenbaum's Organisational Communication Model

		Regulation	Innovation	Integration	Information
Face-to-face:	*Oral*	Directions and requests	Ideas meeting	Selection interview	Induction of new staff
	Written	Job description and performance standards	Reports on courses, visits etc.	Letter of welcome to new recruit	Memorandum
	Non-verbal	Gesture		Gesture	Demonstration of task to be performed
Small groups (three to ten):	*Oral*	Departmental meetings	Problem solving meetings	Coffee break	Training groups
	Written	Agenda	Suggestions after meeting	Invitation to lunch	Organisational handbook
	Non-verbal	Pauses, silences	Seating arrangements	Meeting area conditions	Demonstration

Organisation -wide:	Oral	Meetings of department-tal heads	Strategy group meetings	Address to members of an organisation	Mass meeting
	Written	Organisation chart	Suggestion scheme	House journals	Notice board
	Non-verbal	Style of office for organisation member		House style in stationery etc.	

[Source: Weightman (1990)]

Communication systems within care services

Team Meetings

Good team meetings should:

➢ Have an agenda which is either displayed prominently within the workplace or copies provided for everyone at least a week in advance of the meeting. Many managers put a draft agenda on the notice board inviting staff to add any items they would like to be discussed.

➢ Allocate target amounts of time to each agenda item to ensure that all items are covered and that adequate time is given to each. The chair's role is to let the group know when they are getting close to the end of the time allocated for each item. Many care services have a rotating chair so that each staff member takes on this role.

➢ Be at a time and venue which means that most people can attend and contribute. The time available for team meetings can often be limited as it can be expensive to ensure that all staff are on duty at the same time and that the service is covered.

➢ Have clear boundaries which are maintained. This helps make the most of the time available for the meeting.

Handovers

These are of great value in ensuring that successive shifts have the opportunity to pass on information about the well-being of individuals receiving the service and about operational issues. They also enable the monitoring and handover of medication and any cash, thus helping to ensure that any errors can be tracked. It is a false economy to try to condense handovers into the smallest possible space between

---

shifts or to attempt to dispense with them altogether. Additionally, although it only needs to be minimal, it is good practice to keep a brief record of the handover and who was present.

<u>Supervision</u>

See chapter 56 – supervision should fulfill an important role as a communication outlet.

<u>Service user meetings</u>

These may not always be appropriate as individuals who use the service may not wish to meet to express their views or if the service is delivered to peoples homes they may not be a practical proposition. However, where they do exist, these meetings can be a good means of facilitating communication, both between service users and between staff and service users.

Documentary systems

These recognise that there may be a need to capture information and to pass it on to other members of staff. On one level these are simply the record keeping systems for the service as whole which include care plans, care notes, risk assessments and medication records. On another level there are systems whose main purpose is to promote communication within the organisation.

<u>Diary</u>

The official diary for the service enables workers and others to know what appointments have been made. In domiciliary environments it can be helpful for there to be a diary kept specifically for the individual being supported. If there is relatively unrestricted access to the diary, care should be taken to ensure that it does not contain personal and sensitive information which belongs in the care notes.

<u>Communication Book</u>

This enables messages to be passed within the team and although it can sometimes be quite informal in nature it is essential to ensure that information is passed on and to provide evidence that this has been undertaken. In some workplaces the diary is used instead of a communication book: the main principle being that there is a means of sharing information. Reviewing the communication book or its equivalent should be part of the routine for any member of staff when coming on duty and form part of the handover.

<u>Duty Rota</u>

Although a planning and administrative tool this is also a prime means for communicating to everyone the details of who will be working.

<u>Notice Boards</u>

Notice boards for staff can detract from trying to create a homely environment and in a residential home should ideally be positioned in an office or staff room if available. They may have no or limited relevance in other care settings and would obviously be inappropriate in the home of an individual receiving a domiciliary service. Notice boards for service users can feel institutionalised, but sometimes, if considered carefully and sensitively to service users' communication needs, they can provide a useful means of communicating new information.

Communication with partner organisations

Services do not exist in isolation, and social care workers need to communicate well with a wide variety of people and other organisations.

Communication needs to take into account the different kinds of relationships with each person or organisation, the expectations each has and the type of information which may be required. With all external communication, there is a general need for all workers to communicate in an accurate and timely fashion and to do so with courtesy. The manner of communication is important for a number of reasons and communication with other agencies can have profound implications in terms of services' reputation and credibility. Therefore all social care staff need to be aware of the impact they can have in representing the service professionally.

The prime business of social care is the way in which it supports and relates to people, so services will be judged by the way in which staff relate to all people who they come in contact with. A weak link in the chain of communication can leave a negative impression which can make the difference between whether or not people are prepared to deal more with that service in the future.

When social care workers communicate with others outside their organisation, it is important to maintain an awareness of the impression which can be created of a service. There are, three main reasons for doing so:

➢ to maintain a strong customer relationship - whether a service operates for profit, is a voluntary organisation (i.e.: not for profit and run by a management board who give their time on a voluntary basis) or is publicly funded it is important to maintain a healthy relationship with partners

➢ to fulfil contractual obligations – to individuals or to organisations which have decided to purchase a service (including service users who purchase their own care).

➢ to assist with long term planning of the service.

In Summary

Good inter-personal communication is vital in social care services. However, effective communication within and between organisations is also vital. Facilitating effective organisational communication may require social care workers to develop a different range of knowledge.

24: WRITTEN COMMUNICATION: RECORDING AND REPORTING

Written communication is of vital importance in social care work.

In 1999, a manager quoted in "Recording with Care: Inspections of Case Recording in social Services Departments" said *"My staff are good at what they do, not what they write down"* (Goldsmith 1999). Ten years ago this may well have been a comment made by many social care practitioners and a comment made by many social care practitioners and managers. However, it is now recognized that recording and reporting (writing down!) is an essential aspect of current social care practice. That said, it can sometimes feel like there is a forest of paperwork to get through.

Permanency

Perhaps the key difference between written communication and other methods of communication is that written communication is more permanent than any other form. Whilst what someone has said may be forgotten or confused what is written is permanent – it can be read time and time again perhaps for years! Written work remains "on file" for years and can therefore influence future actions etc. For this reason it is vital that written communication is a skill that staff recognise as important and a skill that staff continually try to develop.

Organisational requirements vary significantly when it comes to recording practice. However, there are some key basic principles to all social care recording practice. These are outlined in the box on page 149. Essentially there are two main areas of knowledge in terms of recording – how to record and what to record.

What To Record

One of the difficulties in record keeping is that different people may choose to record different information and what one person sees as important another may not. Some people may record too much information and others too little. Since the recording of information is so vital to effective care practice, it is important that there is consistency in <u>what</u> is recorded.

As stated, some people may record too much information. In fact this is pointless, no one will have the time to read through reams of information just to pull out one or two key points. On the other hand it is important that sufficient information is recorded so that all relevant information is shared with the team responsible for providing the individual's care and support.

One of the main problems with recording too little information is that the information given will usually focus on problems/difficulties. This will result in the recording being very negative.

Recording should always be balanced and respectful, but getting the balance right can be difficult and is a skill which needs to be developed.

To get the balance of what to record try social care workers should:

> ➤ Match what is recorded to the purpose of the record. Different records require different information. For example, a medication chart and an incident report form will require very different information to be recorded.

> ➤ Record what is important for other staff to know. In a contact sheet or a message book staff will need to record what other staff will need to know to provide the care and support an individual requires. It is important that social care staff record positive as well as negative messages. For example where a person displays aggressive behaviour, in my experience this is always recorded, but where a person displays respectful, thoughtful behaviour this is rarely recorded. This can result in a person being labelled as aggressive because of rare instances of this behaviour.

> ➤ Record information that is not held elsewhere. A great deal of information is recorded in care plans and review notes. In day to day recording staff do not need to repeat this information, they should focus on recording new information rather than repeating what is already known.

> ➤ Check with their line manager if they are unsure.

How to Record Information

Having considered *what* to record it is important to begin to explore *how* information should be recorded. Social care staff should make sure that their recording is always:

Legible

Some people's writing is very difficult to read. It doesn't matter what the quality of the information is if it cannot be easily read by others. If your handwriting is poor, slow down when you write, it may well help.

Factual

Recording should always be based solely on facts, without opinion. Where a particular record asks for opinion (which is rare) make clear that it is your opinion *"in my opinion ……..".*

Where you have observed something the record you make should include only what you have observed and not your interpretation of the information.

Keeping recording factual is vitally important, not least because your opinion might be wrong!

EXAMPLE	
Opinion Based	Factual
Mrs Holden was very depressed today.	Mrs Holden was tearful today, she didn't eat her meal and didn't join in with the afternoon group session.

These two examples show clearly the difference between factual and opinion based recording. There could be many reasons for Mrs Holden's behaviour, she may be feeling ill or may have had an argument etc .... The opinion based record tells us nothing about Mrs Holden's behaviour but in fact gives her a clinical diagnosis, which the social care worker completing the record is not qualified to do.

<u>Concise</u>

Whilst it is important to record everything that is important, recording should be as concise as possible. This means that social care staff will use less of their time in recording and it makes it more likely that the information will be read and understood by others. Remember KISS:

> **K**eep
> **I**t
> **S**hort and
> **S**traightforward

<u>Respectful</u>

It is important that the value base underpins record keeping (as it should all areas of social care work). Therefore the language used to record information is obviously important. Social care practitioners avoid recording in a way which, for example:

> labels people: *"Santokh has challenging behaviour, or, Myra is aggressive........"*

> refers to people in a childlike way: *"Moira had a big tantrum, or, Mr Antoir was really naughty..."*

Where recording is kept to factual information, recording is less likely to be disrespectful.

Correctly Presented

Different agencies will have different requirements in terms of the recording of information. Even within agencies there will be different requirements in terms of different forms of recording, but the following general rules will always apply:

> Always sign and date any recording you make

> If you make a mistake, do not use tippex. Cross out your mistake with a single line ensuring that what you wrote can still be read. Initial the error. This is important because if the records are required, for whatever purpose, in the future it is clear that they have not been falsified.

> Always attribute where the information being recorded came from. If, for example, a service users relative told you something make this clear in the records ("Soriya's mother said that Soriya had a nosebleed yesterday", rather than "Soriya had a nosebleed yesterday"). The formal term for this is giving "providence" to information.

Ensuring Effective Recording

If social care workers keep all of the factors covered in this chapter in mind when they are recording then recording is likely to be effective. One form of written communication has not yet been covered – the recording of messages. In social care, messages often need to be passed on. For example, telephone messages may need to be passed on or messages may need to be passed onto a different shift through communication books etc.

Anton a day service manager was away from the service for the morning attending a meeting. On his return he found a number of messages had been left for him. He was able to respond to all but one, which said:

"Sue phoned she wants you to call her in the next hour. It's urgent".

Anton's problems were:

➢ He knew several Sue's, a Suzanne and a Susan (who were both referred to as Sue) so he didn't know who to phone.

➢ He didn't know when "Sue" had called, he'd been out of the service for three hours so the hour might now be "up".

➢ He had no idea who had taken the message or recorded it.

Although we have not yet specifically covered message taking, the principles outlined in this chapter, if applied, will ensure effective recording of messages.

➢ Be clear (if the message taken had been clear about exactly who had phoned it would have been easier for Anton).

➢ Sign and date the message (if there is any misunderstanding the message can be checked out).

➢ Get the right balance between keeping it brief and giving sufficient detail.

It is easy to see therefore that the principles of good record keeping apply whatever the recording is.

All organisations will have their own requirements in terms of recording. However there are a number of basic principles to good recording practice:

⇔ Handwritten records should be legible and completed in black ink.

⇔ Any errors should be crossed through with a single line and initialled. What was originally written (even if it is a spelling error) should be readable.

⇔ Recording should be contemporaneous (that is written up as soon as possible after the event).

⇔ Records should be dated and where necessary timed.

⇔ Recording should be clear, concise and to the point, expanding on more complex areas.

⇔ Recording should be objective. It should not contain information about the feelings, thoughts, instincts or assumptions of the writer.

⇔ Documentation should be fact based. Where it is felt to be appropriate to include the writer's opinion, this should be made clear. The reason for and need to include opinion should have been discussed and agreed with managers.

⇔ Judgemental language must be avoided.

⇔ Records should give "Providence" – this simply means explaining where the information recorded came from.

⇔ Recording should be accessible to the people it is about (as far as possible).

⇔ Records should be shared with the individual in question.

⇔ Recording practice should be in line with agency and legal requirements (e.g.: in line with the principles of the Data Protection Act 1998).

⇔ Recording must be appropriately stored.

⇔ The rules of confidentiality always apply to all records.

In Summary

It is not unusual for people working in social care to say that too much time is spent on paperwork. This implies that 'paperwork' is a pointless task. However, recording is a vital aspect of modern social care practice. Therefore, written communication is a skill which all social care staff need to develop.

Recording should be completed according to agreed organisational practices, and should be conducted in a way which is respectful to each service user.

SECTION D: SAFEGUARDING

Safeguarding service users from abuse and neglect is a fundamental aspect of effective social care practice. Safeguarding builds on the knowledge covered in previous sections. For example, recent Government publications in relation to safeguarding adults highlight how safeguarding needs to build on empowerment, person centred practices, effective communication and strong multi-agency and inclusive partnership working (Department of Health 2009).

This section will cover some of the key knowledge required for effective practice in safeguarding adults.

25: UNDERSTANDING ABUSE

Understanding abuse and neglect is the first step in effective safeguarding. All social care staff need to develop their understanding in this area for various reasons, including the following:

➢ Service users have a fundamental right to be free from abuse and the fear of abuse

➢ Care staff involved in intimate aspects of a person's life are in a position to identify suspicions of abuse

➢ Care staff may be part of a support package and care plan designed to monitor and reduce the risk of abuse

➢ Disturbingly, much abuse actually stems from the care environment itself. Professional care workers need to be aware and be able to respond to the complex reasons for this

The Right to Freedom from FEAR

Perhaps because of the distasteful nature of abuse, many people do not recognise the extent of abuse in the lives of vulnerable adults. Indeed, the opening comments of the House of Commons Health Committee report on elder abuse begins by stating that *"abuse of older people is a hidden and often ignored problem in society."* (House of Commons 2004).

What is Abuse?

Abuse has been defined as:

➢ *"The violation of an individual's rights which results in injury and/or emotional suffering………… It can be an act against a person or neglect of their needs; and usually involves someone misusing the power they have over someone who is vulnerable." (Bailey 1998)*

➢ *"Abuse may consist of a single act or repeated acts. It may be physical, verbal or psychological, it may be an act of neglect or an omission to act, or it may occur when a vulnerable person is persuaded to enter into a financial or sexual transaction to which he or she has not consented, or cannot consent. Abuse can occur in any relationship and may result in significant harm to, or exploitation of, the person subjected to it". (Department of Health 2000)*

➢ *"A single or repeated act or lack of appropriate action, occurring within any relationship where there is an expectation of trust which causes harm or distress." (Action on Elder Abuse 2006)*

So it can be seen that the term abuse can be defined in many ways. The government have highlighted this in their guidance document 'No Secrets'. However, they say that the starting point for any definition should be:

> "Abuse is a violation of an individual's human rights and civil rights by any other person or persons." (Department of Health 2000)

Abuse can take many forms and these are covered in detail later in this section. However, the key thing to remember is that any violation of a person's rights can constitute abuse. Abuse can therefore range from speaking disrespectfully to a service user to a physical or sexual assault. It is vital to remember that poor care practice can constitute abusive care practice.

The Impact of Abuse

Abuse will have a unique impact for every individual. To understand the impact of abuse, it can be helpful to consider the consequences of abuse in two related areas, that is, the physical consequences and the emotional consequences.

The physical consequences of abuse will be dependant upon factors such as the physical needs of the victim. For example, an assault on a person with brittle bones will have different consequences than for someone with a heart condition. There are also long and short term consequences to consider. A broken bone may cause immediate pain and distress, but the longer term impact may be loss of life skills and independence.

The emotional impact of abuse may result in negative feelings such as fear, anxiety, distress etc… In the long term, these can develop into feelings of helplessness, poor self-esteem and hopelessness and ultimately clinical depression.

How each individual reacts to abuse will depend upon various factors, which include:

➢ Personal coping mechanisms

➢ Perceived likelihood of further abuse

➢ Personal history and previous experiences

➢ Type of abuse

➢ Dependency on the abuser

➢ Relationship to the abuser

➢ Ability to contact help

➢ Perceived options in the situation

Understanding the impact of abuse is helpful in supporting victims, and in providing insight into reasons why victims may behave in certain ways. For example, if a family member or a professional has abused a vulnerable person, it may be more difficult for the person to form a trusting relationship as trust has been betrayed at a fundamental level.

A person who has been subject to prolonged abuse may have their coping mechanisms and self esteem damaged. This can sometimes make it very difficult for victims to request help or recognise that there are alternatives to the situation that they are in.

Understanding the impact of abuse can play an important role in assisting recognition. For example, physical abuse may be hidden beneath layers of clothing, but the emotional impact of stress and anxiety may not.

Research on the impact of abuse on service users has confirmed how destructive it can be. Rushton et al (2000) drew on social workers' perceptions of the effect on the service user. Some of the service users were older people who had confusion. The social workers said that, in respect of some of these people, there was no noticeable effect. This illustrates that abusers picked on very vulnerable people. Most service users were reported to be distressed or very distressed by their experience of abuse.

Barber et al (2000) drew on the experiences of women with learning disabilities who had been sexually abused and concluded that it resulted in poor self image, reduced coping skills and for some, the onset of inappropriate sexual behaviour. More forcefully, O'Callaghan et al (2003) related how people with severe learning disabilities who had been subjected to abuse displayed behaviours consistent with post traumatic stress disorder. The service users lost all confidence and they became very introverted. In various ways they started to display behaviours that challenged services. O'Callaghan et al (2003) also indicated how family members were also profoundly affected by the realisation that their loved one had been abused.

Consistent with earlier research, O'Callaghan et al (2003) commented that the counselling provided to service users did not meet their needs.

What do we Know About Abuse?

Our understanding of the abuse of vulnerable adults is far from complete. However, there is a growing body of research evidence which provides us with some knowledge:

➢ The UK Study of Abuse and Neglect of Older People (O'Keeffe et al 2007), which was commissioned by Comic Relief and the Department of Health reported that:

"Overall, 2.6% of people aged 66 and over living in private households reported that they had experienced mistreatment involving a family member, close friend or care worker (i.e. those in a traditional expectation of trust relationship) during the past year... When the one year prevalence of mistreatment is broadened to include incidents involving neighbours and acquaintances, the overall prevalence increases from 2.6% to 4.0%. This would give a figure of approximately 342,400 older people subject to some form of mistreatment."

(O'Keeffe et al 2007: 3)

This is likely to be an under-estimate because the study did not include people with dementia or those living in residential care.

This study also reported that:

- Neglect is the most prevalent form of abuse of older people in the UK (1.1% of the population)

- Women were more likely to experience mistreatment than men, and women over 85 were the most vulnerable people

- People who had the most significant health conditions were more likely to experience abuse

- 51% of abusers were the person's partner, 49% another person in the family, 13% a care worker, and 5%a close friend. The study did not examine abuse by strangers.

- Those people who were in contact with services were most likely to experience abuse, particularly financial abuse

Crosby et al (2008) report that:

"Indications are that 60–80 per cent of financial abuse takes place in the home and 15–20 per cent in residential care. Over 50 per cent of financial abuse is by a grown-up son or daughter and nearly 70 per cent by a family member. However, since the proportion of financial abuse carried out by family members is comparable to the proportion of financial help given by family members, family members should not be viewed as less trustworthy than other helpers."

(Crosby et al 2008: 9)

Financial abuse in residential settings could either be perpetrated by residents or staff. Residential services need firm policies to address the need for residents' finances to be properly safeguarded.

➢ There is evidence of excessive use of restraint across a range of care services (Bright, 2001). Included in the meaning of excessive restraint is the "chemical cosh", where medication is used to control behaviour in a manner that has no therapeutic justification. Other examples include keeping people in beds that have cot-sides, using furniture to inhibit movement, removing walking aids, etc (Bright 2001).

➢ Many service users suffer multiple abuse (e.g. physical abuse and financial abuse). Amongst older people one study (Brown and Stein, 2000) reported that of all cases of abuse reported:

- 29% involved multiple abuse
- 28% involved physical abuse
- 17% involved financial abuse
- 6% involved sexual abuse

In the same study of all adults with a learning disability where there were concerns of abuse:

- 34% involved physical abuse
- 34% involved sexual abuse
- 13% involved multiple abuse
- 5% involved financial abuse

Of all referrals relating to abuse 6% of them related to adults who had a mental health or alcohol problem and another 6% to adults with a physical disability (Brown and Stein, 2000).

➢ Research by Brown et al (1995) over a four year period clearly showed that most abuse is brought to light through disclosure – the service user saying they are being abused. This emphasises the need to take the service user seriously. It also highlights the additional vulnerability of service users who may not be able to communicate verbally.

 In Summary

Perhaps because of the distasteful nature of abuse, many people deny the extent of abuse in the lives of vulnerable adults. However, it is vital that care workers understand the nature of abuse and have knowledge about the extent of abuse, to ensure that they can effectively identify situations where it may occur. Understanding abuse and following safe care principles will ensure that the likelihood of abuse occurring is minimised.

26: SAFEGUARDING ADULTS AT RISK OF ABUSE: THE LEGAL BASIS

There is a clear and extensive legal framework surrounding child protection. However, the legal basis for safeguarding adults from abuse is much less developed.

The picture is very different across the United Kingdom. Scotland is the country which is furthest ahead since it passed the Adult Support and Protection Act in 2007. This placed adult protection on a statutory basis. In England and Wales, the picture is much more patchy, where there is statutory guidance on the development and implementation of policies and procedures for the protection of adults at risk of abuse (in England this is called "No Secrets" and was published by the Department of Health and the Home Office in 2000; the Welsh Guidance was published by the Welsh Assembly and the Home Office in the same year and is called "In Safe Hands"). At the time of writing, reviews of these documents have been completed and the relevant Government responses are awaited.

The review of "No Secrets" involved 12,000 people and more than 68% of these supported safeguarding legislation. However, there were also arguments against legislation for safeguarding adults, including:

➤ much has been achieved in adult safeguarding without legislation and improvements are felt to be likely to continue

➤ legislation will not necessarily lead to adult safeguarding becoming a priority

➤ the experience in Scotland should be studied over some years before conclusions are drawn

➤ some of the possible new legislative powers would extend the Government's power over peoples lives in a dangerous way

➤ the most effective safeguarding was when it became part of mainstream activity and was effectively part of the choice agenda

(Department of Health 2009: 7)

Whilst it is likely that at some point in the future there will be clearer legislation about safeguarding adults, at present there is very much a "patchwork quilt" effect to legislation which might mean that social care workers need a level of understanding of Acts such as:

➤ *Safeguarding Vulnerable Groups Act 2006*
Covers the system for vetting people who work with children and vulnerable adults in England and Wales.

➤ *Protection of Vulnerable Groups (Scotland) Act 2007*
Covers the system for vetting people who work with children and vulnerable adults in Scotland.

➤ *Mental Capacity Act 2005*
Covers the principles and practices for working with adults who do not have decision making capacity in England and Wales. Also introduces a new criminal offence of ill-treatment or wilful neglect.

➤ *Family Law Act 1996 and Domestic Violence Crime and Victims Act 2004*
Covers protection from domestic abuse in England and Wales.

➤ *Adult Support and Protection (Scotland) Act 2007 and Protection from Abuse (Scotland) Act 2001*

Cover the legal framework for Adult Protection in Scotland.

> *Adults with Incapacity (Scotland) Act 2000*
> Covers the principles and powers for working with adults with incapacity in Scotland

More information about this legislation and other relevant legislation can be found in:

> Social Care and the Law: An NVQ Related Reference Guide for Direct Care Staff (England and Wales)

or

> Social Care and the Law in Scotland: An SVQ Related Reference Guide for Direct Care Staff (Scotland)

One piece of legislation which is United Kingdom wide and is very relevant to safeguarding practice is the Public Interest Disclosure Act 1998.

Public Interest Disclosure Act 1998

This is often referred to as the "whistle-blowers" legislation. It was implemented in July 1999. This Act gives significant statutory protection to employees who disclose malpractice reasonably and responsibly in the public interest and are victimised as a result. If an employee is victimised or dismissed for this disclosure they can make a claim for compensation to an industrial tribunal. There is no cap to the amount that can be awarded.

Whilst it is not a statutory requirement, there is an expectation that organisations will establish their own whistle blowing policy and guidelines. These guidelines should:

> clearly indicate how staff can raise concerns about malpractice

> make a clear organisational commitment to take concerns seriously and to protect people from victimisation

> designate a senior manager with specific responsibility for addressing concerns in confidence which need to be handled outside the usual management-chain

Staff receive the full protection of the Act if they seek to disclose malpractice responsibly e.g.: by following the organisation's whistle-blowing policy/guidelines.

If a member of staff goes to the media or police first they only receive the statutory protection if certain conditions are met.

Policies and Procedures

All organisations providing social care services should have a policy relating specifically to safeguarding vulnerable adults – these may be referred to as POVA (protection of vulnerable adults) policies or safeguarding procedures. Social care staff must ensure that they are familiar with the policies which relate to their working environment.

What Do The Codes of Practice Say?

The Code of Practice for *social care workers* places a responsibility on each member of staff:

- Not to abuse, neglect or exploit service users or form inappropriate personal relationships with them

- Not to discriminate or condone discrimination

- To challenge and report dangerous, abusive, discriminatory or exploitative behaviour

The code of practice for *employers* lays down clear responsibilities:

- To have clear written policies in operation to deal with and report dangerous, discriminatory or exploitative behaviour

- To have policies to minimise the risk of violence or trauma

- To provide the necessary support for workers to follow their own Code of Practice

In Summary

The legal basis for safeguarding adults at risk of harm and abuse is much less well developed than the framework surrounding child protection. In many ways this is only right in that, *"safeguarding adults is not like child protection. Adults do not want to be treated like children and do not want a system that was designed for children"* (Department of Health 2009:6). What it does mean however is that social care staff need to ensure that they are fully familiar with local policies, procedures and protocols and that they follow these. Legal advice should be sought where necessary.

The Social Care Codes of Practice outline clear responsibilities around safeguarding, particularly in terms of the need for thorough policies and professional boundaries.

27: WHO IS AT RISK OF ABUSE?

The short answer to this question is – everyone, but of course there is much more complexity to the answer than this. Media coverage of abuse tends to focus mainly on the abuse of children. However, it is vital to remember that adults are also open to abuse, with some people being more at risk than others.

The broad definition of a 'vulnerable adult', first referred to in the 1997 Consultation Paper "Who Decides?" issued by the Lord Chancellor's Department, is a person:

"who is or may be in need of community care services by reason of mental or other disability, age or illness; and who is or may be unable to take care of him or herself, or unable to protect him or herself against significant harm or exploitation."

The recent Government Review of "No Secrets" involved 12,000 people. 90% of respondents felt that the definition of a "vulnerable adult" needed to be revised and there was a great deal of support for replacing the term "vulnerable adult" with "person at risk." (Department of Health 2009: 8)

It is therefore likely that in coming months references to vulnerable adults will become less common. Nevertheless, there is a clear agreement that some adults are more at risk of (or vulnerable to) abuse than others.

"Safeguarding Adults" published by the Association of Directors of Social Services in October 2005 identifies six aspects of people's lives which may indicate that they are more at risk of abuse:

➢ *Social isolation and lack of inclusion*
In general the more social contacts that an individual has, the more likely it is that others will notice if something is wrong. For example, if person does not attend college other students on the course may notice that he or she is missing, as might the friends of someone who usually joins in a lunch-club or similar activity. Being a member of a social network whether at work, in leisure activities or as a member of a church congregation will make that person just a little more noticeable and increase the possibility that someone will notice if the person is not their usual self.

➢ *Dependency on others for essential needs*
This can include those who require support with shopping, personal care, finances and mobility and therefore includes the majority of those make use of social care services. Paid support staff are sometimes the only people in the lives of service users and although most staff working in the social care field are well-intentioned, there are others who may take the opportunity to abuse their privileged access.

➢ *Poor quality policies and information*
Inadequate policies and procedures can leave individuals unsure about what to do if they are the victim of abuse or suspect that it is occurring to others. This can result in a time delay before action is taken and, in the worst scenario, to nothing being done to protect the person. One of the most shocking aspects of dealing with abuse is that serial abusers will deliberately seek out organisations which they see as not having strong policies and procedures to protect adults at risk.

➢ *Low standards becoming the norm*
This has happened historically in institutional services for people with learning disabilities, mental health problems and some services for older people and occurs

where people lose sight of what they should regard as acceptable and what they would not tolerate for themselves and their loved ones. Accepting low standards as the norm can happen where the setting is geographically or socially isolated as was the case with long-stay hospitals. However, it can also be the case where resources are under strain case where there are staff shortages or where training has not been adequate.

➢ *Domestic abuse being seen as the norm*
Social care workers may provide services to individuals in homes which they share with their families and may become aware of concerns around domestic abuse. As more services are provided to people in their own homes, social care workers may become more aware of behaviour within the home such as bullying. This behaviour may have become accepted within the family but would be unacceptable within any other setting. It remains unacceptable in the home too and should be confronted as it would elsewhere. The Home Office policy document, "Domestic Violence: Break the Chain: Multi Agency Guidance for Addressing Domestic Violence" (2000), makes the point that violent, brutal or threatening behaviour within the home is as serious as a violent assault by a stranger.

➢ *An unhealthy power balance*
As covered in chapter 3, social care workers are in a position of significant power over people who use services. Where there is a lack of understanding of power or a deliberate misuse of this power, there is likely to be an abuse of power.

Other factors can also increase people's vulnerability to abuse. These might include issues surrounding:

Loss and Change

People may also be particularly at risk at certain stages of their lives because of the impact of loss or change, such as:

➢ the onset of mental health problems

➢ acquiring a disability

➢ increasing frailty due to the ageing process

➢ inability of family members to continue to provide care for the person

Low Self Esteem

Self esteem is really the way in which we view ourselves. Where a person is described as having a low self esteem or poor self image it basically means they "feel bad" about themselves. Where someone has a "healthy" self esteem it means that they are confident and "feel good" about themselves. Even though self esteem is about our psychological well being it can have a profound effect on our physical health.

It is important that care staff support service users to feel good about themselves. People in receipt of care and support are more likely to have a poor self image and self esteem and they may feel dependent and even worthless. Negative feelings like these will then have a negative impact on a person's health and well being. It will also leave people much more at risk of abuse and self harm.

Communication Differences

Where there are significant challenges in terms of communication different risks of abuse increase. For example, a person with limited or no verbal communication may be especially vulnerable to abuse, not least because they may lack the means to disclose the abuse. This reinforces the need to listen to more than words and to develop effective methods of communication wherever there are differences in communication.

In Summary

Everyone who is in receipt of care services is potentially vulnerable to abuse, although some people are more at risk than others.

28: FORMS OF ABUSE

Abuse is often divided into different forms or types. However, these categories are not exclusive. For example, rape is a physical assault as well as a sexual assault.

A great deal of abuse is accompanied by emotional abuse (though this can also occur in isolation). For this reason, we begin with a closer look at emotional abuse.

Emotional Abuse

This includes the use of words and actions as weapons against a vulnerable adult that does not necessarily encompass physical harm. Examples of emotional abuse include racist or sexist taunts and discrimination, shouting, abusive language, belittling, mocking, threatening and bullying.

Emotional abuse can also include removing sources of comfort and reassurance, encouraging disruption and unhappiness in a person's life or preventing participation in activities that are important to social and emotional well-being.

<u>Examples</u>

➢ Lena Onsola is a resident in a social services residential home for older people. Lena is gay, though her partner is now deceased. A number of the female care staff are unhappy about helping Lena with her personal care. When they do assist her, they make their dislike clear with "jokey" comments such as "No wonder you couldn't find a man with a body like that" and "Don't get excited when I wash you, you're not my type".

➢ Prathibha is the only black service user attending a day service for people with learning disabilities. During lunchtimes, when staff are busy, a number of service users call Prathibha a "dirty cow" and refuse to sit with her to eat their meals.

➢ Ralph has a diagnosis of schizophrenia. He lives independently on a local housing estate. Other residents on the estate call him "mad" and "mental" and cross the road when they see him.

POTENTIAL INDICATORS OF EMOTIONAL ABUSE

➢ Anxiety
➢ Sleeplessness
➢ Reluctance to get up
➢ Withdrawal and self isolation
➢ Anger
➢ Distress/tearfulness
➢ Fears and phobias
➢ Low self esteem
➢ Comforting behaviour such as rocking
➢ Weight loss or gain
➢ Anti-social/destructive behaviour
➢ Sudden changes in behaviour

Physical Abuse

Physical abuse includes any action that causes or is intended to cause physical harm to another. For example, kicking, punching, pushing, slapping, scalding, burning, biting. Most physical abuse would come within the remit of criminal law. However, particularly when dealing with vulnerable people, "rough handling" and deliberately poor administration of care tasks (such as lack of physical sensitivity when handling dressings, catheters, and lack of sensitivity and concern when helping someone to eat etc.) would also constitute physical abuse.

Examples

➢ Mary has been caring for her mother Elsie for some time and is finding this increasingly stressful. Elsie is becoming more confused and has a tendency to repeat the same questions again and again. Mary has hit Elsie several times to try and stop Elsie asking questions.

➢ Varsha dislikes certain food, so she often keeps her mouth closed when staff are trying to assist her to eat her meals. Staff get concerned about Varsha not eating and loose patience with her. They force food into her mouth, using their hands and cutlery to prise open her mouth.

POTENTIAL INDICATORS OF PHYSICAL ABUSE

➢ Various injuries which may not tally with the explanation given
➢ Repeated injuries
➢ Explanations for injuries that change over time, or are over elaborate
➢ Physical evidence of injuries, bruises etc. which have been acquired at different points in time
➢ Injuries such as cigarette burns, finger tip bruising or bites
➢ Inappropriate clothing intended to cover injuries
➢ Unwillingness to undress or show parts of the body where there may be injury
➢ Reaction to a particular person or people of a particular gender etc.
➢ Changes in appetite and weight
➢ Anxiety
➢ Agitation
➢ Distress/tearfulness

Sexual Abuse

Sexual abuse includes any sexual act carried out against a person's wishes, or when that person is unable to consent. This would include rape, touching sexual parts of the body, inserting objects into sexual organs, forcing the person to perform sexual acts, filming or photographing a person against their will for sexual purposes.

Sexual abuse can be categorised into contact and non contact abuse:

➢ Non contact sexual abuse can include any sexual abuse where physical contact does not take place e.g. sexual harassment, teasing, the taking of photos, the showing of pornography against a person's will etc.

➢ Contact sexual abuse is abuse where physical contact takes place: e.g. touching of the breast, genitals, mouth etc., masturbation, of one or both persons, penetration of the mouth, vagina or anus by a penis or other object.

Examples

➢ Mrs Wegierska was widowed several years ago. She moved into a residential service shortly after the first signs of confusion were noticed. In the service is another resident Mr. Astbury. Mrs Wegierska has been calling Mr Astbury her husband. Recently Mr Astbury has been taking Mrs Wegierska into his bedroom and having sex with her. Mrs Wegierska thinks Mr Astbury is her husband. She is not able to consent to this contact.

➢ Mark, a support worker, forces Christina who has a learning disability to look at pornographic magazines.

➢ Alan is a mental health support worker. When Eva, a service user, becomes upset and starts to cry, Alan takes advantage of the situation and tells her she'll feel better if she has sex with him.

POTENTIAL INDICATORS OF SEXUAL ABUSE

➢ Injuries to genital areas or breasts that do not tally with explanations given
➢ Repeated injury to the above
➢ Urine or genital infections
➢ Unexplained injury or bleeding from anus or genitals
➢ Unexplained discomfort or unwillingness to urinate or defecate
➢ Overly sexualised behaviour
➢ Sexually explicit drawings/art work
➢ Sudden, unexpected, behaviour changes
➢ Avoidance of a certain person/people
➢ Low self esteem
➢ Difficulties in relationships
➢ Changes in eating patterns

Financial Abuse

This includes all issues around the misuse of finances, property or belongings of a person, including:

➢ Robbery and fraud

➢ Spending of allowances or savings of a person against their will, or without their knowledge or informed consent

➢ Misleading people about how the money will be spent, or the relevance of expenditure

➢ Disposing of property against a person's will or without a person's knowledge

➢ Displacing a person from their property

Examples

➢ Shortly before Christmas, Lena a care assistant, agrees to go shopping for several residents to get their Christmas presents. She buys cheap presents for the residents and uses some of their money to do her own shopping.

➢ Susan lives at home with her parents. She has learning disabilities and receives a variety of benefits. Susan's parents use this money for themselves and provide very little for Susan, who never has any money.

POTENTIAL INDICATORS OF FINANCIAL ABUSE

➢ Unexplained withdrawals from savings accounts
➢ Lack of finances to pay bills
➢ Unexplained arrears or debts
➢ Possessions going missing or being sold
➢ Sudden and unexplained change in lifestyle
➢ Sudden and unexplained withdrawal of money from accounts
➢ Unusual interest by another in the individual's finances

Institutional Abuse

Any of the types of abuse described can and do occur within institutions. However, institutional abuse itself refers to the abusive practices and behaviours that can occur on a widespread basis within an institution, and that are considered "acceptable". Examples of institutional abuse include:

➢ Uniform treatment of all service users

➢ Possessions and clothes being used by anyone in the service

➢ Service users forced to follow routines that benefit the service and not the service user, e.g.: set bed times

➢ Expectations that staff can impose punishments or "withhold privileges"

Example

Monica (a care assistant) has already assisted Mr Patel to have a shave using his electric razor and he has gone to have his breakfast. Monica then goes to support first Mr Mathers and then Mr Gardner. Monica takes Mr Patel's electric razor and shaves both men before putting it back in Mr Patel's room. This is common practice in the service as it saves time.

POTENTIAL INDICATORS OF INSTITUTIONAL ABUSE

➢ Anxiety
➢ Loss of confidence
➢ Submissiveness
➢ Low self esteem
➢ Weight loss, changes in appetite etc.
➢ Difficulty in / anxiety about making independent decisions

Neglect

Neglect can be defined as failing to attend to the key needs of people who are dependent upon others. Neglect can be divided into two types, direct and indirect. Direct neglect is when a person knowingly and deliberately withholds something which should meet a person's essential needs. Indirect neglect is where the perpetrator does not actively mean to cause harm, but is neglectful for other reasons. For example, this could be due to lack of information about the implications of their actions, or a lack of awareness about alternative means of addressing an issue. People can also neglect themselves – which is covered in more detail in chapter 29.

Examples

➢ Mrs Roberts is a frail older woman. Mrs Roberts is incontinent and needs assistance during the night to ensure she is comfortable. Following a change of staffing the night care assistant feels she needs to concentrate on the laundry and other domestic chores. The night care assistant leaves Mrs Roberts all night.

➢ Fred is becoming doubly incontinent at night. His daughter feels that this is avoidable. To try and manage the situation, she refuses to give Fred anything to eat or drink from 4.00 in the afternoon until the following morning.

POTENTIAL INDICATORS OF NEGLECT

➢ Anxiety
➢ Physical appearance of neglect and unkemptness
➢ Weight loss
➢ Prone to illness due to lack of warmth or nutrition
➢ Submissiveness / lack of confidence
➢ Low self esteem

Medication Abuse

The manipulation of medication provides many opportunities for abuse. This can include withholding key medication or giving someone too much medication. Medication abuse can mean that medical conditions do not respond to treatment, a lack of pain relief, drowsiness or poisoning.

Example

Mr Nazim is considered by staff to be always complaining. There have been various arguments with staff and recently they have occurred late in the evening. Mr Nazim takes various tablets prescribed for him. He also has some sleeping tablets that are PRN and can be taken if he requires. The sleep-in staff decide to give him the sleeping tablets on a regular basis (at the same time as he takes his early evening medication) to make sure that he doesn't "cause trouble".

POTENTIAL INDICATORS OF MEDICATION ABUSE

➢ Medical conditions not responding to treatment
➢ Chronic medical conditions failing to stabilise
➢ Lack of pain relief
➢ Over medication may result in drowsiness, or poisoning

In Summary

Abuse is often divided into different forms or types. Abuse can be physical, emotional, financial, sexual and institutional. Neglect and misuse of medication also constitute abuse. Abuse is almost always related to an abuse or misuse of power.

29: UNDERSTANDING SELF NEGLECT AND SELF HARM

It is not uncommon for people receiving care services to neglect or harm themselves. There can be a whole host of reasons for this as we will cover. Understanding this area is important for care staff for a variety of reasons, including the following:

➢ Care staff are likely to be a part of a support package. Where a person is neglectful of themselves or engages in self harm this is likely to be addressed to some extent in the person's care plan. To play an active role in such a care plan staff should have an understanding of this area.

➢ Care staff can be uncertain about their role in responding to self neglect and self harm. Having an increased understanding can help with this.

Self neglect and self harm are behaviours that are widely seen in a negative light. This is understandable. However, it is very important that staff do not convey negative or judgemental attitudes to service users who self neglect or self harm.

What is Self Neglect?

Whilst self neglect is different from a situation where a service user experiences neglect by a carer or staff team it is arguably linked in many ways - research evidence indicates that in all cases of active abuse almost a half of them also involve the service user self neglecting. In cases where a service user was neglected by carers or staff teams McCuren and Jenkins (1992) found that almost two thirds of the service users also neglected themselves.

This is borne out in Mowlam et al's (2007) study into the effects of abuse and neglect of older people. They report that self harm and self neglect may be a response to the emotional distress, decrease in confidence, clinical depression, suicidal thought, social isolation and loss of independence which abuse can engender in the victim. Critically, respondents in their study usually experienced a combination of impacts (2007:44) and they found that people who experienced long term abuse were more likely to experience self harm and self neglect, as well as worsening physical health as a result of the abuse.

There are a whole range of behaviours that constitute self neglect. These include:

➢ Not eating adequately
➢ Not attending to personal hygiene tasks (e.g.: not using the toilet appropriately, not bathing or washing)
➢ Not changing clothing
➢ Not taking medication

    (This list is not exhaustive)

Why Does Self Neglect Occur?

There are many reasons that people neglect themselves. These can include:

➢ Depression – people see no point in caring for themselves

➢ Low self esteem – people can have a poor view of themselves and therefore see no reason to care for themselves

➢ Lack of motivation – people may have little to look forward to

➢ Abuse – self neglect may be a sign that a person has been abused

➢ Control – if people have little control over their life they may only be able to control their food intake, their personal hygiene etc. and may therefore choose to exert their control by not caring for themselves

➢ Mental health problems at that time

➢ Confusion (possibly a temporary state) or dementia

➢ Living alone and being isolated

➢ Having alcohol or drug problems

➢ Decreased physical abilities resulting in a loss of motivation

There are many dilemmas surrounding self neglect. Since people have a right to make choices, care staff may allow a person to neglect themselves. However, staff have their "duty of care" to consider and therefore need to address self neglect. Where there are concerns of self neglect, staff should discuss these as soon as possible with their line manager and strategies will need to be devised to deal with the neglect.

Self Harm

What is Self Harm?

The term "self harm" is an umbrella term for a number of behaviours, which might be used as coping mechanisms to deal with psychological pain and expressing difficult experiences. In general, self harm can be seen as an action by an individual that results in physical harm or that has an adverse impact on their own health or wellbeing. The following can be described as self harmful:

➢ self injury

➢ self poisoning (e.g.: overdose)

➢ eating disorders

➢ alcohol and substance misuse

➢ burning

➢ self punching

➢ engaging in sedually dangerous behaviour

➢ 'reckless' behaviour (without due regard for safety)

➢ Over exercising

In the general population it is arguable that behaviours such as self-cutting are more common than is actually reported. Individuals who engage in self harm make it clear they distinguish between self harm and attempting suicide.

However, there are other examples of self harm that, to one extent or another, are socially accepted. These include consumption of alcohol that results in health problems as well as the use of drugs, whether prescribed or illegal, which result in health problems.

Why do People Self Harm?

The reasons why any one individual will engage in self harm are complex and unique to each individual. The reasons for self harming behaviours (which can be of concern to social care professionals) cannot be glibly explained by use of the term "attention seeking". When the self injurious behaviour is engaged in away from staff or relatives the individual will often seek to conceal the behaviour.

A more useful way to view self harm is to see it as the way by which a person gives physical expression to their own sense of pain, hurt or bewilderment.

It is as if a person's sense of emotional hurt, (be it rejection, violation, abuse or other experiences) is so great and the pain is so real, that the person can only comprehend it if there is a physical origin. Put another way, the creation of a physical source of pain is a sign and symbol of the emotional hurt and pain that the individual is experiencing.

In some cases there may be a metabolic origin for the self injury (due to chemical imbalances in the brain e.g.: serotonin in the neurotransmitters). There are a small number of rare syndromes where self injury is often reported e.g.: Rett Syndrome. In these cases the origin of the self injurious behaviour could again be metabolic.

Research indicates six main reasons why people engage in self harm:

1. Relief of feelings.

➤ To bring relief from tension and stress, like a safety valve.

➤ Freeing unwanted and distressing feelings – e.g.: grief.

➤ To feel clean.

➤ To block painful thoughts, memories and worries.

➤ To bring physical pain in order to counteract the emotional pain.

➤ To express feelings of anger.

2. Self punishment.

➤ Having the need to punish themselves due to feeling of self hatred.
  "The badness I feel becomes unbearable. I can't take it any more so I cut. The relief is instant. It's like I've got what I deserve. The badness drains away."

3. To Gain Control.

➤ To gain some control over their own lives.

➤ Getting out of a difficult situation for a while.

➤ To prevent worse things happening.
  "It's like a control thing. How deep, how often, where I cut – it's all down to me. It's my body and I'll decide what to do with it."

4. As a means of communication.

➤ To demonstrate an outward sign of their inner distress.

➤ Trying to communicate when thoughts and feelings cannot be verbalised.

5. As a form of comfort.

➤ Creating a "haven" – a situation of comfort and security, being cared for.
  "I like looking after my cuts. It's the one time I can be really nice to myself. Then I curl up in bed and just snuggle down and go to sleep."

6. In order to feel "real" or "alive".

(Wilkins, 1995. Arnold, 1995. Base et al 1988).

Responding to Self Neglect and Self Harm

Reducing the risk of self neglect is based upon empowering individuals and promoting a positive self image and self esteem. Where people feel good about themselves they are much more likely to take care of themselves.

In response to self harm staff teams need to be positive to the individual and develop a positive care plan. This care plan should be developed by a multi-disciplinary team since there will be health issues related to any individual who engages in self harm.

The level of assertive action will be dependent on the person's situation and their own outlook and personality. Some individuals can be supported so that they stop engaging in self injurious behaviour. Others may well continue to engage in it, but through support the behaviour can be self managed so that it does not adversely affect other aspects of their life and lifestyle. This approach is sometimes referred to as harm minimisation.

The Playfield Institute and the Scottish Government working with a range of other organisations have developed some useful guidance on responding to self harm. Whilst this is designed for staff working with young people the advice which is summarised in the following points can be usefully employed in working with people of all ages:

<u>What you can do</u>

➤ It is always advisable to seek the advice of a mental health specialist if you discover a person is self harming.

➤ Listening and caring is the most important thing you can do to help. It might not seem much, but showing that you want to know and understand can make a lot of difference.

➤ Seeing the person behind the self harm is important to show that you care about the whole person and not just the self harm.

➤ Accepting mixed feelings is very helpful. The person might hate their self harm, even though they might need it. It helps the person a lot if you accept all of these changing and conflicting feelings.

➤ Help the person find further support. They may need help in addition to what you can give – you can support and encourage them in finding this.

➤ Show concern for the person's injuries. By offering the same compassion and respect you would show for any other injury, you are showing the person that their body is worth caring about.

➤ It is important to recognise how hard it may be for the person to talk to you. It may take a lot of courage for a person to discuss their self harm and their feelings and it may be difficult for them to put things into words. Gentle, patient encouragement can help.

➤ Help the person find alternatives to self harm. Some people find it helpful to develop a list of alternatives to their self harm. Young people who have self harmed have said that their most successful alternatives are:

- Hitting a punch bag to vent anger and frustration

- Hitting pillows or cushions and having a good scream

- Going outdoors for a walk

- Any form of physical exercise

- Writing down thoughts and feelings on paper and possibly ripping them up

- Keeping a diary

- Calling and talking to a friend

- Creative alternatives, like art

- Looking at self help websites

- Using a pen to draw on their skin in the place they might usually cut

- Holding an ice cube against their skin instead of cutting

What not to do

➤ Don't "tell the person off" or punish them in some way. This can make the person feel even worse, so could lead to more self injury.

➤ Don't blame the person for your shock and upset. You have a right to feel these things but it will not help if you make the person feel guilty about it.

➤ Don't jump in with assumptions about why the person is self harming. Different people have different reasons and it is best to let the person tell you why they do it.

➤ Don't avoid talking about it. Avoiding talking about it won't make the self harm go away, but will leave the person feeling very alone.

➤ Don't try to force them to stop self harming. Doing things like hiding razor blades or constantly watching the person doesn't work and is likely to lead to harming in secret, which can be more dangerous.

➤ Don't ask a person to promise not to self harm. This will not work, but is likely to put a lot of emotional pressure on the person and can set them up to feel guilty.

➤ Don't treat the person as mad or incapable. This takes away their self respect and ignores their capabilities and strengths.

➤ Panicking and overreacting can be very frightening for the person. It is better to try and stay calm and take time to discuss with them what should be done next.

(Playfield Institute et al 2008)

In Summary

Safeguarding adults and having an understanding of self neglect and self harm are linked in a number of ways. Clearly in safeguarding adults and promoting their well being, social care staff need to work to reduce the incidence of self harm. It is also clear from research that self harm and self neglect may be a response to abusive experiences. For these reasons, understanding self harm is often a requirement for various social care qualifications.

30: PREVENTING ABUSE

"You know, sometimes it feels like this. There I am standing by the shore of a swiftly flowing river and I hear the cry of a drowning man. So I jump into the river, put my arms around him, pull him to shore and apply artificial respiration. Just when he begins to breathe there is another cry for help. So, back in the river again, reaching, pulling, applying, breathing and then another yell. Again and again, without end, goes the sequence. You know I am so busy jumping in pulling them to shore, applying artificial respiration that I have no time to see who the hell is upstream pushing them all in".

(McKinlay 1981, cited in Pillemer and Suitor 1990)

Prevention depends on accurately identifying why abuse occurs in the first place and then establishing work based practices that aim to counter (and if possible eliminate) those factors.

White et al (2003) have sought to identify the environments and cultures that promote or at least tolerate abuse. They identify various factors that services should be conscious of and the preventative options that services need to consider:

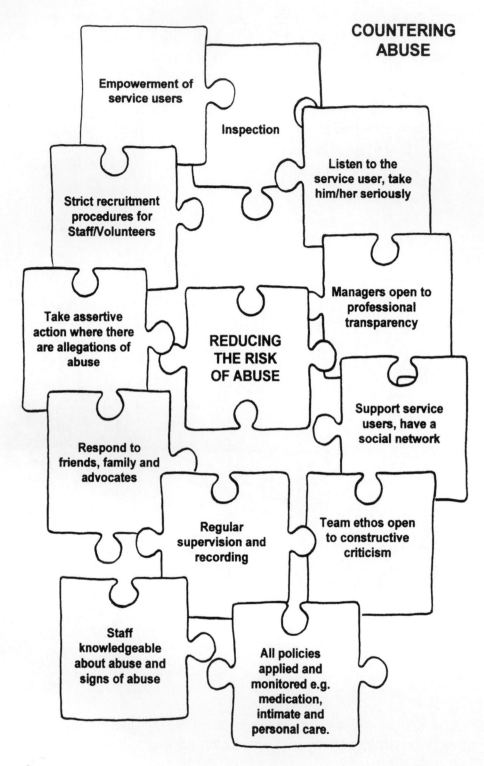

COUNTERING ABUSE

Empowerment of service users

Inspection

Listen to the service user, take him/her seriously

Strict recruitment procedures for Staff/Volunteers

Take assertive action where there are allegations of abuse

REDUCING THE RISK OF ABUSE

Managers open to professional transparency

Support service users, have a social network

Respond to friends, family and advocates

Regular supervision and recording

Team ethos open to constructive criticism

Staff knowledgeable about abuse and signs of abuse

All policies applied and monitored e.g. medication, intimate and personal care.

➤ *Management*
  Managers need to know what conditions are like on a day to day basis. Staff must receive guidance and practice needs to be monitored through good quality supervision. Managers themselves need good practice skills and must be able to recognise poor or abusive practice and be willing to challenge this.

  Where managers have an authoritarian style and are controlling of staff and service users, this may promote a culture of oppression and abuse. Therefore, managers need to cultivate a participatory, democratic style of management as part of a protection from abuse strategy.

➤ *Staff development and support*
High levels of sickness, staff turnover and resultant staff shortages are reported to contribute to vulnerability. This is because both new staff who are inexperienced and long standing team members are called on to work long hours with consequential stress.

The way in which new staff are introduced to the service, the induction they receive and availability of guidance are all important. Additionally, all staff need a sense of achievement in their work. Staff who work with service users who can be aggressive or challenging or who work with service users who engage in limited direct feedback may need additional support to sense that their work is seen and valued.

➤ *Staff attitudes and behaviours*
The importance of staff having positive professional values towards all service users has been repeatedly conveyed. This requires countering views which excuse poor practice because "she would never notice".

Sexist and homophobic views could increase the risk of sexual abuse being tolerated or unrecognised. Infantilising service users through using pet names and other practices and the use of teasing and jokes at the expense of service users all increase the risk of abuse.

➤ *Boundaries*
Since many conventional boundaries are broken in social care practice (for example, in providing intimate personal care) staff need to be supported to recognise what their role is and where the boundaries are. There is some evidence that where a close relationship builds up between a service user and staff member there is an increased risk of abuse, especially where the relationship is exclusive.

Consideration also needs to be given to situations where staff are related to each other within the same team or in a personal relationship with another team member. In such situations supervision, monitoring and accountability are all important.

Staff need to have a sense that they are there to support service users. Whatever the needs of staff are they should be met outside the service.

➤ *Staff training and competence*
Staff need to be competent in a range of areas. Crucial amongst these are awareness and understanding of abuse and challenging behaviour. It is also important that staff apply good practice in intimate care, record keeping, handling service users' money, control and restraint, sexuality, supporting communication and coping with personal feelings of stress and anger.

Staff who work with individuals who are aggressive or have behaviour which challenges may need additional support. When working with service users who have a history of aggression it is important staff know the positive responses expected. Otherwise, informal care plans can be generated which can be punitive. See chapter 47 around violence at work.

Just because a staff member has been on a training day relating to, say, control and restraint, this does not mean responsibility has been discharged as all staff members need to apply best practice on a daily basis.

➢ *Power and organisational climate*
Staff are powerful in relation to service users. Where staff feel powerless in relation to the organisation, they may use the power they have to the detriment of the service user. This could be mirrored by service users. Within a group of service users some individuals seek to exert power over vulnerable individuals.

Cohesive staff teams can be the means by which a service develops positively. However, a staff team that has a culture which tolerates or encourages abuse can be so powerful that attempts by individuals to challenge this can result in victimisation and intimidation. Services need to promote transparent and professional cultures actively and have effective whistleblowing procedures in place. Support and protection must be provided for staff who whistleblow.

➢ *Isolation*
Isolation is related to a range of risk areas. If service users have few contacts outside the service there is an increased risk of abuse. A malevolent member of staff may use the claim of upholding a service user's right to privacy to increase the service user's sense of isolation.

Individual workers or a group of workers can become isolated, especially night staff and staff who work a lot of evenings and weekends. Staff must not be free to set their own rota so that they work only certain (quiet) times or with chosen others or without supervision. Management time needs to be spread across all times that the service is staffed, even if it involves only visits.

Entire services can become isolated. Residential services particularly are notorious for imploding and for becoming inward looking. It is vital that services welcome new ideas, have contact with outside professionals and respond to advice and comments from others.

➢ *Service conditions, design and placement planning*
Poor conditions, which can include the rationing of essential items, convey that service users are not valued. This can be masked from other professionals (e.g.: inspection officers) by conditions temporarily improving when visits are expected (e.g.: a shift is fully staffed whereas it is usually allowed to be short). How service users are grouped together and the activities they engage in (or lack of activities) can increase the risk of abuse. Planning of activities and groups needs to be done with the aim of minimising risks.

➢ *Empowerment of service users*
The empowerment of service users must also be part of an abuse prevention approach. Giving service users accessible information about the expectations they can rightly have in terms of how they are addressed, their right to make choices, take risks and the freedom to meet with others should all be made clear. Also, the right of service users to complain should be made clear.

Additionally, family members and friends should be informed about their rights to advocate for the service user, as well as what support they could enquire about e.g.:

an advocacy organisation.

Other prevention practices are well known but need to be expressed. These include applying strict recruitment procedures for staff and volunteers and taking immediate assertive action when an allegation of abuse is made.

➢ *Individualised care*
Within services there needs to be individualised care that addresses areas of vulnerability of each service user.

Social care workers should identify the particular areas of vulnerability of the service users they support through person centred care or person centred planning (see chapter 8). Then through care planning and review meetings, plans should be put in place to reduce the risks associated with the person's vulnerability. This may have been largely addressed through a social worker's or care manager's assessment and care plan. However, when service users first begin to access services, they are potentially vulnerable to additional risks (so these are unlikely to have been addressed by a social worker).

➢ *Establishing a culture where concerns can be picked up*
Services should try to develop a culture where members of the care team are able to build warm and empathic relationships with those they are providing a service to. By getting to know service users well, workers can create a safety net where apparently small changes or possible causes for concern are picked up quickly and acted upon. This also increases the likelihood that if a problem or concern occurs, the person will tell someone about it. It takes a great deal of courage for someone to decide to tell another person that they have been abused or ill treated, and the person may well have to search for the right moment to do so. The time they have chosen may not be easy for the worker (particularly if they have other duties to undertake), but it is important that the worker listens carefully to what the person has to say and demonstrates that they are taking the matter seriously. If the person feels that he or she has not been heard, it may be even more difficult for them to speak out again in the future.

Policies and Procedures

One of the ways in which social care services seek to reduce the risk of danger, harm and abuse occurring is through the development and implementation of policies and procedures. These can often markedly reduce the likelihood of danger, harm and abuse occurring in the first place. Examples of this include policies around the handling of service users' money.

This also explains why other policies have been developed e.g.: policies relating to providing intimate personal care, risk assessment procedures etc. A vital aspect of reducing the risk of danger, harm and abuse is therefore the need for all workers to follow all policies and guidelines carefully.

Good Care Practices

Following good practices can also reduce the risk of danger, harm and abuse occurring. For example, treating people with respect and dignity and working within the professional value base increases people's self esteem. This in turn increases people's abilities to protect themselves and recognise danger, harm and abuse.

Empowerment

Empowering service users is a key aspect of effective safeguarding. The Government recognises this and states:

"Safeguarding must be built on empowerment – or listening to the victim's voice. Without this, safeguarding is experienced as safety at the expense of other qualities of life, such as self determination and the right to family life."

(Department of Health 2009:5)

Complaints procedures can help to empower people, and therefore make them less vulnerable to danger, harm and abuse. Knowing that service users have access to an effective complaints procedure may also prevent potential perpetrators from abusing.

Informing people about their rights can again empower people and reduce the risks of abuse occurring.

Multi-Agency Working

Effective multi-agency working and information sharing is also a key aspect to preventing abuse and reducing the risks for service users.

It is therefore clear that the areas covered in the other sections of this publication all contribute to effective safeguarding.

In Summary

In safeguarding practice the prevention of abuse is the main priority. Preventing abuse is a fundamental aspect of every social care worker's role. Many factors are involved in abuse prevention, but following the key principles of social care practice (as covered in section B) is probably the most effective method of abuse prevention.

31: DETECTING ABUSE AND DEALING WITH DISCLOSURES

If care staff understand the nature of danger, harm and abuse and why it can occur then the likelihood of it occurring is minimised. Likewise if service users, carers and the general public are more informed about danger, harm and abuse they will be more aware and risks will be reduced. However, abuse will still occur even with the best prevention strategies in place and social care staff therefore need to know what to do where abuse is taking place.

Detecting Abuse

One thing we do know is that people who experience difficulties in communication are more at risk of abuse. Since most abuse comes to light because the victim verbally discloses (see later) it is likely that a significant amount of abuse goes undetected. Social care staff must therefore remain vigilant when working with very vulnerable service users and be aware of any changes in a person's behaviour. The service user may say things that appear out of place or their behaviour may change in a way that raises concern. They may refer indirectly to an abusive situation e.g.: if a service user was physically abused so that their hand hurts, then they may just refer to their hand hurting. The main skill lies in not jumping to a conclusion about whether abuse has occurred or not, but in "listening" fully to what the person is communicating. However, it is equally important to recognise these signs as potential indicators of abuse.

"The worst thing you could possibly do is refuse to think about it!"

(Bailey 1998)

Often people do not disclose abuse for a variety of reasons, including:

➢ Fear of the abuser

➢ Fear of not being believed

➢ Communication barriers

➢ Feelings of guilt

➢ Confusion

Awareness of the signs and symptoms of abuse together with sensitivity and a commitment to addressing the barriers to effective communication can help to address these factors. The major signs and symptoms of abuse are covered in chapter 28, with the following table summarising these.

Where a social care worker has any concerns or suspicions that a service user may have been abused (is or being abused) they must report their concerns to their line manager immediately. They must not try to address their suspicions in any way but must report their concerns and get guidance on what to do next.

POTENTIAL INDICATORS OF ABUSE

PHYSICAL SIGNS

May include:
- Injuries
- Pain
- Unexplained accidents
- Infections

EMOTIONAL SIGNS

May include:
- Distress
- Tearfulness
- Anxiety
- Fear
- Agitation
- Lack of self worth
- Low self esteem
- Compliance
- Anger

HEALTH RELATED SIGNS

May include:
- Changes in appetite and weight
- Deterioration in health
- Sleep disturbance

BEHAVIOURAL SIGNS

May include:
- Any sudden changes in behaviour
- Comfort behaviours such as rocking
- Unusual responses to individuals or people of a particular gender etc.
- Wetting/Soiling

OTHER SIGNS

Can include aspects such as:
- Sudden lack of funds
- Loss of possessions
- Changes in communication
- Hints or full disclosure

ALWAYS REMEMBER THAT JUST BECAUSE A PERSON IS DISPLAYING ONE OR MORE OF THE SIGNS OF ABUSE IT DOESN'T AUTOMATICALLY MEAN THAT THEY ARE BEING ABUSED.

Recording Suspicions

Social care workers should always record suspicions accurately. Recording potential signs and symptoms is important as a picture can be built up to aid in the detecting of abuse.

IT IS VITAL THAT WORKERS DO NOT TALK ABOUT ANY SUSPICIONS TO THE PERSON THEY SUSPECT IS A VICTIM, OR THE PERSON THEY SUSPECT IS THE ABUSER. THE WORKER'S ROLE IS TO RECOGNISE THE SIGNS OF ABUSE, TO RECORD THESE FACTUALLY AND TO REPORT SUSPICIONS TO THE RELEVANT MANAGER. IT IS **NOT** THE WORKER'S ROLE TO INVESTIGATE THE SUSPICIONS.

Social care workers should remember:

➢ Never to ignore the signs and symptoms of abuse

➢ To record potential signs accurately

➢ To report any suspicions to managers

Disclosures of Abuse

A significant amount of abuse is discovered because the victim declares that it is happening. A disclosure can take various forms as identified by Bailey (1998):

Full Disclosure

A full disclosure is where the victim tells a person directly that they are being abused. The person usually tells someone they trust, who may well be a social care professional. A full disclosure may be totally unexpected and so may come as a real surprise.

Partial Disclosure

A partial disclosure is where the victim hints to a person that they are being abused. However, they may change the subject quickly and may seem reluctant to give details.

Indirect Disclosure

An indirect disclosure is where the victim talks about abuse in a general sense or with regard to someone else. They may be looking for the person's response and trying to find out how they would respond if the victim declared the abuse that they were experiencing.

Responding to Disclosures of Abuse

When a person discloses abuse, it is important that social care staff pass this information to their line manager, or the senior member of staff on duty immediately. It is also important to record accurately what the person said.

Any disclosure should be followed up with an investigation – these are almost always multi-agency as covered in the next chapter. Investigations should never be undertaken by individual care staff. The way that the disclosure is handled and the recording and reporting of the disclosure will be vital in terms of the progress of any investigation.

Sensitive interpersonal skills are required in order to support a person who discloses abuse (i.e. says that they are being abused). These skills include:

➤ Believing the person

➤ Showing concern

➤ Listening effectively

The Do's and Don'ts of Disclosures

Where abuse is disclosed a social care worker <u>should</u>:

✓ Listen

✓ Believe

✓ Stay calm

✓ Allow the person to talk

✓ Reassure the person that they are doing the right thing by telling someone

✓ Tell the person that they believe them

✓ Tell the person that they need to pass this information on

✓ Record accurately the date, time and place of the disclosure and what was said (using the person's own words as far as possible)

✓ Report the disclosure to their manager immediately.

They <u>should not</u>:

✗ Ask any questions that may be 'leading'

✗ Appear shocked, horrified, disgusted etc.

✗ Pressurise the person

✗ Ignore what they have been told

✗ Promise to keep what they have been told a secret

✗ Put opinions in their recording

✗ Pass judgement on either the victim or the abuser

✗ Confront the alleged abuser

The importance of good record keeping

If someone has disclosed abuse or the possibility of abuse, it is very important that a clear and accurate record is made of what has taken place. Making a note at the time will probably distract from the work of supporting the person and he or she may find this off-putting, but this must be done at the first possible opportunity.

If anyone who is involved with a disclosure is making notes for their own records, they must bear in mind that these may be needed for any subsequent investigation or for a Court case. Any rough notes made at the time must therefore be placed in

the service user's file.

Records should contain the following:

➢ The date, time and where the person disclosed the information

➢ The date, time and place of the alleged incident disclosed by the person or witnessed

➢ The name of anyone else who was there when the alleged incident took place or anyone else who was present when the person disclosed the information

➢ What the person said in his or her own words

➢ Any other information which is relevant to record without going into unnecessary detail

In making records the principles of good record keeping as covered in chapter 24 must be employed.

Preventing "Contamination" of an Investigation and any Evidence

Where an individual discloses abuse social care staff need to think about not 'contaminating' evidence or hindering the investigation process. A worker should not stop someone recalling events but they also need to keep in mind that it will be someone else's role – possibly the Police – to investigate and find out more information. To pursue too much detail at this stage risks compromising any subsequent investigation and could mean that the person could be needlessly distressed by being asked the same questions again.

The social care worker will need to ensure that emotional and practical support is provided to the individual who may have been the victim of the alleged abuse. They need to ensure that the organisation's procedures on dealing with abuse and their Local Authority's guidelines on Protecting Vulnerable Adults are followed and also that the appropriate personnel are notified according to your procedures.

Preserving Evidence in the Case of Immediate Reporting to the Police

If a criminal offence such as assault or a sexual offence has been committed, the Police will need to be notified. Who should do this will be indicated in local procedure.

The person concerned is likely to be very distressed and may well want to have a bath or shower for reasons of cleanliness and because they feel "dirty". The worker will need to reassure the person and comfort them until the Police arrive. The worker will need to explain to the person what will be happening as far as they are able to, which may not be easy, particularly if the person is distressed by the fact that the Police are involved. Similarly, the person may wish to change their clothes, but this must not take place until the Police have arrived. Some people may be unhappy and distressed about Police involvement as it may heighten any fears they may have about events spiralling out of their control and it may also prompt fears of retribution by the abuser.

It is also important to ensure that the person is not given anything to drink until the Police arrive as they may wish to take a swab from the person's mouth.

The scene of the incident should also not be disturbed. Do not strip the bed, wash bedclothes or disturb any items in the room. Do not allow anyone else to go into the room until the Police arrive.

If there are any tissues, condoms or other material contaminated by blood, semen or other body fluids either leave these in situ, or if this is not practical, put them in a clean envelope or glass.

Ensure that the person who has disclosed the possible abuse and the alleged abuser are apart and under no circumstances have one worker supporting both people.

<u>Healthcare emergencies where abuse is suspected</u>

Should the individual be injured or unwell as a result of the incident the social care worker should:

➢ Give the person first aid treatment but remember to inform the emergency services what you have done

➢ Call an ambulance

➢ Notify the Police who will arrange for a Police surgeon to examine the person

➢ Follow organisational local procedure and the policy for the Local Authority area.

In Summary

Social care workers may well suspect that abuse has occurred or is occurring. In this case it is vital that they inform their manager and that they pay particular attention to their recording.

In other situations it may well be that a service user who is being abused discloses this to a social care worker. In this instance social care staff must consult with a manager and follow organisational policies and local procedures.

In both situations it is vital that social care workers take care to avoid the potential contamination of evidence.

32: INVESTIGATIONS OF ABUSE

Investigations will usually be multi-agency since different agencies and professionals can offer a range of skills, knowledge about a specialist area (such as the law or medicine), different knowledge about the individual concerned and different resources and means of support. It is this combined multi-agency working that can offer a holistic approach in both detecting abuse and in formulating a way to best support and protect the person.

The role of social care staff and social care managers is limited in the investigation of abuse. The role of care staff will be in contributing to the overall process of multi-agency investigation. The manager's role will be to manage their input into this. Objective verbal and written communication, with vigilant regard for facts such as dates and times, will be the principle way in which managers and staff teams contribute to the investigation of abuse.

The Responsibilities of Social Care Workers

The responsibilities of social care workers in this area can be summarised by three points (ROC):

Report   - They must always report any concerns or disclosures to managers.

Observe   - They need to make careful observations and record these accurately.

Care Plan   - They need to be fully aware of a person's care plan and work to it carefully.

A Manager's Responsibilities

A social care manager's responsibilities in relation to this area can be summarised by four points (CAMS):

Collate   - They need to collate all the information which they receive from staff members and pass this on where necessary. It may be that individual staff don't have enough of the "jigsaw", but that when the manager reviews what all staff are saying, they can recognise patterns of behaviour which may indicate abuse.

Advise   - Managers should keep the individual and the staff team advised about the investigation process and progress (as far as confidentiality allows), and advise staff about their role and the limits to this.

Monitor   - Managers should monitor the work of staff (for example, are they recording effectively?), and observe the service user themselves, if possible, to monitor the situation fully.

Support   - Managers should support the individual, as well as the staff working with the individual who may find the situation distressing.

Investigation outcomes

In some circumstances, investigations can culminate in court proceedings. All recording may then be used as evidence. The quality of recording and the way that disclosures and later behaviours of service users are handled is of vital importance and will have a significant impact on the outcome of any case.

For example, if a social care worker had asked a leading question - such as "He hit you, didn't he?" or later say something like "You're acting like this because of the abuse, aren't you?" this would make anything the service user had said inadmissible in court – seriously jeopardising the case. It is therefore vital that workers have some awareness around how to avoid the contamination of evidence in investigations.

In Summary

Social care staff may be asked to contribute to investigations of alleged abuse, particularly with regards to recording and reporting. However, investigations should be carried out by specialist workers on an inter-agency basis, following local policies and procedures.

SECTION E: SOCIAL CARE PROCESSES

There is a clear process to social care which involves assessment, planning, intervention and review. This section will explore this process and some of the underpinning models and theories. Recent developments in the sector around the personalisation agenda are impacting on this process so this section concludes with an exploration of personalisation and social pedagogy.

33: THE SOCIAL CARE PROCESS

Social care and social work is generally seen as having a clear process. Taylor and Devine (1993) referred to the "basic helping cycle" and this is often seen as the basic process of social care.

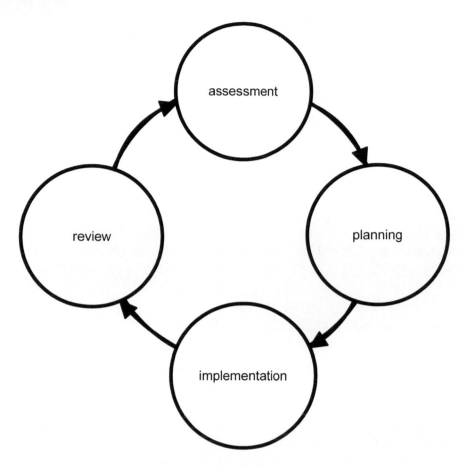

Others describe on this idea in slightly different ways:

➢ The ASPIRE model (Sutton 1999)

AS	-	Assessment
P	-	Planning
I	-	Intervention
RE	-	Review and Evaluation

➢ The ASIRT model (Thompson 2005)

AS	-	Assessment – which acts as the basis of an action plan which informs the:
I	-	Intervention – assessment sets the objectives for the intervention.
R	-	Review – assessment becomes the baseline from which the review/evaluation operates.
T	-	Termination – assessment objectives are considered in terminating intervention.

More recently however, some writers have started to dispute this, claiming that assessment can be an end in itself and doesn't necessarily lead to any intervention – therefore the "cycle" is not always followed. If the assessment is good enough, then some people will be able to act on it for themselves and will not require further services. The assessment then IS the service which is provided.

"While assessment is sometimes viewed as preceding intervention, increasingly assessment is being seen as a service in its own right rather than as a prelude to service delivery."

(SCIE 2003:2)

The idea of assessment as a service in itself, not necessarily as the beginning of a wider process, fits neatly into current models of personalisation (see chapter 40), where following an initial assessment an individual may well be provided with direct payments or an individual budget so that they can "plan and intervene" for themselves.

As a result of the personalisation agenda and *"social care policy being at the forefront of the party political agenda."* (Maxwell 2009) the traditional process of social care presented in this chapter is under significant scrutiny at present. However, some people still present a clear argument supporting the social care "helping cycle". For example, Maxwell (2009) argues:

"Moreover, it is the processes employed and adapted by the sector that can be both improved for now, and placed at the forefront of a new, revitalised care service."

Social care workers might be involved in part or all of the social care process or helping cycle. Whatever level of involvement a social care worker has, it is important for them to understand each component part of the process. The remainder of this section therefore works through each part of the helping cycle process in turn.

In Summary

A four stage process is often seen as the basic social care process. This is being adapted by significant changes in the sector but understanding the basic "helping cycle" is still important for social care professionals.

34: ASSESSMENT

Historically, assessments were carried out by social workers and social care workers only became involved with a service user when they began receiving services at the planning or implementation stage of the helping cycle. However, practices are now changing and assessments might be carried out by a range of professionals including social care workers. Indeed, self assessment is becoming much more common.

Whether social care workers carry out assessments themselves or not, it is important that they have a clear understanding of assessments because:

➢ even where they do not carry out the assessment themselves, they will contribute significantly to the process

➢ they should understand how a service user might experience an assessment

➢ they will be able to make more effective use of the assessment findings where they understand the process

The Assessment Process

In considering the assessment process, Milner and O'Bryne present a useful five stage model of assessment (1998):

Stage 1: Preparation – which might include deciding who to see, what the purpose of the assessment is, what information will be needed etc.

Stage 2: Data collection – the worker gathers the necessary information.

Stage 3: Weighing up the data – the worker weighs up the information to reach an answer to the key question "is there a problem and is it serious?"

Stage 4: Analysing the data – the information is interpreted to gain a fuller understanding so that ideas for intervention can be developed.

Stage 5: Utilising the data – this stage is used to finalise judgements. The data will be used to evidence judgements and recommendations for intervention.

Models of Assessment

In research published in 1993, Smale and Tuson (et al) identified three different models of assessment which are still seen as the three main models of assessment in social care services:

➢ *The Questioning Model*
Here, the worker holds the expertise and follows a format of questions, listening to and processing the answers. The use of this model means that the assessment process largely reflects the worker's agenda.

➢ *The Procedural Model*
Using this model, the worker gathers information to make a judgement about whether the service user fits the criteria for service provision. It is likely that a range of

checklists will be used. The use of this model means that the assessment process largely reflects the agency agenda.

> *The Exchange Model*
In this model, workers view people as experts on their own problems. The emphasis of this model is on exchanging information. The worker follows what people are saying rather than trying to interpret what they think is meant. The worker should help the service user to identify internal resources and potential. In this way the practitioner can consider how best to help service users mobilise their own resources in order to reach goals which are defined by the service user. The use of this model means that the assessment should reflect the service user's agenda.

Smale et al make it clear that the exchange model is their preferred model. Working to this model however requires a great deal of skill. It means more than merely sharing assessments with service users. The model asserts that people in need and their family and friends will always know more about their problems and how they affect them than workers. However, the model recognises that workers will have expertise in the process of problem solving. The aim of the worker should be to involve people in arriving at a compromise for ensuring needs are met. Rather than "making" an assessment the worker should manage the process.

Whilst making clear that they favour the exchange model, Smale et al acknowledge that workers can often feel pushed into the procedural model of assessment when they feel overwhelmed by agency pressures, eligibility criteria and the scarcity of resources. However, they point out that the exchange model can still be useful in these situations as long term and more stable solutions are likely to be reached, and because inner resources can be maximised so that resource provision can be limited to specific areas (if needed at all).

Smale et al accept that the questioning model is the most likely to be used when risk is the main emphasis of the assessment. This is likely to be because specific answers to questions will be needed and to some extent the worker's agenda will need to be addressed.

It is our view that many social care workers begin the development of their assessment skills by using a questioning or procedural model. Often workers can be so overwhelmed by the paperwork that they focus on the accurate completion of this – leading them away from an exchange model. As worker's confidence grows, they should be able to work more towards an exchange model of assessment.

In Summary

This chapter has outlined the process and some key models of assessment. There are, of course, a number of approaches to assessment and specific issues around risk assessment, which are covered in the next few chapters.

35: ASSESSMENT: SERVICE LED, NEEDS LED AND OUTCOMES FOCUSSED APPROACHES

Service Led Assessment

Service led assessment is where the assessment is led in terms of what services are available or where there is an over-emphasis on matching needs with service provision. The Social Care Institute for Excellence (Crisps et al 2003) have noted that assessments are often limited to the provision of already available options rather than the identification of new services. They argue that the process of assessment should also identify options for the service user which are not already in existence.

Unfortunately, whilst all Government policy is clear that assessments should not be service led, it is clear that there is still some very poor assessment practice which is service led. For example, a recent social care assessment I read stated "Mrs Dawson needs to go to a day centre." In what way is this a need? Perhaps Mrs Dawson needed the opportunity to interact with others, the opportunity to engage in an activity which might motivate her to get up and dress herself etc but these needs could be met in a range of ways – not simply through going to a day centre. The social care assessor had clearly muddled up Mrs Dawson's needs with what she thought might be available, potentially missing out some of the key issues.

"Needs Led" Assessment

In recent years the emphasis in social care has been on needs led assessment. Many would argue that as the people carrying out assessments are often employed by agencies with limited resources that assessment can never be truly needs led. There are further arguments that the concept of need in itself is not clear, so it is worth developing an overview of theories of need.

There are a number of theories of need. Perhaps the most well known of these is Maslow's hierarchy of needs.

Maslow's Hierarchy of Needs

Maslow (1970) argues that all humans have a hierarchy of needs. We first need to satisfy basic biological needs (e.g.: food, warmth etc) and then we are successively drawn to meet higher needs.

Originally Maslow created a pyramid of needs with five levels. He later extended this to seven levels.

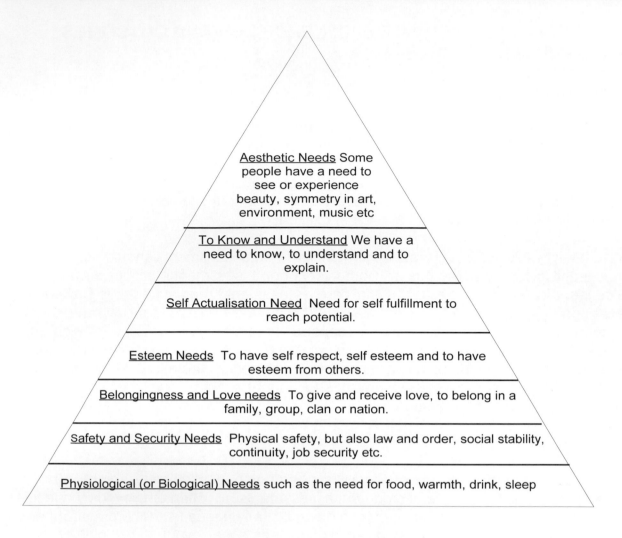

The people have a need to see or experience beauty, symmetry in art, environment, music etc

The Strength of the Needs

Maslow argued that each level of need was a very powerful motivating force for each person.

At first, we are preoccupied with meeting our physiological (or biological) needs. If our need for food, water, warmth etc is not being met, then all the other 'higher' needs are unimportant. We must satisfy our biological needs. Once we are in a situation where our biological needs are largely or fully met, we start to experience a craving for safety and security. The more fully our biological needs are met, the stronger is our desire to establish safety and security. The safety and security needs are not just about being free of the fear of being physically attacked. It also refers to our need for stability, order and routine. This includes social and economic stability.

Once the safety and security needs are largely or fully met, then our need for belonging and love becomes as intense as the two preceding needs once were. We crave the opportunity to love and to be loved, to belong to someone else and to be part of a wider group or community.

When we satisfy or largely meet our need to love and be loved, the importance of our need for self esteem starts to rise. This need includes being able to achieve tasks, being competent, independent and having personal strength. Additionally, we need respect from others in the form of prestige, status – even fame. Maslow noted that basing self esteem solely on the opinion of others was inviting insecurity. We need a sense that self esteem is based on deserved respect from others rather than celebrity or unwarranted adulation.

The need for self actualisation increases as our need for esteem is satisfied. Maslow assumes that all people will experience this need. How this need is satisfied will be an expression of our individuality. For one person, it will be through being an ideal mother; for another person, achieving a physical, athletic goal; for yet a different person, developing a new invention etc.

In his later writings, Maslow then added on two higher stages. In some respects they are extensions of the self actualisation stage rather than entirely new stages.

In the first of the two new stages (the sixth stage of the whole pyramid) Maslow argued that we have a need to know, to be curious to seek to understand our world. People who enter into boring and unstimulating lifestyles are at risk of developing mental health problems.

The second of the two new stages (the seventh stage of the whole pyramid) is the aesthetic need. Maslow recognised that this need may only be felt by some people. However, for these people the need to experience beauty, symmetry and idealised harmony was so strong that Maslow felt it should be considered a need.

Maslow made it clear that people did not need to work through the stages in a methodical, rigid manner. A person could be seeking to meet their needs from two or three stages at the same time. However, a person would only be able to increasingly devote their personal resources to a higher stage once a lower stage was largely satisfied.

Perspectives on Maslow's Hierarchy of Needs

Maslow's Hierarchy of Needs has been a very significant standard in seeking to explain human motivation and the human condition. It is incredibly popular.

Within psychology, it has been difficult to generate research that can adequately test the theory. Some psychologists like the theory so much they have developed it further, either by increasing or reducing the number of stages. Other psychologists have pointed out its weakness and the way there are individuals who do not follow the staged progression.

Maslow's Hierarchy of Needs and Services

There are too many services that only support service users as far as level two. Some services don't even get as high as level two (safety and security). Very few service users are actively supported to have their needs around love and belonging met. Additionally, the use of labels in services cuts across upholding a person's self esteem and their sense that others respect them as competent people.

Human Needs Theories

Whilst Maslow's hierarchy is perhaps the most well known theory of need, there are others. A number of writers have developed Maslow's ideas. One of the most well known is John Burton who has developed Maslow's hierarchy to apply it to theories about human conflict. Burton sees human needs not as a hierarchy but more as an emergent collection of human development essentials. These needs do not have a hierarchical order. Rather, they are sought simultaneously in an intense and relentless manner (Burton 1990).

Burton and other human needs theorists categorise needs in areas such as:

➢ Safety/security

➢ Belongingness/love

➢ Self esteem/personal fulfilment

➢ Identity

➢ Cultural security

➢ Freedom

➢ Justice

➢ Participation

Bradshaw's Taxonomy of Need

First developed by Jonathan Bradshaw in relation to the needs of older people, this was entitled a taxonomy of social need (see 1972). However, it is now probably more widely used in terms of health care than social care.

Bradshaw refers to real need. He believes this to be a combination of four types of need:

➢ Normative need. This refers to needs which the expert/professional defines – these needs tend to be based on the professional's view of societal "norms".

➢ Perceived/felt needs. This refers to needs felt by the individual – in a way a self assessment. This type of need is sometimes referred to as a "want" rather than a need.

➢ Expressed need (demand). This refers to the needs expressed by people – this can be seen as felt need converted into expressed need when the person seeks assistance.

➢ Comparative need. This refers to the comparison that people make in defining needs – do we need what others have? etc. This is often referred to in understanding poverty – the concept of comparative poverty recognises that people may perceive themselves to be poor in comparison with others but this would not necessarily be viewed as "real" poverty.

Bradshaw claims that each of these areas of need overlaps and that it is perhaps somewhere in the overlap that "real need" can be found. (Glendinning et al 2005)

Acquired Needs Theory

Proposed by McClelland (e.g.: 1961) this theory is also known as learned need theory or the three need theory. The idea is that we all have needs which fall into three general categories:

➢ Achievement (coded as N-Ach)

➢ Affiliation (coded as N-Aff)

> ➢   Power (coded as N-Pow)

McClelland proposed that a person's specific needs are acquired over time and are shaped by life experiences. He goes on to say that most people feel that one of these needs is more important than the others. As such, he says which one of these is most important to us most affects our behaviour. Thus, he states that there are three types of people:

> ➢   Achievers

> ➢   Affiliation seekers

> ➢   Power seekers

This theory of need has been particularly influential in terms of understanding people at work and within organisations.

Outcomes Focussed Assessment

The concept of needs led assessment is now being complimented by outcomes focussed assessment. This has been developed by research carried out at the University of York. This approach is based on the social model of disability and empowerment (Harris et al 2005). The outcomes model is becoming more and more influential in social care.

The approach identifies outcomes in three dimensions:

> ➢   outcomes involving change – for example, improving self confidence, self-care skills or changes to accessibility of environments

> ➢   outcomes that maintain quality of life (or slow down deterioration in quality of life) sometimes referred to as maintenance outcomes.

> ➢   outcomes that are associated with the process of receiving services – such as feeling valued, being respected, feeling listened to etc.

Harris et al (2005) have developed an outcomes framework which categorises outcomes into four areas – in many ways these four areas could be seen as needs. The three dimensions of outcomes could be applied to any of the four areas in the framework.

Autonomy Outcomes	Personal Comfort Outcomes
➤ Access to all areas of the home ➤ Access to locality and wider environment ➤ Communicative access ➤ Financial security	➤ Personal hygiene ➤ Safety/Security ➤ Desired level of cleanliness of home ➤ Emotional well-being ➤ Physical health
Economic Participation Outcomes	**Social Participation Outcomes**
➤ Access to paid employment as desired ➤ Access to training ➤ Access to further/higher education/employment ➤ Access to appropriate training for new skills (e.g.: lip reading)	➤ Access to mainstream leisure activities ➤ Access to support in parenting role ➤ Access to support for personal secure relationships ➤ Access to advocacy/peer support ➤ Citizenship

The outcomes focussed approach is seen as a user centred approach which involves the practitioner acting more as facilitator than assessor.

Research carried out by the Social Policy Research Unit (Harris et al 2005) identified that many professionals find an outcome focussed approach to be an improvement on needs based assessment.

 In Summary

Needs led assessment has historically been the most influential approach to assessment. However, outcomes focussed approaches are now growing in popularity. Whichever approach is used within a particular area, assessments should never be service led.

36: THE STRENGTHS PERSPECTIVE AND RESILIENCE

The Social Care Institute for Excellence (2003) have made clear that very often assessment practice focuses on identifying *"deficits or difficulties rather than strengths."* They go on to clarify that holistic assessment practice involves incorporating the strengths perspective. This links very closely to current themes in social care practice such as active support and personalisaiton. That said, the strengths perspective is not "new". It has been developing for many years (arguably at least 40 years) with different writers contributing to its formation from their own fields. It is partly a reaction against two features of traditional social work and the provision of health and social care:

1. An increasing medical classification and diagnosis of individuals leading to labelling of large sections of society. This labelling is negative and has a deterministic theme (e.g.: you had a traumatic childhood <u>therefore</u> you will be a terrible parent and your children will end up in care).

2. Assessments of needs have always been weighted towards listing people's deficits, vulnerabilities and negative past experiences. In the current environment where demand for services is increasing but the resources available have barely increased, then there is an increased focus and heightening of service users' lack of capability and risks. That is, there is much more focus on what a person cannot do than on what a person can do.

In both of these suggestions, there is a structural or bureaucratic bias against recognising people's strengths, abilities and resilience. Professionals may be led to make use of a language that is pathologising and alienating in order to ensure that service users have access to services. See page 33 for discussion of the ways in which labelling is used to ensure people can reach the threshold required to access services.

Saleebey (1996) generated the following comparison of professional pathologising against the strengths perspective:

Pathology	Strengths
Person is defined as a "case"; symptoms add up to a diagnosis.	Person is defined as unique; traits, talents, resources add up to strengths.
Therapy is problem focussed.	Therapy is possibility focussed.
Service user accounts are filtered by a professional to aid the generation of a diagnosis.	Personal accounts are the essential route to knowing and appreciating the person.
Professional is sceptical of personal stories and explanations.	Professional knows the person from the inside out.
Childhood trauma is the precursor or predictor of adult dysfunction.	Childhood trauma is not predictive; it may weaken or strengthen the individual.
Professional devises treatment or care plan.	Focus is aspirations of individual, family or community.
Professional is the expert on service user's life.	Individual, family or community are the experts.
Possibilities for choice, control, commitment and personal development are limited by label/diagnosis or condition.	Possibilities for choice, control, commitment and personal development are open.
Professionals' knowledge, skills and connections are principal resources for	The strength, capacities and adaptive skills of the individual, family or community are

service user.	the principle resources.
Support is centred on reducing the effects of symptoms and the negative effects of emotions or relationships	Support is focussed on getting on with one's life, affirming and developing values and commitments and making or finding membership in a community.

The strengths perspective argues that personal qualities and strengths can come out of and be formed by difficult life experiences. Resilience, independence, loyalty to one or more people can arise due to a painful or traumatic personal experience. People can develop great insight into their own situation.

An important source of strength can be cultural, community or personal stories or narratives. Cultural or community accounts of origins, development, migration and survival can provide inspiration and meaning (Saleebey 1996).

Most professionals will probably say that they already apply the strengths perspective to their work. The counter to this is that many professionals only pay lip service to the strengths perspective. This is because the strengths perspective calls on the professional to move away from the objective, concrete and tangible. The strengths perspective calls on the professional to connect with the individuals and families they work with in a manner that recognises hope, aspirations, spirituality, identity and belonging. The connection needs to be rooted in a true sense of equality.

The strengths perspective recognises that individuals and families have already been subjected to a range of demanding life events. Additionally, if people have had contact with health and social work services for some time they could have internalised the ideas of deficiency and needs. It is in addressing this that the professional's skills are called upon to work creatively with the service user and this can be very demanding. Individuals who have lived with grinding poverty or are on guard due to intimidatory and unpredictable racism are not going to automatically refer to the way they have benefited from their life experiences. The social care worker is required to enable the service user to recognise the talents, resources, adaptive skills and support network the service user or family has.

Resilience Perspective

The resilience perspective is closely related to the strengths perspective. Often resilience is seen as one aspect of the strengths perspective.

Resilience refers to supporting people develop their own reservoir of skills, abilities and knowledge. This personal reservoir includes the person's social support network. Ideally the individual's sense of the resources they have should be developed in depth (e.g.: strengthening existing family relationships or friendships) and across a broad range (the person is supported to try new experiences both so that they acquire new skills, but also so that they meet new people).

The resilience perspective recognises that individuals can have difficulties in one area of their life. One of the ways a person overcomes a difficulty is by drawing on other aspects of their life either directly to problem solve, or indirectly so that the person has a sense that in other areas of their life they are doing well.

Development of the Strengths Perspective

Each branch of social care and social work has developed its own literature on recognising people's strengths. For example:

In mental health services, the recovery model is closely related to aspects of the strengths perspective:

➢ The focus on wellness rather than illness

➢ The recognition of a person's individuality

➢ The de facto acknowledgement of the effects of the person's mental health problems but a recognition of the fact that this doesn't stop the person getting on with life

➢ Maintaining a sense of hope

In learning disability services, the strengths perspective (although not called that at the time) can be seen as far back as the 1960s.

➢ Jean Vanier has consistently talked about how much he learned from people with learning disabilities who he lived with, the strengths of people and the way his life has been enriched by living with people with learning disabilities (e.g.: Vanier 1988)

➢ Wolfensberger has been ambivalent towards professionals due to their failure to recognise the strengths of people with learning disabilities (e.g.: Wolfensberger 1988)

➢ Numerous other writers have championed the importance of engaging with people with learning disabilities as true equals and to recognise the way society benefits (e.g.: Brandon 1997, Neufeldt 1990, Williams 2006 etc).

In children's services the strengths and resilience of black families has been focussed on by various researchers who have been concerned by the way services have applied institutional racism in their work with black families:

➢ Owusu-Bempah and Howitt (1999) have discussed how black children can develop a positive sense of self in spite of racism and the importance of family relationships generally

➢ Hylton (1997) discusses survival strategies used by black families who experience racism including the importance of the whole (wider) family and spirituality

➢ Dutt and Phillips (2000) convey the importance of recognising the strengths of black families

These are just examples, but it is sufficient to say that the strengths perspective has advocates in all areas of social care and social work.

Limitations and Critique of the Strengths Perspective

There is no acknowledgement of reluctant or resistant service users. Some service users don't want contact with services. Also, some service users are not honest with social workers or social care staff. Due to this, many workers adopt a sceptical approach to what service users say. The worker may take the service user's account seriously, but they then test it, either through further questions or by seeking independent confirmation from someone else. Such professional scepticism cuts across the strengths perspectives sense of values. In theory the worker needs to generate an environment where the service user or family member feels they can be honest. However, if the service user or family member declares they have harmed a child or vulnerable adult, then the worker will have to initiate various actions.

The extent of illness or life trauma is minimalised. There is no intention to gloss over difficulties in a person's life. Cousins (1989) said that one should not deny the verdict (medical diagnosis, assessment etc) but one should defy the sentence. A radical social perspective would question the societal move towards increased labelling. Rather than being defined by a label, it can be more productive to discuss with the person in what ways their hopes and aspirations are being restricted or limited. What are the practical impacts? What are the impacts on motivation, outlook and personal ambitions? Then move from there.

The strengths perspective presents both a challenge and an opportunity. To apply the strengths perspective fully, workers must move away from bureaucratic, deficit led assessments. Workers need to engage with the service user or family in the language of hope, aspirations and redemption (good things come out of painful experiences). Social care workers could practice re-framing statements about problems into being ones about learning from difficulties.

Ironically, the opportunity is that in a time of increasingly restricted services, if workers can engage with an individual or family and support them to identify the strengths and abilities they have in themselves and their support network, they will leave the service user or family with something to build on.

In Summary

The strengths perspective has an important role to play in the social care processes of assessment and planning. In many ways it links to a number of the basic principles covered in Section B. For example, focussing on strengths is a key part of being person centred and integral to active support.

37: RISK ASSESSMENT

Risk assessment is a key aspect of social care practice. To understand the concept of risk assessment and the theoretical underpinning to this, it helps to understand that risk assessment is generally carried out in terms of two areas:

➢   The risks a person poses to others (dangerousness)

➢   The risks a person is subject to (vulnerability)

Whatever the focus of the assessment, the purpose is generally for the assessment to inform plans about intervention – generally referred to as risk management strategies.

<u>The Risks a Person Poses to Others</u>

In these situations risk assessment views risk as wholly negative and the focus is on accurately assessing the risks posed such that they can be avoided. Examples of this form of assessment are drawn from assessment of offending behaviour by workers in the criminal justice system, or assessments by workers in mental health teams where a person is felt to pose a risk to others.

<u>The Risks a Person is Subject to</u>

Risk assessment in these situations doesn't necessarily focus on risk as wholly negative. There is a recognition that risk taking can be positive – e.g.: in increasing skills, developing confidence etc. Here the focus is on identifying risks and then deciding which risks are acceptable to the person and which are not acceptable.

The assessment should lead to strategies for risk management which focus on balancing the benefits of risk taking with any potential harm.

Interestingly, it can be argued that risk assessment in terms of child protection and, to an increasing extent, adult protection combine aspects of dangerousness and vulnerability assessments. For example, a risk assessment may explore the "dangerousness" of the situation and the risks a person is exposed to.

Two basic techniques are used in risk assessments:

➢   Actuarial Assessment

➢   Clinical Assessment

Actuarial Assessment

This is developed from insurance industry methods for risk calculation and is basically about a statistical calculation of risk. The focus is on probabilities which are expressed in numerical terms – usually percentages or scores and sometimes a traffic light system of red, amber and green.

Actuarial assessment is seen as more accurate than clinical assessment but there are always problems with statistical measures. The approach is reliant on research findings about groups and it can be difficult to transfer learning from generalised information to individual situations. Therefore, the more infrequent the risk, the less accurate the actuarial prediction will be.

Actuarial assessment is limited in terms of risk management solutions in that this type of assessment provides a prediction about likelihood rather than offering any understanding about the risks and possible effects etc.

Clinical Assessment

Clinical assessment is a much more individual assessment method. It is undertaken by workers on a case by case basis. Clinical assessment is based on a professional judgement of risk and as such can be value based and subjective. Clinical risk assessment has a poor record of accuracy.

It is largely accepted that there are two forms of error with clinical assessment – false negatives and false positives, as covered later in this chapter.

Despite the unreliability of clinical assessment, it does have some strengths in that this individualised form of assessment can offer more than simple probability predictions. This type of assessment can provide an analysis which offers an understanding of the nature of risk and ideas for risk management strategies.

Holistic Risk Assessment

Recognising that neither of these two approaches are wholly effective, writers now promote an approach which combines the positives of each method (e.g.: Limandri and Sheridan, 1995, Kemshall, 2002). This holistic approach combines probability predictions and ideas about the nature of the risk. These combined methods are often referred to as "second generation" assessment tools (Monahan and Steadman 1994). Kemshall sees the holistic approach to risk assessment as essential to individual case work. She sees this approach as highlighting areas for significant intervention and change as part of the care management process (Kemshall 2002).

Brearley's Model of Risk Assessment

Brearley first described his framework for risk assessment in 1982. Since then, it has become arguably one of the most influential models of risk assessment in adult social care services. It is probably so popular because it brings together an approach for risk assessment and risk management. Brearley's model is based on a clear definition of danger, risk, hazards and strengths, as follows:

➢ Dangers: undesirable outcomes

➢ Risk: the chance of some kind of loss or the occurrence of an undesirable outcome as a result of a decision or a course of action

Social care work can focus too narrowly on potential losses, therefore missing the potential for gain or growth. Competent professional practice involves weighing up the pros and cons of both possibilities, which Brearley describes in terms of hazards and strengths. He sees a hazard as an existing factor that introduces or increases the possibility of an undesirable outcome. He identifies two types of hazard:

➢ Predisposing hazards: these are factors in the person's background, such as their experiences and personality which make the undesirable outcome more likely

➢ Situational hazards: these are factors specific to the current situation, which make an undesirable outcome more likely

Brearley's distinction between the two types of hazard is useful because it helps the worker to focus on those aspects of the risk situation which may be more open to intervention and change. Some 'hazards' can be changed, but some can't

➢ Strengths: Building on the strengths model, Brearley recognises that strengths are often overlooked in risk assessment. He identifies strengths as any factor which reduces the possibility of an undesirable outcome occurring. Brearley identifies that there is a real danger in focussing too narrowly on hazards and that in recognising and building on strengths this danger is minimised. This may seem an obvious requirement of holistic, person centred assessment, but it is one which can easily be neglected in the pressured environment of working with risk.

Listing hazards and strengths provides a way of quantifying the balance between them. Social care practitioners then need to identify what other information can be obtained to help them analyse the whole situation before reaching a conclusion and making a judgement about the decisions to be made.

Conclusions and Decisions in Risk Assessment

No risk assessment process can be totally accurate. As previously stated both actuarial approaches and clinical approaches are not "fail safe".

It is generally accepted that there are two types of inaccuracies – false positives and false negatives. The following table taken from Walker and Beckett (2005: 86) clarifies this.

True and false positives and negatives

True positives	Situations identified as high risk where the harmful event actually occurs in the absence of protective intervention.
False positives	Situations identified as high risk where the harmful event actually would not occur even in the absence of protective intervention.
True negatives	Situations identified as low risk where no harmful event occurs.
False negatives	Situations identified as low risk, but where the harmful event does nevertheless occur.

This table is helpful in that it illustrates how, when carrying out a risk assessment and planning intervention, a worker can "go wrong" in two ways. For example, let's take a situation where an older person moves into residential accommodation because a risk assessment has concluded that there are too many unacceptable risk to them remaining in their own home. Using the concept of true and false negatives and positives there are 2 potential outcomes:

True Positive   -   If the person would have remained in their own home, they would have been harmed ie: the assessment and intervention was "right".

| False Positive | - | If the older person had remained at home, they would not have come to any harm ie: the assessment and intervention was "wrong". In actual fact, since the move will in itself cause loss and distress, the older person will experience "harm". |

In another situation, a person remains in their own home because a risk assessment has concluded that there is a low risk of harm. Again there are two potential outcomes:

| True negative | - | The person remains at home and comes to no harm ie: the risk assessment was "right". |

| False negative | - | The person remains at home and comes to harm ie: the assessment was "wrong". |

Understanding the concept of true and false positives and negatives helps to illustrate the double bind that social worker and social care professionals often find themselves in. "Damned if you do, damned if you don't." This has led to various discussions about decision making, and as a result of these Carson (1996) introduced the concept of defensible decision making.

Defensible Decision Making

In recognition of the fact that risk assessment is a highly fallible process, with no guarantee of certainty, Carson argues that the key skill is to arrive at decisions in a manner that a reasonable body of co-professionals would also have followed. This makes the decision defensible if brought to account.

Aspects that make up a defensible decision include the following:

➢   all reasonable steps are taken

➢   reliable assessment methods have been used

➢   information is collected and thoroughly evaluated

➢   decisions are recorded

➢   staff work within agency policies and procedures

➢   staff communicate with others and seek information they do not have

The Hindsight Fallacy

Introduced by Macdonald and Macdonald (1999) this concept is in common language ("in hindsight…" "with the benefit of hindsight…" etc). When a negative result occurs – for example a risk assessment has concluded a low risk and then a person comes to harm, the assumption is that a serious mistake has been made. However, this is not always the case. The risk assessment may have led to a highly "defensible decision".

"….a bad outcome in and of itself does not constitute evidence that the decision was mistaken. The hindsight fallacy is to assume that it does."

Walker and Beckett (2005) conclude that it is vital when reviewing outcomes to recognise situations where there were risk indicators that should have been noted (a mistake was made) and situations where the significance "could not have reasonably been seen without the benefit of hindsight." (2005: 87).

Approaches to Risk / Intervention Strategies

Having considered the main approaches to risk assessment and the potential outcomes of risk assessment, we can move on to look at some of the main intervention approaches. The main intervention approaches can be categorised into:

➢ risk elimination

➢ risk reduction

➢ risk minimisation

➢ risk management

Risk Elimination
Risk elimination refers to an approach which seeks to completely eliminate risks. This is a practically impossible aim in social care work. There are, however, a few examples where a risk is entirely influenced by one environmental factor and where this environmental factor can be changed.

Risk Reduction
This approach seeks to "reduce" the risks or the likelihood of identified risks occurring.

Risk Minimisation
This approach is most often referred to as harm minimisation. Essentially, this approach is about minimising the impact of the risk.

Risk Management
Risk management approaches seek to "manage" risks rather than attempting to eliminate them. Risk management strategies are usually devised on a case by case basis using aspects of risk reduction and risk minimisation.

Risk Averse Approaches

A number of social care services are seen as having a "risk averse" culture. That is, they seek to adopt a risk control rather than a risk management approach. Walker and Beckett (2005) identify the key differences in risk control and risk management as follows:

➢ Characteristics of the risk control perspective

Definition:	risk is negative – danger, threat
Priority principles:	professional responsibility and accountability
Practice priorities:	identification (assessment scales) and elimination (procedural, legalistic)

➢ Characteristics of the risk management perspective

Definition:	positive – risk is part of life, balancing risks and benefits is part of individual's development, being self-determining and personally responsible

Priority principles: self determination, anti oppressive practice

Practice priorities: solution focussed, partnership practice, empowerment

It is widely recognised that services have often in the past been too protective of people. Services have always sought to minimise or eliminate any risk of harm, be it emotional, mental or physical. It is now accepted that the attempt to eliminate all risk undermines people's dignity and inhibits opportunities for personal development and growth. Often care environments that reduce risk as much as possible result in impoverished environments. Effective practice in risk assessment within care environments is about balance.

The answer to over protection is not to throw any sense of service responsibility to the wind and claim that whatever happens to people upholds their dignity. The aim should be for services to support people to take measured risks, the tasks being, at the time first initiated, at the top end of someone's present capability. If the task is successfully completed the person's sense of confidence and self esteem should be notably enhanced. If the person is not successful, whilst there is a risk that their confidence and self esteem is knocked there should be support to assist people through this. The person still has the sense that at least they tried it even if it wasn't successful.

A SHIP IN A HARBOUR IS SAFE, BUT THAT'S NOT WHAT SHIPS ARE BUILT FOR

In any programme that is intended to maintain or extend a person's level of independence, but which involves risk, there must be planned steps which enhance the person's skills and control the level of risk. In essence, services should actively use risk assessments in a constructive manner. As people are supported to develop and extend their skills the risks associated should be evaluated to see if the person can extend their level of independence.

Risk taking is an integral part of daily life and is a significant route to supporting service users to maintain a sense of achievement and fulfilment. If risk is handled in a planned and conscious way, it can be a great springboard for all.

Risk Compensation

It is widely accepted that people adapt their behaviour based on their perceptions of risk. For example, where people feel that they face significant risk, they will ensure that they employ safety conscious behaviours. Where people feel "safe" in the knowledge that risks are minimised, their behaviour will adapt to their perception of risk, so that they may place themselves at heightened risk. People are in essence lulled into a false sense of security. This is widely demonstrated in research relating to road safety – for example, cyclists wearing helmets will take more risks because they feel "safe" wearing helmets.

In devising risk management strategies, it is important to address potential behaviour changes created by risk compensation. As a straightforward example – many social care organisations have made a conscious decision not to provide self defence training for staff because of fears that staff will adapt their behaviour and place themselves in more risky situations. They may stay and "fight" rather than seek to leave when faced with an incidence of violence and aggression when in fact leaving is always the safest and most preferable option. Keeping safe is more about being equipped with knowledge and information about risk and being able to identify risk than knowing what to do in terms of self defence.

Understanding the concept of risk compensation is important in terms of discussing risk management strategies with service users. How will they ensure they contribute to the strategy through their behaviour etc?

In Summary

Risk assessment is vital in social care practice. There are a number of approaches to risk assessment which social care workers need to understand. Effective risk assessment should identify appropriate risk management measures as opposed to seeking to eliminate risk. A vital aspect of empowerment and good practice in social care is to recognise the dignity of risk and supporting service users to manage risk.

38: PLANNING INTERVENTION

Once a person's needs have been assessed and ideas generated about ways and methods of supporting that person, many services will agree a care plan or support plan. It is important that a clear plan is in place for a range of reasons:

➢ service users will be clear about what they can expect in terms of support

➢ family members and other informal carers will understand how a service user's needs are to be addressed

➢ care and support staff will understand their role in the service user's life

➢ the input of all professionals will be clearer, therefore improving partnership working

➢ inspectors can be clear that a service is working towards agreed and measurable goals

The Department of Health (2002) suggests that care plans should include the following:

➢ A summary of identified / eligible needs indicating the intensity, instability, predictability and complexity of needs, the associated risks to independence and the potential for rehabilitation.

➢ A note about whether or not the service user has agreed the care plan and a reason where this was not possible.

➢ A note on whether or not the user has consented for care plan information to be shared among relevant agencies and a reason where this was not possible.

➢ The objectives of providing help and anticipated outcomes for users.

➢ A summary of how services will impact on identified, eligible needs and associated risks.

➢ The part the service user will play in addressing needs, including the strengths and abilities they will bring to this.

➢ Details of managing risk as appropriate. Where it has been agreed that service users will accept a certain degree of risk, this must be written into the care plan.

➢ Details of what carers are willing to do and related needs and support.

➢ A description of the level and frequency of the help that is to be provided, stating which agency is responsible for what service.

➢ Details of any contributions to care costs that service users are asked to make.

➢ A nursing plan (integrated not attached) where appropriate.

➢ The name of the person co-ordinating the care plan and the contact number.

➢ A contact number or office in case of emergencies and a contingency plan if things go wrong.

➢ Monitoring arrangements and a date for review.

We would offer the following guidance on the planning process:

What is the Need / Problem / Issue?

Outlining the need or the presenting issue, as identified in the assessment process, is important so that the service user and everybody involved in their care knows why the plan is being put into place. It is important to keep focus on an agreed number of issues so that the service user is not overwhelmed and to prioritise which needs should be addressed in the first instance (in line with the theories of need explored earlier), plans do not need to be lengthy to show they are thorough. Sometimes, brevity can show more care in being appropriate to the person's needs.

What are the Aims and Objectives?

Translating identified needs into aims and objectives is perhaps where the skills and expertise of a social care worker are most necessary.

"The translation of 'needs' into 'aims' should take account of the strengths and limitations of the service user and the situation, something which is often harder for the person receiving help to see. You are offering your knowledge and skills to help the service user."
(Taylor and Devine 2004)

Clarification on aims and objectives is sometimes required. A dictionary definition includes:

Aim: direct at, point out; direct one's ambition; purpose

Objective: the point to which operations are directed; the point to be reached; goal

The easiest way to think about this is that the aim is what the service user ultimately wants to achieve. The objectives are the steps which will be taken to reach the aim (the ultimate goal).

Research suggests (Taylor and Devine 2004) that no more than three aims should be addressed in one intervention. However, there might be a series of objectives related to each aim.

The major new emphasis in care planning is on specifying the expected results of the care – known as the outcomes. Being clear about the criteria for measuring outcomes is also important in care planning. That is, achievable aims should be outlined – the outcomes of which can be measured.

What is the Planned Outcome?

This question is about identifying which changes are achievable with each person and supporting the person and everyone involved in their care to recognise that change is possible. Change could entail very small steps, and planning these outcomes in stages can be a helpful way of ensuring possible solutions are broken down into specific outcomes for that individual. For one person an outcome could be independent shopping, and for another it might be around re-learning self care skills. The idea is that the plan is person centred and relevant to that individual at that specific time. In an age where many services are often subject to funding reviews and contracting processes and the growth of the personalisation agenda, people have the need to see that services deliver specific outcomes. A planning tool which demonstrates this process in action can be a helpful way of services demonstrating precisely what progress they aim to make with each person. This is because talking in vague terms of "support" may not be enough to convince some funders and individuals in charge of contracting their own care. Being more specific is also more supportive and will enable service users and their networks to have "ownership" of the plan.

How will we Measure this Outcome (Indicators)?

If any outcome is specific, then the plan needs to be able to show how everyone will know that change has been achieved. What are the indicators of very small changes for people? If the outcome is around the person being able to access activity provision in their community, then how many activities per week is a reasonable measure of success for this person? If the outcome is around improving the person's self care skills, then how will everyone know that progress has been made? Is this about the person brushing their teeth without support or about them making a cup of tea safely and independently?

What Will the Service do to Achieve this Outcome?

This is about clarifying what the service's role is, and also what it is not. How many hours of care support is being put in? Who will be providing specific work on each identified area? What other resources could be available within the service for the service user and their carers to choose from? Also, what other agencies and services are involved in working with the person's care team (e.g.: Occupational Therapist, Social Worker, GP)?

What is Expected of the Person?

Care plans which focus only on service provision can have the air of "doing to" people, rather than enabling and empowering users of services in line with the principles of active support, as explored in chapter 13. Person centred care planning should always identify what the service user will need to do in order for them to achieve the outcomes, as this enables changes to be owned by the person rather than the service. This could involve looking at the person committing to change by attending appointments in the community, being open about the barriers they may face along the way, or committing to working with the care team on the agreed areas.

When will we Review if the Outcome has been Achieved (Milestones for Review)?

All plans need a review timescale to be built in, so that changes are recorded and further actions identified. This can be particularly important where changes have not been as expected as this can sometimes mean that a different type of support is needed to enable the person to make the progress they hope for in that area. Setting milestones where review will occur enables the whole care team, including the person's carers, to maintain focus when things might be challenging, and ensures that reviews do not drift when a busy workload for the service can occur. Milestones will be different according to the nature of each presenting need or issue, and according to the support which is put into place.

Care plans should always be discussed and agreed openly with the whole care team, including the service user and their carers. It can be useful sometimes to have a draft of a plan ready prior to a discussion taking place, but in this instance, it is vital that people are enabled to challenge the content of their plan. After all, it is their plan, and again must link with the principles of person centred care and active support.

Keeping the Planning Process Person Centred

Whilst this chapter has provided some guidance on care planning and planning processes, it is vital to remember that planning should always be person centred.

The Department of Health makes this clear, stating that:

"Care planning should be responsive to – but not prejudiced against – the age, living circumstances, geographic location, disabilities, gender, culture, faith, personal relationships and lifestyle choices of service users. Care planning should build on the strengths and abilities of individuals, and the part they can play in addressing their needs. It should address external or environmental factors that have caused the need to arise or will hamper the resolutions of need if not addressed."

(Department of Health 2002: 24)

The way in which a care plan is presented should reflect this perhaps it needs to be presented in a pictorial way, for example. Social care staff need to remember that plans are about and for service users and not services.

In Summary

Planning care and support is a vital aspect of the social care process. Social care workers have a duty to follow care plans and should have an understanding of how the process works.

39: REVIEWS

Reviews are an essential part of the social care process. If the review stage is missed, then support offered to an individual is likely to "drift", plans are likely to go out of date and outcomes are less likely to be achieved.

Guidance from the Department of Health (2002) recommends that a review should take place within three months from when social care services are first implemented or when major changes to a care plan are put in place. After this, they recommend that reviews are held at least annually and more frequently if circumstances dictate.

This guidance states that the purpose of a review is to:

➢ establish how far the support has achieved the outcomes set out in the care plan

➢ reassess the needs and issues of individuals

➢ help determine a service user's continued eligibility for support

➢ confirm or amend the current care plan, or lead to closure

➢ comment on how individuals are managing direct payments where relevant.

Review Meetings

Often reviews take the form of a meeting where everyone involved in providing support to the service user is represented. Usually, the care plan forms the basis of the discussion and it is amended as a result of the discussion.

A record should be made of the review and the care plan should be updated. If a "case" is closed following a review, then the reasons for the closure should be recorded.

A review record should include the following:

➢ A review of the achievements of the care plan objectives – by assessing the realism of the original plan and its continuing relevance, checking it against the perceptions of the user and carer and those of the service providers

➢ Reasons for success or failure of the plan

➢ An analysis of whether current services have been both cost effective and of the right quality

➢ Reassessment of the current needs of the service user and carer

➢ A consideration of whether the eligibility level remains the same – workers should extend, reduce or withdraw services as appropriate and provide a full explanation for the service user and / or their representative

➢ Re-evaluation and revision as appropriate of the original care plan objectives – setting new short term objectives for each service provider, bearing in mind the wishes of the user and carer

➢ Re-definition and re-negotiation of the service contacts as necessary

➢ Re-calculation of the cost and revision of the budget, subject to management approval, for the period leading to the next review

➢ Identification of areas where service quality is deficient

➤ Agreed date for next review

The review record should be shared with the service user and subject to confidentiality constraints, other contributors to the review.

(Adapted from Social Services Inspectorate and Department of Health 1991)

In Summary

Reviews are an essential part of the basic process of social care and social care practitioners should be fully involved in the review process.

40: PERSONALISATION

The idea of personalised care is nothing new, and links closely with the development of Direct Payments and the ideas of person centred active support. If we argue that social care provision should be tailored around individual's needs and self directed by the user of services, then the agenda around personalisation is a logical step. However, the government's White Paper *Putting People First: A shared vision and commitment to the transformation of Adult Social Care* (HM Government 2007) represents a "sea change" in terms of how social care services are to be structured, commissioned and delivered.

Social care is a high priority area in politics as more people live longer with complex health and social care needs. Central to the White Paper is a bold value-based vision:

"Ensuring older people, people with chronic conditions, disabled people and people with mental health problems have the best possible quality of life and the equality of independent living is fundamental to a socially just society."

(HM Government 2007: 2)

In practice, this should mean that as well as holding personalised budgets, people should be supported to:

> *"live independently;*

> *stay healthy and recover quickly from illness;*

> *exercise maximum control over their own life and where appropriate the lives of their family members;*

> *sustain a family unit which avoids children being required to take on inappropriate caring roles;*

> *participate as active and equal citizens, both economically and socially;*

> *have the best possible quality of life, irrespective of illness or disability;*

> *retain maximum dignity and respect."*

(HM Government 2007: 2-3)

This document focuses on improved multi agency working and early intervention and mirrors change in children's services. The focus on "re-ablement" (people getting better quicker after a change in their needs) and on improved access to information and advocacy services is, however, more specific to adult social care transformation.

Personalised budgets and changes to the process of social care

Key to the vision of personalisation is the idea of more people taking on responsibility for their own budget to meet their own social care needs. Previously, when an adult with social care needs received an assessment from the local authority, they would be offered services which could meet their assessed needs. These services could include a Direct Payment so the person could employ staff to provide the care required. From 2011 on, the person assessed will be told **how much money** their personal budget for care is instead, so that all of the decisions about how this care will be provided will rest with the person as a matter of course, rather than as one of the many options.

This will mean that the process of assessment, care planning and delivery of social care services will change fundamentally. Instead of care being there as a "safety net" for the most vulnerable in society, access to effective social care is cast as a basic human right. The idea is that what precisely is effective for each person is different, so in practice there is a need for:

➢ greater choice of provision. It will no longer be acceptable for people to receive no services and fall through gaps in provision when the list of available options does not match their needs. Instead, the person should receive support or advocacy to find some provision which *does* meet their needs

➢ linked with this, people should be seen as individual people with choices, preferences, lifestyles and cultures of their own , and not as a de-personalised or indistinct group of "vulnerable adults" with "needs" as this goes against the value base of social care, and also can lead to people *becoming* vulnerable or de-valued

➢ universal care provision to change in terms of considering its accessibility and inclusivity

➢ care to focus more on the key principles of individuality, cultural sensitivity and active support

➢ care to be provided which provides more than the basics (medication, assistance with using the toilet etc) and which enhances the person's life and choices

➢ greater competition in the "market" for consumers (i.e.: service users) to purchase the care which they want to receive

All of this presents a challenge, not just to local authorities and those commissioning services, but to:

➢ Social care workers – to consider how practices and cultures within the care setting meet the needs of individuals; champion their choices; cast them as the purchaser or customer (as opposed to a passive "receiver" of care); and actively promote their rights and individuality. See the Skills for Care "New Types of Worker" web site (www.newtypesofworker.co.uk) for more information on the challenges for workers

➢ Service users – to understand what is available, and how a budget can be used to commission services is one issue. Managing this process in practice may involve several people and some individuals may need more support than others through this process. It may also be harder for some people to complain about poor care or to "de-commission" a service if it does not meet their needs, as many people need a high level of empowerment to be confident enough to do this.

➢ Carers – to feel confident that the service user is empowered and that the provision is effective. Carers may also be entitled to a personal budget to meet their own needs as a carer for time off or access to opportunities. This may mean that the carer and the "cared-for" person both have to manage budgets and processes, which could become a challenge in itself.

➢ Providers – to ensure provision is effective (as described above) and flexible enough to meet changing needs and individuals. If provision is not effective at meeting individual requirements, people will not choose that provider. Many large care agencies and independent organisations have gone through changes and re-branding to ensure their provision appeals to individual service users who can commission services, as well as to retain large local authority contracts.

➢ Adult Social Workers – following several years where the role has been in many areas described as "care manager", this will change again to one which focuses more on assessment, eligibility for budgets, and advocacy for individuals seeking to develop provision which meets their own personal needs. Changes to the process of assessment and delivery of social care services take time to occur and to be evaluated.

Resources for Social Care Workers

The website www.personalisation.org.uk is a useful resource and contains information about topics such as brokerage of services, managing finance, involving carers and wider family, and equalities issues.

Skills for Care's New Types of Worker web site (www.newtypesofworker.co.uk) shares how the role of workers in social care is changing and new settings within which social care will be delivered in order to maximise choice and independence.

The Transforming Adult Social Care website hosted by the Social Care Institute for Excellence, www.tasc.org.uk, has lots of useful information on how the transformation of Adult Social Care is being implemented in different areas, innovative practice, and how choice and control will be linked to resource allocation systems.

In Summary

The personalisation agenda represents a fundamental change in how social care needs will be assessed and how services should be commissioned by individuals so their needs are met. It is vital for social care workers to keep up to date with developments in this area, and for everyone working in social care to consider the challenge of personalisation as a means of integrating values and principles into all social care processes.

41: SOCIAL PEDAGOGY

Social pedagogy has a long history within many European countries – particularly Denmark, France, Italy, Germany and the Netherlands. It has not really been practised within the UK, but is now a growing field of interest with Government policy in relation to children's services referring more and more to social pedagogy.

The historical roots of social pedagogy are about working with children taking an individual educational approach. However, it is now widely used as an approach in working with adults within the European context. It is therefore very likely to be used as an approach in adult services in the future.

ThemPra (2009) state:

"Social pedagogy is an approach covering the whole lifespan of people, and with recognition to lifelong learning as well as social pedagogues' person and care centred value base, social pedagogy has become the preferred way of working with adults as well. Considering the need for improvement in adult services – for refuges, prisoners or older people in care, to mention but a few – England would benefit from conceiving social pedagogy in the broadest possible way and striving to implement it across all welfare services."

Essentially, social pedagogy is about educating people (children and adults) in a way which recognises their role as active learners, so that they can take a full and healthy role in a diverse society. There are key issues within the concept of social pedagogy around diversity, inclusion and opportunity as the social pedagogue (professional, educator or social care worker) seeks to provide opportunities and learning for those excluded or disadvantaged within society.

Cameron states that:

"The social pedagogue works with the whole person, and supports their all-round development. Pedagogues employ theories, professional knowledge, and creative and practical skills with groups and on an individual basis. They acknowledge uncertainty and constantly review situations and decisions, in dialogue with colleagues. Human rights and participation underpin social pedagogy."

(Cameron 2007)

The idea of social pedagogy then is similar to schools' provision around Personal, Social and Health Education (PSHE), which is sometimes now referred to as Citizenship or SEAL (Social and Emotional Aspects of Learning). The differences between a teacher of PSHE and a social pedagogue, however, are around the focus in social pedagogy on the individual's needs as a learner, and on the practitioner's approach to their role. The concept of social pedagogy also applies equally to work with adults as well as children. This is because the role of the pedagogue:

➤ focuses on the individual, even when working in group settings

➤ seeks to promote and model positive social relationships

➤ applies knowledge from across the range of disciplines as described above

Application to Social Care Practice

In social care and social work, it is easy to see how social pedagogy applies in how "direct work" is practised with individuals or groups of service users. Rather than there being a set "curriculum", this work tends to focus on addressing specific issues to meet individual needs. This could include life story work (see page 54), therapeutic work, or discussion about different ways of tackling a difficulty the person is facing.

The ThemPra Society describe how central the relationship between the pedagogue and learner is as this is seen as central to creating trust and to learners feeling empowered and enabled to learn. Again, this is unlikely to feel new to most people working in social care, but the idea is that through this relationship, trust is built, which in turn enables the person to feel safe to learn and to discuss and reflect on challenges and issues as they present in their life. The relationship between the person and the professional needs to be authentic (so the person knows that the professional genuinely cares about their well being as well as just being someone who is paid to be in their lives), but built upon professional standards and boundaries.

Alongside this process of reflection upon issues which naturally present as learning opportunities, the pedagogue seeks to provide positive learning experiences which enable the person's learning to occur. This learning can take place in any setting or environment and is not about worksheets or formal teaching, but instead is about the whole person ("holistic learning"), their needs, rights, choices and relationships with others. Positive learning experiences are crucial to social pedagogic practice because:

"The power of experiencing something positive - something that makes us happy, something we have achieved, a new skill we have learned, the caring support from someone else … raises our self-confidence and feeling of self-worth, so it reinforces our sense of well-being, of learning, of being able to form a strong relationship, or of feeling empowered."

(ThemPra 2009)

The key concepts of social pedagogy are therefore about:

➤ Promoting each person's well being

➤ Holistic learning

➤ Positive, empowering and professional relationships between the pedagogue and the person accessing services

➤ Empowerment

It could be argued that everyone working in social care takes on the role of a social pedagogue at some point. Most of us probably don't call it that! However, as social care is subject to increasing professionalisation, and the concept of social pedagogy gains momentum in the UK (as it is already doing in parenting work, residential child care and family support – see www.socialpedagogyuk.com), more social care workers are likely to encounter the term.

Social pedagogues in Europe are generally qualified with a degree in social pedagogy and it is interesting to note that the first degree in social pedagogy in the UK has recently started.

Whilst it is unlikely that social care workers will be qualified as social pedagogues they may find that taking a social pedagogical approach is useful in their work and that they find social pedagogy a useful way of describing their professional expertise.

In Summary

Social Pedagogy offers social care workers a way of describing the professional application of their skills. Social care workers are often involved in working with service users in an educational capacity to enable them to access opportunities and relate to others positively. Social pedagogy allows workers to examine how they use their skills to enable others to grow, develop and learn, and is likely to continue to grow in the UK as a field.

SECTION F: HEALTH AND SAFETY

The background knowledge in relation to health and safety is referred to in almost every vocational qualification, probably because working in a way which promotes health and safety is part of everyone's role whatever field they work in. This is no less so for social care workers.

Since the knowledge required in this area is very "concrete" and can be quite detailed, it is often considered a "boring" area, and social care staff can "switch off" whenever health and safety is mentioned. However, this aspect of work is vitally important – as is the knowledge underpinning this area.

42: HEALTH AND SAFETY: THE LEGAL FRAMEWORK

The legislation covering most of the other areas referred to in this book differ across the UK because of the different legislative arrangements in England, Wales, Scotland and Northern Ireland. However, health and safety legislation is UK wide – largely influenced by European directives. This chapter will outline the key legislation covering health and safety in the workplace.

The Health and Safety at Work Act 1974

This Act is the main piece of legislation which applies to this area. It places a general duty on employers to ensure health, safety and welfare of all employees "as far as reasonably practicable."

Under the Act, employers have a duty to:

➢ ensure the health and safety at work for all employees

➢ provide and maintain equipment and systems which are safe and not a risk to employees' health in terms of use, handling, storage and transport of articles and substances

➢ provide information, training and supervision relating to health and safety at work

Managers have a duty to:

➢ maintain a safe working environment for all staff

➢ ensure that all staff adhere to policies, procedures and instructions

➢ provide training for staff practices and work methods

➢ explain hazards and safe working practices to new employees before they start work

➢ report/record all accidents

Employers have a duty to:

➢ ensure the health and safety at work for all employees

➢ provide and maintain equipment and systems which are safe and not a risk to employees' health in terms of use, handling, storage and transport of articles and substances

➢ provide information, training and supervision relating to health and safety at work

The Health and Safety at Work Act 1974 is an example of "umbrella legislation" in that since 1974 there have been successive regulations which have expanded its scope, clarified responsibilities and responded to new circumstances as they have arisen without changing the overall principles of the original Act.

The Health and Safety regulations which relate most specifically to the social care sector are:

Safety Representatives and Safety Committees Regulations

If an employer recognises a trade union and that union has either appointed or is about to appoint safety representatives then the employer must consult those representatives on matters which will affect the employees they represent.

The roles of trade union safety representatives appointed under these Regulations are:

➢ to investigate possible dangers at work, the causes of accidents and general complaints by employees on health and safety and welfare issues and to take these matters up with the employer

➢ to carry out inspections of the workplace particularly following accidents, diseases or other events

➢ to represent employees in discussions with health and safety inspectors and to receive information from those inspectors

➢ to attend meetings of safety committees

An employer must set up a safety committee if two or more trade union representatives ask for one.

Health and Safety (First Aid) Regulations

These Regulations require employers to provide adequate equipment, facilities and personnel to enable first aid to be given to employees if they become ill or are injured at work.

The Regulations do not oblige employers to provide first aid for members of the public, though the Health and Safety Executive strongly recommends that employers make provision for them.

Workplace (Health, Safety and Welfare) Regulations

These Regulations complement the Management of Health and Safety at Work Regulations, and cover the management of workplaces. Duties are placed on both employers and employees (in the sense that both have control over a workplace). The main requirements created by these Regulations are:

➢ the workplace, equipment, systems etc must be maintained in an efficient state

➢ enclosed workplaces must be ventilated by a sufficient quantity of fresh and purified air

➢ a reasonable temperature must be maintained inside buildings and a sufficient number of thermometers must be provided

➢ lighting must be suitable and efficient

➢ workplaces must be kept sufficiently clean

Manual Handling Operations Regulations

These cover what is often referred to as "moving and handling". The Regulations contain the following main requirements:

➢ suitable and efficient assessment of all moving and handling should be made, if the handling cannot be avoided

➢ risk reduction strategies must be considered by employers to reduce the risk of injury to the lowest level reasonably practicable

➢ employers must provide reasonable information about moving and handling

➢ employers must review assessments where there is reason to suspect that circumstances have changed, and then make any necessary changes

➢ employees must make full and proper use of any system of work provided by the employer

Reporting of Injuries, Diseases and Dangerous Occurrences Regulations

These Regulations are often referred to as RIDDOR. The Regulations require the reporting of work-related accidents, diseases and dangerous occurrences. Employers, self employed people and people in control of work premises have duties under the Regulations to report:

➢ deaths or major injuries at work

➢ work related injuries which result in people being away from work for over 3 days

➢ work related diseases

➢ dangerous occurrences at work

Health and Safety (Consultation with Employees) Regulations

Any employees not in groups covered by trade union safety representatives must be consulted by their employers under these Regulations. An employer can choose to consult them directly or through elected representatives.

Elected representatives of employees have the following roles:

➢ to take up with employers concerns about possible risks and dangerous events in the workplace that may affect the employees they represent

➢ to take up with employers general matters affecting the health and safety of the employees they represent

➢ to represent the employees who elected them in consultations with Health and Safety inspectors

Employers may choose to give elected representatives extra roles.

Management of Health and Safety at Work Regulations

These Regulations place a duty on employers to assess all health and safety risks associated with their work, and to introduce procedures and practices that minimise the likelihood of any identified risks occurring.

Additionally employers have to provide training for staff:

➢ when they start work

> when their work or responsibilities change and there are new or greater risks

> periodically if needed - for instance if the skills do not get used regularly

The training must be during working hours and not at the expense of employees.

Control of Substances Hazardous to Health Regulations

These Regulations are often referred to as COSHH.

The Regulations cover substances which can cause ill health. Any substances such as cleaning materials, waste products, fumes etc are covered.

In order to comply with the Regulations employers must:

> assess the risks to health arising from work

> decide what precautions are needed

> prevent or control exposure to substances hazardous to health

> ensure that control measures are used and maintained

> monitor exposure of workers to hazardous substances and where assessment shows that health surveillance may be needed to carry out such surveillance

> ensure that employees are properly informed, trained and supervised

Product Liability

Product liability is established under Part 1 of the Consumer Protection Act 1987. Product liability means that under the Consumer Protection Act 1987 a manufacturer is liable for injury caused, or property that is damaged, due to faulty equipment that they have provided. The manufacturer is also responsible for providing information about the safe use of the equipment. Hence instructions are often stuck to equipment as well as being provided in leaflets or booklets. Product liability could apply equally to hoists, other aids and adaptations as well as an office chair.

If the equipment is not faulty and is used satisfactorily then liability for its safe use transfers to the employer.

Provision and Use of Equipment Regulations (PUWER)

These Regulations impose a range of duties on employers (and to a limited extent to the employees who use the equipment). Aspects include:

> The initial state of the equipment

> Use of equipment for the proper purpose

> Suitability of equipment

> Maintenance

> Inspection

> Training staff in its use

The scope of these Regulations has been interpreted very broadly so that it includes cupboards and curtain rails as well as equipment that is subject to heavy usage. The employer's liability is strictly applied. Even if the equipment was regularly inspected and then it unexpectedly fell and injured a staff member the employer is still liable. The employer would not be liable for negligence if the equipment was satisfactorily maintained and inspected, but they would still be liable for any injury under these Regulations.

Lifting Operations and Lifting Equipment Regulations

These Regulations apply to lifting equipment used at work. Lifting equipment would include hoists, stairlifts and through floor lifts. The Regulations impose a range of duties on employers and to a limited extent on staff who use or supervise the use of the equipment. Duties include:

➤ Ensuring adequate strength and stability

➤ Positioning and installation

➤ Marking of safe working loads

➤ Organisation of lifting operations

➤ Examination and inspection

➤ Reporting defects, and acting on these reports

There is no set guidance as to how frequently lifting equipment should be inspected. This is partly dependent on whether the equipment is exposed to conditions that could cause it to deteriorate so that dangerous situations could arise. Some hoist manufacturers recommend a thorough examination of their hoists every six months. Against this the Health and Safety Executive have published a document recommending that hoists are inspected at least every twelve months. The implication is that some manufacturers could have a conflict of interests. (That is because they can charge a care organisation every time their trained inspectors go out on a visit.) What is clear is that the time scales for thorough inspections should be drawn up by a competent person who is aware of all relevant facts.

Food Safety Act 1990

This Act applies wherever food is supplied other than within a family situation. Therefore, all social care settings which involve the supply of food must comply with hygiene and other food safety requirements.

This Act is a wide ranging piece of legislation which strengthened and updated existing laws relevant to food safety. The Act sets out a number of requirements about food produced for human consumption:

➤ food provided must not be injurious to health

➤ it must not be unfit to eat

➤ it must not be contaminated

The Food Safety Act and all food legislation is enforced through environmental health officers and trading standards officers who are employed by local authorities.

Environmental Protection Act 1990

This is a very wide ranging piece of legislation, much of which is probably not relevant to social care staff. Some sections, however, may have a direct bearing on your work. For example, section 34 of the Act places a duty of care on anyone who "*produces, imports, carries, keeps, treats or disposes of household, commercial, or industrial*" waste.

In addition, the Environmental Protection Act contains the main legislation for England and Wales on statutory nuisance. A variety of definitions of statutory nuisance are outlined within the Act. However, those which may be most relevant to care staff are:

➤ any premises in such a state as to be prejudicial to health or a nuisance.

➤ noise emitted from premises so as to be prejudicial to health or a nuisance.

Corporate Manslaughter and Corporate Homicide Act 2007

This Act received Royal Assent on 26th July 2007. It amends case law and generally the Law of Negligence.

Most of this Act came into force on 6th April 2008 and it basically does just one thing: it creates a new offence of Corporate Manslaughter, or in Scotland, Corporate Homicide. The differing terminology is simply in order to fit with existing legal structures on each side of the border. The Act is, aside from this, UK wide legislation.

The offence of Corporate Manslaughter/Homicide is not new, but has always been wrapped up in a mass of case law and other legislation known collectively as the Law of Negligence. In the old system, a company could only be convicted if one high up individual, known legally as a "controlling mind" could be seen as almost personally culpable for the death of a person through the company's activities. Years of accident investigations have shown that fatal incidents, and indeed corporations, do not work like that. There is usually a string of events that lead to an incident.

The new Act therefore redefines the offence and the causes required to be present for a case of Corporate manslaughter to be brought. It happens like this:

➤ A death occurs. Obvious really, but if someone is "only" severely injured, standard health and safety legislation still applies.

➤ The death does not have to be an employee of the company concerned, but it does have to result from the way that company's activities were managed or organised.

➤ Also, the death must have arisen from a gross breach of the company's duty of care to the victim.

➤ Lastly, the organisational failings that led to the death must have been somehow authorised by senior management. That is to say, practices that were authored, agreed to, or known about by senior management. Senior management does not just include Directors either.

Please also note that this Act does not introduce any new duties on organisations but does, interestingly, extend to organisations engaged in illegal activities. The Act applies to any business in the UK or foreign businesses operating in the UK from partnerships upwards. Single traders are not covered. Crown Bodies and government organisations are covered including the Prison Service and the Army.

In order that certain people doing dangerous jobs can get on and do them without their employers being paralysed by legislation, there are certain exemptions where charges under this Act may not be brought. Some are "comprehensive", e.g.: soldiers in battle and training, while others are "partial" which is where some aspects of social care come in.

Partial Exemptions

While social work and probation departments are still covered by this Act in their duties as employers and occupiers of buildings, they are exempt from prosecution under this Act when their staff are carrying out statutory inspection functions and other frontline aspects of their jobs. It is difficult to see how this will work in practice and it will be shaped by case law but if, for example, a social worker visits a house to investigate a claim of abuse and is killed by a client then, provided their employer had not failed in their duties as an employer, no charge can be brought against the employer under this Act. Other occupations subject to partial exemptions include lifeboat crews and mountain rescue teams, which rather puts the job into perspective, doesn't it?

Policies and Procedures

Social care workers need to have a working knowledge of their agency's policies and procedures in order to carry out their responsibilities in terms of health and safety. As a minimum workers will need to be familiar with the policies and procedures covering the following:

➢ Communicable diseases/ infection control policy

➢ Confidentiality and information disclosure

➢ Control of exposure to hazardous waste (based on COSHH regulations)

➢ Fire safety policy

➢ Hygiene and food safety

➢ Record keeping and access to files

➢ Health and safety

➢ Moving and handling

➢ Dealing with accidents and emergencies

➢ Responding to abuse.

The above list is drawn from the National Induction Standards for Social Care (TOPSS England updated 2005).

Policies and procedures are necessary in all sectors, but perhaps more so in social care for various reasons, including:

➢ Legal compliance: Legislation (for example National Minimum Standards) require services to have policies and procedures in specific areas.

➢ Good "business" sense: Having policies and procedures (particularly those relating to human resources issues) make good business sense.

➢ Consistent practice: Clear policies and procedures will ensure consistent practice in a staff team and staff will be aware of minimum standards for their practice.

➢ Managerial accountability: Good quality policy and procedures protect managers in terms of their accountability for the actions of staff.

The Royal College of Nursing (2006) developed a useful framework for evaluating health and social care policy. The framework provides for principles *"against which we can evaluate service and policy developments, consultations and initiatives across health and social care settings and sectors."*

(RCN 2006:2)

These principles were updated in 2008 and provide a useful framework for the review and evaluation of policies, procedures and systems.

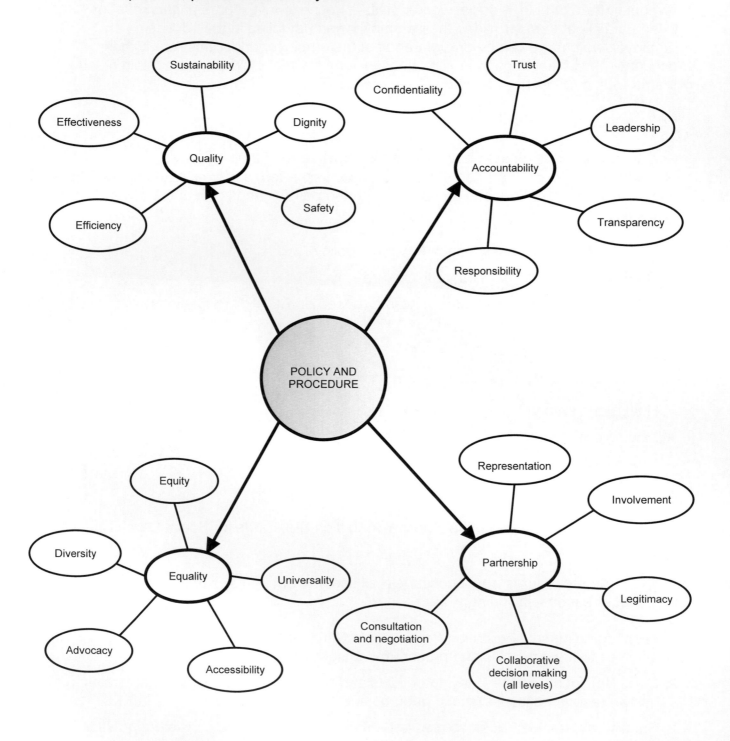

It is important that all services have policies and procedures which reflect national legislation and good practice guidelines in this area. Individual workers may not have much control over the nature of an organisation's policies, particularly if they work within a large provider of services. However, all workers should be:

➤ aware of the legislative context in which they operate

➤ aware of the policies and procedures, which guide their work

➤ up to date in relation to necessary training to enable them to put policy safely into practice.

In Summary

We all have responsibilities in terms of health and safety at work. It is important for social care practitioners to be aware of these responsibilities and to have at least a basic understanding of the law which informs this area of practice.

43: RISK ASSESSMENT

Risk assessment theory and practice is covered in chapter 37. In this chapter we will explore risk assessment in the context of health and safety. However, this should be read alongside chapter 37.

The Management of Health and Safety at Work Regulations place a legal responsibility on employers to carry out risk assessment as the first step in ensuring a healthy and safe workplace. Risk assessments should identify possible hazards, assess the likelihood of harm resulting and identify what measures could be taken to manage the risks.

Hazard and Risk

It is worth spending some time clarifying the associated concepts of hazards and risks since these are key words within health and safety risk assessment.

➢ A hazard is an activity or substance which has the *potential* to do harm.

➢ A risk is the likelihood of harm occurring.

Everything that people do exposes them to hazards. However, it is the way that people do things or the way that people use substances that determine the risk.

In health and safety the aim of making a risk assessment is to identify the potential hazards, to identify the seriousness of these hazards and to assess the associated risks.

As a basic example, whenever we go up or down stairs there is a possible hazard that we might fall. However, the likelihood of this depends on who is going up / down stairs and how they do this.

In the social care sector the employee's workplace, in practice, can be a variety of different locations which may include the homes of those they are providing a service to. By extension then, risk assessments must take into account the different locations that social care workers may be working in.

In assessing the extent and nature of the risk, workers will need to take into account the severity of the risk and the likelihood or probability that it will occur. This is often represented as a calculation where both severity and probability are given a numerical value and multiplied to form the risk factor.

In this way the worst possible outcome is balanced against the probability that this outcome will occur. For example, an individual who can have prolonged epileptic seizures may have epilepsy which is well controlled by medication. The worst possible outcome from a prolonged seizure may conceivably be death. However, this may be balanced by the fact that the medication controls the epilepsy so well that it has been several years since the person last experienced a seizure. Therefore, although the severity is high, we can justifiably assess that the probability of a seizure occurring is very low.

Risk Assessments in Health and Safety

The Health and Safety Executive (2006) identify five steps in undertaking a risk assessment.

Step 1   **Identify and document possible hazards**

These are usually environmental hazards which might be in the home of the individual being supported such as very hot water coming from a bath tap, or in the external environment such as a busy road nearby.

Step 2   **Identify who might be at risk of harm and what form the harm might take**

The hazards do not present a danger in themselves but individuals may be put at risk by the actions they take. An individual may be at risk of scalding if he or she decides to take bath in water which is extremely hot. Someone crossing a busy road who has relatively poor pedestrian skills may be at risk of being struck by a car and being injured if they take insufficient care.

In each of the above examples it is not just the person who is being supported who may be at risk. Any visitor lacking the necessary skills may be at risk of scalding whilst other road users may also be at risk of injury if involved in an accident.

Step 3   **Evaluate risks arising from hazards and determine whether any existing precautionary measures are sufficient**
Someone who lacks the ability to run a bath unaided and judge the safety of the water temperature may be at significant risk of injury or even death from scalding unless steps are taken to protect them.

One option might be to have a mixer system installed which gives a controlled, lower water temperature. This can be quite costly to install, but it removes the possibility of scalding although the problem would still remain should the individual need to access a bath in a different location which does not have this system. Alternatively, a member of staff could help the person to run the bath supporting them to do as much as possible for themselves and ensuring that the water temperature is safe.

A person with poor pedestrian skills may benefit from a programme being devised to help them to improve their skills. This could include progressively reduced degrees of supervision with the aim that the person becomes fully independent.

In both the above instances the degree of risk can be reduced by providing supervision and additional support where necessary. The amount of supervision over time might be reduced as the person's competence grows.

Step 4   **Complete a risk assessment**

Under the Regulations there is a requirement that risk assessment documentation is completed if the organisation employs more than five people. In fact under the Care Standards Act 2000 there is an expectation that risk assessments will be completed in all cases and it is regarded as good practice within health and social care organisations.

The risk assessment must record significant hazards, assessment of risk and reasonable precautions which can be taken. This documentation must be recorded carefully and must be accessible to all workers who might have to use it. It must be dated and available for future inspection if required.

Step 5   Review the assessment periodically and update if necessary

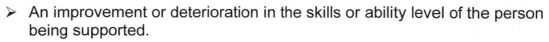

Risk assessments will require review at regular intervals (at least annually) and as circumstances change. Examples of changes which may signal the need for an earlier review include:

➢ An improvement or deterioration in the skills or ability level of the person being supported.

➢ A change in the service user's environment.

➢ A change in health or in level of impairment requiring more or less support.

➢ A change in service level not influenced by the above.

The review date should be accurately recorded on the risk assessment.

Aside from the legal requirement to produce and use risk assessments, there are further reasons to do so:

➢ They provide a measure of protection to the individual and to others who may be either directly or indirectly at risk.

➢ They provide protection to workers, which may be quite literally by safeguarding them from a possible consequence of taking the risk, or by ensuring that the service and workers can justify any actions taken in respect of the risk.

➢ They can also help to protect other people, including the general public who may be exposed to risk.

There is a danger of health and safety and risk assessment in particular being associated with the more "traditional" aspects of health and safety, such as fire precautionary measures, moving and handling and COSHH (Control of Substances Hazardous to Health) to the exclusion of risks connected with the choices and behaviours of the people using a service. All social care staff should be able to see the connection between health and safety and risk management and all aspects of the service which is provided, rather than seeing it as something which is the province of health and safety specialists.

Identifying Risks in Services and the Community

Identifying risks is a responsibility of all workers. However, just because a risk is identified, it does not necessarily mean it can be eliminated.

The type of risks that a worker need to be conscious of will be determined by their work role and type of service.

In a community based team the risk areas could include:

➢ Risks to service users (e.g.: Mental health issues, risks of falls, etc)

➢ Vulnerability to abuse

➢ Lone working and risk of violence (either from a stranger or service user or carer)

➢ Stress

In a domiciliary service the risks could include:

- Trips and falls
- Risk of abuse (in respect of vulnerable service users)
- Other risks to service users (e.g.: fire)
- Stress
- Manual handling
- Lone working and risk of violence

In a care home or day centre the risks could include:

- Manual handling
- Risk of violence to staff and service users
- Risk of abuse (of vulnerable service users)
- Trips and falls
- Fire
- Stress
- Handling of medication
- Handling and preparation of food
- Risk of infections
- Risks to service user (e.g.: leaving the building alone)
- Other work related risks (e.g.: use of disinfectants)

Field workers in the community may need an added awareness around the risks during a home visit.

These lists are by no means exhaustive.

Responding to risk is not just the responsibility of managers or any worker on their own. As already stated, health and safety is a joint responsibility. All services and teams should maintain an open dialogue around health and safety, including risk assessment and reviews of everyday practices. Service users should also be involved in discussions as appropriate.

Some risks will need the involvement of the whole team, and other risks will need discussions with line managers and other agencies.

Promoting a Positive Culture

If a service operates within the model of active support, as covered in chapter 13, it should be well on the way to promoting a positive culture in relation to risk.

Taking some risks is a daily occurrence for everyone and must be necessary if people are to take a full and active part in their communities. Government Guidance makes this clear:

"The possibility of risk is an inevitable consequence of empowered people taking decisions about their own lives."

(Department of Health 2007)

Most people are able to balance risk against possible benefits and will take any necessary precautions to help minimise risk. It may not be quite so easy for the people that social care workers support to achieve this balance for themselves. This is where support will be required. It is where the key dilemmas will occur and where getting the balance right is perhaps the most difficult. Sometimes when providing support, social care staff can be anxious to eliminate any identified risk of harm which can mean that a decision is made that a particular choice cannot be supported. As previously covered, this should only occur in extreme circumstances and where risk assessments clearly indicate the reasons why the person's choice cannot be supported.

Risk assessments are designed to ensure that those making decisions are aware of all the risk factors and have considered any precautionary measures which might help to reduce identified risks. Their purpose is not to inhibit choice and prevent people making choices which may carry a degree of risk, but to raise awareness in order that decisions can be made with the full knowledge of possible consequences and some anticipation about measures which might be taken to reduce this.

The impact of a risk assessment can sometimes be to prevent people undertaking activities which would be expected to bring pleasure and satisfaction in the lives of people being supported. The aim should be the opposite - to take preventative measures to actively reduce the possibility of the person being at risk. Key reasons why some organisations may be "risk averse" and over-reluctant to provide positive active support to people in taking risks might include:

➤ A wish to protect the individual from harm. This is natural when working with vulnerable people and is the object of Safeguarding Adults policies, but services are now designed around the individual to an increasing extent with the aim of supporting them to be as independent as possible. An important aspect to personalising services is recognising the dignity of risk.

➤ Fear of putting the organisation at risk of litigation. Once again this is understandable in that the media regularly carry stories of legal action being taken against allegedly negligent organisations. There are also more and more advertisements by organisations promising to help individuals to claim compensation.

➤ Fear of being blamed if things go wrong. This arises if the employee has little management support when dealing with issues of risk and often where there is a perception that managers will rush to take disciplinary action against staff members should an error occur.

These feelings may be argued away as simply being unproven assumptions, but from the perspective of a lone worker or someone working as part of a small team (perhaps in people's own homes and away from a base) they may seem justified. The key to feeling secure in supporting people to take reasonable risks lies in the culture within the organisation. This in turn rests upon the efforts of managers to demonstrate that they value their staff and are prepared to support them when necessary. Staff will not feel able to contribute to a positive culture around risk unless they themselves feel that they are listened to and that their views are respected by their managers. This kind of supportive culture brings benefits to all elements of managing the service – not just the management of risk.

Maximising Service User Involvement

Values should always inform social care practice. Involving service users in discussions about health and safety conveys respect as well as the fact that service users have a responsibility to maintain certain standards around health and safety if they are able to.

The discussion with service users could relate to what to do following an accident supporting the service user to maintain their own personal hygiene, or assisting them to follow accepted guidance on handling food safely.

Discussing matters with the service user conveys to both the service user and colleagues that such involvement is a key aspect of good practice.

Duty of Care

A positive risk taking culture sits alongside the duty of care which social care workers have. The duty of care is defined as:

"An obligation placed on an individual requiring that they exercise a reasonable standard of care while doing something (or possibly omitting to do something) that could foreseeably harm others."

(Department of Health 2007)

It is vital that the duty of care is not used as a reason to deny the dignity of risk taking. The need to get the balance right has been made clear in various professional Codes of Conduct. For example, the code of practice for social care workers says that workers must *"promote the independence of individuals while protecting them as far as possible from danger or harm."*

Having a clear understanding of the concepts covered in this section will help to make a judgement to get the balance right.

In Summary

Risk assessment is the first steps in health and safety. All social care workers need to understand the process of risk assessment. It is vital that risk assessments are not used to deny service users opportunities within a risk averse culture. They should be used to support people in a way that recognises the dignity of risk taking and minimises potential risks.

It is vital that all social care workers acknowledge and address service users rights to make informed choices and decisions about actions which may involve elements of risk. The duty of care is not in itself a sufficient reason to deny the fact that there is dignity within risk taking.

44: SPECIFIC ISSUES IN HEALTH AND SAFETY

Moving and Handling

Back pain is a major cause of job related illness in Britain. It is therefore very important that social care staff look after their own back.

The Spine

The spine has three main functions:

➢ support the human skeleton

➢ to protect the spinal cord

➢ enable us to move freely.

The spine is made up of 33 bones (vertebrae). Twenty four of the bones can move, which in turn enables us to move. The other bones are fused together, four in the coccyx at the very end of the spine. Five bones are fused in the sacral region (just above the coccyx). The sacral bones connect the spine to the pelvis.

Firstly, "arms" of each vertebra connect with "arms" of the vertebra above and below it. These joints are known as facet joints. At these joints the bone is covered in cartilage, a strong but slippery lining which enables the bones to rub against each other (in the joint) without causing friction.

Secondly, the main body of each vertebra does not connect with the main body of the vertebra above and below it. Instead a disc is sandwiched between the main body of each vertebra and its neighbouring vertebra.

This disc is made of a strong fibrous casing which has a thick gel-like substance in the middle. This acts as a cushioning pad or shock absorber when we lift objects or run or bend etc.

Thirdly, ligaments ensure that joints remain together. Whilst they are not elastic, they do have some give.

Fourthly, there are several layers of muscles, some of which control our posture and others which enable us to bend and straighten up.

Pressure on the Spine

When anyone bends down from the waist to lift an object, the back is under a great deal of pressure. The discs are compressed and the back muscles have to pull their body weight, the weight of any object and pull against gravity. Bending at the waist to lift an object can easily result in back injury.

Added to this risk, when people are lifting objects they often twist their body. This will put more pressure on both the discs and the back muscles.

Since so many people have suffered from back problems due to lifting, two main strategies have been adopted to address this.

Firstly – only engage in manual moving and handling where it is unavoidable. Wherever possible, use other means to assist a person to move (e.g.: hoists).

Secondly – where manual moving and handling is necessary, use techniques that have been found to reduce the risk of people developing back problems.

<u>Moving and Handling Techniques</u>

Every social care service where moving and handling is required will have developed techniques and should provide staff with training on these. The best way to learn about moving and handling techniques is to learn through watching the techniques being applied and then by rehearsing these techniques and receiving feedback from the member of staff who is providing the training. Once the technique is satisfactory, workers can then apply it in line with the service's expectations.

Handling Food Safely

In many social care settings, social care practitioners will be involved in food preparation and handling. Even if they do not prepare food, it is likely that they will handle food in one way or another. Being aware of how to reduce the risk of food poisoning occurring is very important, whatever a worker's professional involvement with food will be.

<u>Food Poisoning</u>

Food poisoning is caused by certain types of bacteria growing and multiplying in food. Whether someone who eats a certain food will become ill with food poisoning is dependent on several factors. For some food poisoning bacteria to have an adverse effect, there needs to be a great deal of the bacteria in the first place. Some types of food poisoning bacteria appear to need only a low level of exposure to cause illness.

Additionally, a person's own resistance to the food poisoning bacteria can determine whether a person will actually develop food poisoning. Some groups of people are more at risk than others. These include older people and people who are already ill.

Food poisoning can cause abdominal pains, vomiting, diarrhoea and fever. The person can become ill soon after eating the food with food poisoning bacteria or several days after. The onset of the actual symptoms can be quite sudden.

There are several key strategies to reduce the risk of food poisoning. One key strategy is the prevention of cross-contamination. This has several aspects to it:

➢ Health of the staff handling the food

➢ Cleanliness. A clean environment and effective hand washing markedly reduce the risk of cross-contamination markedly

➢ Separate storage. Ensuring foods are stored separately and that they are appropriately covered

Another key approach is temperature control of the food.

Health of Staff Handling Food

Staff who handle food have a legal obligation to inform their manager of certain illnesses. The manager can then assess the risk to the safety of the food when they have all the relevant information, and they can then decide on any relevant action. This may require the person to be excluded from their food handling responsibilities until they have definitely recovered from their illness.

Staff who handle food should notify their manager if they:

➢ have been suffering from vomiting or diarrhoea

➢ have cuts or sores that are infected (red, swollen, pus-containing)

➢ feel unwell

➢ were ill on a holiday they have just returned from

➢ someone in their household is suffering from vomiting or diarrhoea

Cleanliness

This is a crucial aspect of reducing the likelihood of food poisoning occurring.

➢ Before handling any food, hands should be thoroughly washed. If you handle raw meat, poultry (including raw eggs) or fish, wash your hands after preparing them

➢ Surfaces should be cleaned immediately after use, this includes chopping boards, work tops etc

➢ Wash all utensils thoroughly in hot water and detergent. Regularly change the water. Rinse all the washing up and it is best left to air dry. Try to use tea towels as little as possible. When using a dishwasher, make sure the correct amount of salt and detergent are used. Avoid using a tea towel on the crockery and cutlery when removing them from the dishwasher

➢ Drawers and cupboards (where crockery, cutlery and utensils are kept) should be kept clean

➢ The fridge / freezer should be cleaned regularly

➢ Wash root vegetables as the first part of their preparation. Bacteria from the soil can lie on the surface of the vegetables

Storage

➢ Store food separately in covered containers or ensure that they are carefully wrapped in film or foil. Never reuse foil or film.

➢ Store raw meat, fish and poultry below cooked foods and other foods so that there is no chance of the raw foods dripping onto the cooked foods.

➢ Try to avoid overfilling the fridge – it can be difficult to keep a fridge at the required temperature if it is too full.

➢ Don't put warm or hot food directly into the fridge. This can cause the fridge temperature to go above 5°C. Allow the warm / hot food to cool first.

> Do not store food in an opened tin can in a fridge. Transfer the food from the can into a container and cover the container.

> Store raw eggs in the fridge and keep eggs and vegetables away from cooked and ready to eat foods at all times.

> Be aware of how long food is stored in the fridge. Advice on how long food can be safely stored in a covered container in a fridge varies. It can depend on the type of food itself. In most cases, services have developed their own guidelines.

Temperature Control

Food poisoning bacteria grow more quickly in food at temperatures between 5°C and 63°C. Above 70°C most bacteria are killed. Below 5°C food poisoning bacteria do not grow or grow only slowly. Some bacteria die at temperatures below 5°C.

The general advice is if food is to be served hot it should be kept piping hot until it is served. If it is to be served cold it should be kept cold until it is to be served. The longer that food is kept at room temperature, the more time there is for food poisoning bacteria to grow.

Fridges and freezers must operate at the correct temperature (below 5°C for fridges and 18°C for freezers). Many food jars need to be stored in the fridge and for a limited time period. This is indicated on the jars label.

When cooking meat, fish and poultry, ensure it is thoroughly cooked in line with the produce recommendations.

Infection Control

Within care services there are, various aspects of the work which mean there are potential risks to health.

Since social care work often involves personal care, there are immediately risks of infection passing from the service user to the staff member. The risk of infection is increased given that one staff member often supports various service users and that the service users are potentially in a group at greater risk of developing infections (e.g.: older people or people who are already ill). Additionally, service users and staff are often in close proximity and are likely to use some shared facilities e.g.: bathroom / toilet.

At one time or another individuals can become ill. Some illnesses cannot be transmitted to other people e.g.: cancer, heart disease etc. There are a variety of illnesses that can be passed on to others (that are "communicable"). Within care services staff should be able to work in ways that reduce the likelihood of communicable illnesses or diseases being passed on to other people.

If two people in a service develop the same communicable disease at the same time (or one soon after the other), this could be considered an outbreak. For some communicable diseases, one person having the infection can be a cause for concern in its own right (depending on what the infection is) and so be considered an outbreak. Managers of the service have the responsibility to notify local health and environmental health staff of outbreaks of certain communicable diseases and to take action to control (stop) the disease being spread to others.

How people can become infected

Within social care settings there are four potential ways that infections can be passed on:

➢ inhalation (breathing in minute droplets / particles of infection)

➢ ingestion (eating foodstuffs that carry the infection)

➢ direct contact with the skin or mucous membranes

➢ through the skin (e.g.: being pricked by an infected needle, contact with open wounds)

Inhalation

Communicable diseases that can be contracted through breathing in bacteria include:

➢ Tuberculosis

➢ Shingles, Mumps, Rubella

➢ Methicillin – resistant staphylococcus aureus (MRSA)

➢ Influenza

Ingestion

Communicable diseases that can be contracted through a person eating or drinking the infection include:

➢ Food poisoning bacteria e.g.: salmonella, E-coli 0157, listeria etc

➢ Dysentery

➢ Typhoid

Contact with the skin

Communicable infections that can be acquired by contact with the skin include:

➢ Scabies
➢ Impetigo

Contact through the skin

Infections that can be transmitted either by the skin being pierced or through already open wounds include:

➢ Hepatitis A

➢ Hepatitis B

➢ Illnesses that cause diarrhoea (e.g.: Dysentery)

➢ Human Immunodeficiency Virus (HIV)

Preventing the spread of infection

There are a variety of work practices that should be applied by staff in order to prevent infection. Additionally, if a person develops a communicable disease in a service, the managers of the service may need to introduce other measures (hopefully only until the risk of further infection has passed).

Washing your hands

Evidence consistently indicates that the single most important work practice that should be observed by staff is effective hand washing. Social care staff should wash their hands:

➢ before and after each contact with a service user

➢ after handling clinical waste (body fluids, incontinence wear), linen or emptying bins or handling any bags intended for disposal

➢ before handling food, eating or drinking

➢ after using the toilet

➢ after removing protective gloves and aprons

➢ after blowing their own nose

➢ after contact with animals

Gloves and Aprons

It is important to note that hands should be washed after providing intimate personal care or after dealing with body fluids, even when gloves have been worn since gloves do not provide 100% protection.

Considering this, gloves and aprons should always be worn whenever it is necessary. They do reduce the risk of infections being spread. Always remove and dispose of the apron and gloves after you have provided personal care (or dealt with a body fluid spillage or whatever the task was).

Effective hand washing

➢ Nails should be kept short

➢ Remove any jewellery

➢ Use running water – a wash basin filled with water with a plug in quickly becomes a growth area for bacteria

➢ Wash hands and forearms with water

➢ Apply soap and work over your fingers, hands (back of hands as well) and forearms thoroughly. This should be for at least 15 seconds and areas often missed include the thumb, finger tips and the skin between the fingers

➢ Rinse hands and forearms

➢ Dry hands using disposable paper towels. Shared towels can result in cross contamination

Aspects related to hand washing

Use hand washing facilities close to the place where you have carried out the activity, and immediately after you have completed the activity.

General cleaning and disinfection practices

High standards of general cleanliness are part of infection control practice. On the whole, cleaning of hard surfaces etc, should consist of using hot water and detergent. The use of disinfectants should be kept to a minimum. There are several reasons why disinfectants should only be used sparingly:

➤ Various disinfectants can be caustic or corrosive or can taint food

➤ Most disinfectants should only be applied if diluted with water, getting the right water to disinfectant ratios adds a complicating factor

➤ Most disinfectants constitute a potential hazard to health

➤ On the whole, disinfectants only work if the surface has recently been cleaned with hot Water and detergent

➤ Hot water and detergent are generally effective enough

Cleaning equipment

Different mops, buckets and cloths should be used in specific locations and should not be used in other areas. For example, a mop bucket used to clean a toilet floor should not be used to clean a kitchen floor. Where items are used such as mops and buckets, these should either be colour coded or clearly labelled.

Cleaning routine

Each service should have an established cleaning routine and a system for ensuring it is adequate and maintained. This should also indicate what cleaning tasks are required to be carried out in specific rooms.

Laundry

Having established routines for cleaning linen safely is part of infection control practice.

Central to any system of laundry is a washing machine (to state the obvious). To disinfect linen it is essential that the wash cycles include heating the water to 65°C (for ten minutes) or 71°C (for three minutes). If clothing needs to be washed (because it was soiled with body fluids) then it should be washed at the highest temperature possible but which does not result in any damage to the clothes (this could often be 40°C). Some services may wash soiled clothing in very diluted disinfectant (in the machine).

When sorting used linen or foul linen, do not place it onto the floor or other furniture. Before stripping a bed have in the room the necessary linen bags and place the linen into the relevant bags.

When red alginate bags are used (for foul linen) you should be instructed about their use. The red alginate bag can be placed directly into a washing machine (without the need to take the linen out – hence reducing handling).

Once linen is washed, it is recommended that it is dried, ironed and stored in a separate area.

Single use items

Various items are single use only and this must be observed. Simple examples of this include gloves and aprons.

Individuals with special needs

Some service users have special needs such as having a urinary catheter. Only staff who have been trained in catheter management should be actively involved in assisting a service user with their catheter.

Spillage of body fluids

Whenever there are spillages of body fluids they must be cleaned up quickly and safely.

Any body fluid is a potential source of infection and so staff must respond in a way that protects themselves and other people.

Staff need to have clear information about how body fluid spillages are to be dealt with.

Staff must wear disposable gloves and apron before attempting to clean up a body fluid spillage.

Body fluid spillages must be disposed of in the correct way.

Any items or surface area in contact with body fluids should be thoroughly cleaned or disposed of (if the item is disposable) as necessary.

Specimen collection

A service user may be asked by their doctor to provide a specimen of urine, faeces or sputum. When staff need to support the service user in collecting or handling a specimen it is important that this is done safely and correctly.

Staff should be trained in how to support a service user to provide a specimen. Aspects of any approach to collecting a specimen correctly and safely include the following:

➢ consult the service user about what is required and ensure they give their free consent

➢ only use the specific, sterile specimen containers. Make sure it is securely closed

➢ keep handling to a minimum

➢ avoid storing the sample, pass it on the laboratory (or GP surgery) as soon as possible

➢ wear gloves and aprons when taking specimens

➢ staff should wash their hands before taking the specimen, after taking the specimen and after each time the container is handled

Waste management

The service you work in will already have in place an established procedure on how waste is managed. Any procedure will have various aspects to it. These aspects include:

> acknowledging that there are different types of waste

> identifying the different types of waste and the way they are to be dealt with and disposed of

> putting waste in the correct bags or bins and ensuring that they are filled and sealed in line with good practice requirements

> handling any bags with care in line with manual handling guidelines

> responding promptly to any accident or incident in a safe and effective manner

> being aware that waste must not be discarded in public areas but must be placed in a designated area (bin or container) until this is removed from the service

Preventing through immunisation

The risk of contacting some communicable disease can be reduced by individuals being immunised. One of the most significant immunisation campaigns in recent years relates to immunising people against influenza. Various at risk groups are recommended to be immunised. One at risk group is people aged over 65.

People in an "at risk" group should be supported to see their GP to discuss immunisation.

Managing an outbreak of diarrhoea and vomiting or any type of communicable disease

When a person has a communicable disease there are various actions that must be taken. Their actions will be initiated and co-ordinated by the management of the service and exactly what measures are introduced will depend on the nature of the disease and medical advice.

Aspects of managing an outbreak include:

> medical treatment for the person who has the communicable disease

> enhanced preventative measures introduced by the management and applied by all staff. This could include more thorough cleaning using disinfectants for the length of the outbreak

> reinforcement of the need for effective hand washing and for using gloves and protective aprons

> consultation and advice from Health staff responsible for infection control and possibly Environmental Health officers of the local council. This advice to be applied by the service

> for some communicable diseases staff may be required to have treatment themselves (e.g.: if a service user has scabies)

 In Summary

There are a range of specific issues in terms of health and safety which can relate to social care practice. Every service should have relevant policies and guidelines for staff and training on these should be provided. Staff have a legal responsibility to follow these policies and guidelines. It can be useful for social care staff to understand the reasons behind these policies and procedures.

45: RESPONDING TO EMERGENCIES

One of the key skills of competent social care workers can be to remain calm in a crisis and not to add to the sense of drama or crisis by panicking or by getting angry or irritated. Workers in a day centre or residential care home might hear shouting or screaming. One general guide is to walk towards the sound of the screaming or shouting, and then find out what is happening. A worker may need to introduce some order or agree with the immediate support team how the situation should be handled.

If a worker is the first person at an emergency scene (or the first person who appears able to act), then their response should include the following:

➢ Assessing the emergency

➢ Maintaining their own and other people's safety

➢ Summoning help

➢ Supporting any "casualty"

➢ Understanding their own limitations

➢ Handing over the "casualty" to the emergency services and giving them relevant information

➢ Seeking appropriate support if required

➢ Completing the appropriate paperwork

Working through each of these in turn:

Assessing the Emergency
It is important the worker remains calm and tries to think rationally. Trying to gauge any casualty's condition is helpful.

There may be environmental clues to why the emergency has occurred (e.g.: a wire cord from, say, a vacuum cleaner lying across the floor).

Maintaining one's own safety
If there is anything the worker can do to make the area safe, then they should do so.

Summoning Help
If the emergency situation occurs in a care home or a day centre, the worker will usually need to call for the manager on duty. It will usually be up to the senior staff member to either call the emergency services or delegate that task to a staff member.

If the incident occurs in a service user's own home, then a worker may well be working alone. The worker should be able to contact the emergency services while with the "casualty".

Supporting any Casualty
If the person is conscious, the worker should inform them what has been done, ask them what happened and find out how they feel at the time.

Handing over the Casualty to the Emergency Services
When the emergency services arrive, the worker should inform them about:

➢ What they know about the cause of the emergency and when it happened

➢ The casualty's name and relevant personal information

➢ What actions the worker has undertaken

➢ Any changes in the casualty's condition that they have observed e.g.: when did they become unconscious?

Records

Recording has been covered in chapter 24. The guidelines given there relate equally to health and safety records. All organisations will have guidelines in relation to health and safety records, particularly in terms of the recording of accidents, incidents and emergencies. It is important that workers are aware of and follow these.

Being Clear about Your Role

In all aspects of social care, workers should be clear about their role and responsibilities, to work within this framework and not to exceed their role (or competence). It is never more important than in terms of dealing with emergencies at work. If a worker exceeds their role in an emergency, they may well put their own safety and perhaps even their life (and the lives of others) at serious risk.

It is difficult in a publication of this kind to explore potential emergencies in any detail. Social care workers will know what sort of emergencies will occur in their own work role and should also be familiar with which policies and protocols are in place to give guidance on the management of these emergencies.

In Summary

On occasions social care workers will need to respond to emergencies. The nature of the emergencies will clearly vary and training and advice cannot be given to cover every eventuality. However, staff should follow the guidance provided in this chapter. They must also be aware of their agency's policy and procedure and follow this at all times.

46: MANAGING VIOLENCE AND AGGRESSION

This section considers the broader aspects of recognising potentially volatile situations and basic strategies for managing such situations. The principles underpinning this section are:

➤ No service user should suffer injury or abuse
➤ No member of staff should suffer injury or abuse in the course of their work

Understanding violence and aggression

There may be a range of reasons why a person is aggressive. Understanding why a person has been violent or aggressive is important as it may help to prevent future instances. The following explanations of why someone may be aggressive is by no means exhaustive but may help to use as a checklist.

Defensive behaviour

If a person feels threatened they may become aggressive as part of their defence. People requiring care may feel threatened by a range of situations including being provided with assistance with basic care tasks.

Increased dependence

People may be embarrassed or frustrated by a decline in their abilities and increased needs. Therefore, people may be angry about increased dependence.

Shock

People may be surprised or alarmed by approaches, especially if they have a sensory impairment.

Misunderstanding

People may misunderstand events or situations, especially if they have dementia and this can obviously lead to aggression.

Mental health problems

A range of mental health problems may lead to violence and aggression. For example, people may experience paranoia (sometimes referred to as paraphrenia), which is basically extreme suspicion.

Reality confrontation

Where a person has dementia or confusion and they are faced with reality either during moments of lucidity or through an unskilled use of methods such as reality orientation, they may become aggressive:

"Exposing an elderly disorientated person to the painfulness of a present which is characterised by a loss of persons, places and things can result in anger as they attempt to seek security and pleasure in a reassuring past". (Stokes 1987)

Stress

Aggression is a possible consequence of extreme stress.

Emotions

A whole range of emotions may lead to aggression – including fear, anger, confusion, loss etc.

Pain

If a person is in pain, especially if they are not able to express this, they may become aggressive or violent.

Communication

Essentially, when a person is aggressive or violent, they are trying to communicate something to care staff. The more that this "message" is ignored, the more potential there is for further aggression and violence.

Recognising the warning signs

There are often a number of warning signs preceding aggression. These may include:

➢ adopting a tense posture

➢ threatening gestures

➢ agitated appearance

➢ rise in volume of voice

➢ verbal threats

➢ sweating

➢ changes to skin colour

Strategies for managing aggression and minimising risk

As the saying goes "prevention is better than cure". Good care practices, if always followed, will help prevent incidents of violence and aggression. For example, communicating effectively can minimise misunderstandings which may lead to aggression.

The remainder of this chapter considers the skills needed to manage incidents of violence and aggression if they do occur.

Practical measures

➢ Consideration will need to be given to other vulnerable people within the situation. (E.g.: Can they remove themselves from a potentially volatile situation?)

➢ Familiarise yourself with security arrangements at your place of work

➤ If you are in a position to remove yourself, to allow the person to calm down, this is often the best policy!

➤ Ensure you are familiar with the means of requesting urgent assistance, such as alarms

➤ Always ensure that you know where the nearest exit is, and that you are able to reach it

➤ Provide alternatives (e.g.: "why don't we sit down and have a cup of tea together and talk about what's wrong?")

Interpersonal techniques

➤ Respect the person's personal space

➤ Try not to mirror the stance of the person who is becoming irate (naturally, people will mirror the body language of whom they are with)

➤ Try and keep your own body language relaxed, even if you don't feel it!

➤ Keep your voice calm and quiet

➤ Allow the person who is upset to air their problems, but encourage them to do so in a more appropriate environment, if other vulnerable people are involved

➤ Provide practical support, such as information about the complaints procedure

Personal Security

➤ If you feel uncertain, unhappy or nervous about a situation or dealing with a particular person, share your concerns with your line manager and request support

➤ Always take threats of violence seriously

➤ Always report and document threats and incidents of violence

Supporting others

Incidents in any social care service have an impact on both staff and service users. Fear, anger, anxiety and guilt are all strong emotions that can arise. Whilst such emotions are difficult, they are a natural and essential part of coping with a crisis and should not be denied. During an emergency, the focus of professional social care staff is in protecting others and minimising risk i.e.: dealing with the emergency in a professional manner. However, after an event, others may need support which may need to be offered in a variety of appropriate ways.

 In Summary

It is important to remember that following good care practices will reduce the likelihood of violence and aggression. However, social care workers may well need to deal with incidents of violence and aggression. They should always do so appropriately.

47: VIOLENCE AGAINST SOCIAL CARE WORKERS

In 2001 the Department of Health published a document called "A Safer Place". This was developed by a taskforce set up to look into violence against social care staff.

The document is essentially an audit tool for managers to consider whether their organisation minimises the potential for workers to be subject to violence or abuse.

The document defines violence and abuse against social care workers as:

"Incidents where persons are abused, threatened or assaulted in circumstances relating to their work, involving an explicit or implicit challenge to their safety, well-being or health. This definition is taken to include verbal abuse or threat, threatening behaviour, any assault (and any apprehension of unlawful violence), and serious or persistent harassment, including racial or sexual harassment, and extends from what may seem to be minor incidents to serious assault and murder, and threats against the worker's family".

It goes on to cover various principles including:

➢ Violence, threats and abuse to workers are unacceptable

➢ Good policies need to be developed, in consultation with service users, workers and other relevant people

➢ Managers and environments should maximise workers safety

➢ Good quality risk assessments should be developed and these should be kept under regular review

The document outlines various responsibilities that managers have towards staff and the type of actions they can engage in to uphold these responsibilities. One of the management responsibilities is to ensure that all staff are aware of what they should do to reduce the risk of violence occurring in the first place and what to do once a situation starts to develop.

Organisations should provide social care workers with information to enable them to work through the following steps:

➢ Identify potential risks

➢ Avoid potentially dangerous situations

➢ De-escalate

➢ Disengage

➢ Call for help

➢ Use appropriate physical interventions

Since social care staff work in a wide range of areas it is difficult to give examples that apply to all staff. Therefore, what follows is bound to be limited. Staff do need to develop their own sense of risk awareness and to plan what to do if a situation becomes dangerous.

Identify Potential Risks

In terms of identifying the behaviour an individual may engage in, the biggest single indicating factor is previous behaviour. If a person has been violent in the recent past, there is a risk that they could be violent at some point in the future.

If an individual is on the whole reasonable but once they drink alcohol they become aggressive, then the consumption of alcohol is a risk factor. If a person is in group care (at a day centre or residential care home) and the presence of a certain service user triggers an aggressive cycle, then that would be a risk factor.

In some neighbourhoods extreme right wing parties have gained some local support. Where there are local clusters this is a potential risk factor for staff who are black or Asian or for staff who are seen as gay.

Avoid Potentially Dangerous Situations

Having a sense of the potential risks should lead the worker to seek to minimise the likelihood of an aggressive incident occurring. Once a potential risk is identified, ways of managing this should be included in a care or support plan plan. The service user should also have been consulted about what response staff will be required to take.

If two particular service users in the same room results in a difficult situation can the two service users be supported to engage in activities in different rooms?

If a home care worker arrives at the home of a man and it soon becomes clear he has consumed alcohol and this is a known risk factor, then it could well be written into his care plan that at this point the care worker leaves.

Within care plans there could be comments about what staff should or should not do in order to reduce the risk of dangerous situations arising.

De-escalate

In some situations it may be possible to calm a situation down which has started to become of concern. Aspects of de-escalation include the social care worker remaining calm, listening to the person and, wherever possible, acknowledging that the service user has a point and recognising that the person's concern can be pursued through normal routes e.g.: complaints procedures etc.

Disengage

Staff need to be aware that leaving a potentially dangerous situation is a legitimate and responsible action to a threatening situation.

A staff member may enter a situation that they quickly perceive is potentially dangerous. In order to keep open the option of leaving the staff member needs to consider practical aspects such as remaining near the door.

Call for Help

Staff should be aware of how to summon assistance. This is usually easiest when an incident occurs in a service or office. Home care staff working alone are the most vulnerable, and must know how to call for help.

Use Appropriate Physical Intervention

Any staff who are expected to use physical intervention will receive training as to what is expected, what physical interventions are acceptable. They will rehearse applying these in training.

One common feature of such training is to convey that using physical interventions should be the option of last resort.

If any staff member is in a situation that is so threatening that they are actively concerned for their own well being then there is a common law right to use reasonable and proportionate force for the purpose of self defence. However, leaving the situation wherever possible is always the most appropriate action.

Applying an Effective 'No Violence Against Staff' Policy

In emergency situations where a service user is agitated or angry, one of the options is for staff to retreat. There are situations where support staff do not like this option. I have known support staff to follow an agitated man into his bedroom in a care home – where the service user promptly hit the support worker.

Creating space for the service user, allowing them to calm down in their own time is, arguably, one of the stronger options. It could also be helpful to consider the idea that anger can be an expression of powerlessness, so attempts could be made to look at ways of enhancing the service user's control over aspects of their situation in order to avoid repeat incidents.

A worker might visit a service user in their home with a decision from the organisation that they will not like. Sometimes it may be helpful to ask them to have a family member with them. It's not unusual for a family member to be an ally! The worker could start the discussion by giving the service user a complaints form and then at the end of the meeting they could help them to fill it in if they want to do that. This can help the service user to see that any anger they have should be channelled into procedures and to de-personalise the issue.

Setting the ground rules is important. In offices and workplaces there are often posters stating that violence is not tolerated. Such statements can also be included in information given to service users. However, this should be balanced – service users have a right to be listened to and respected.

Training for staff is one of the measures used by organisations to communicate a no violence policy. Training that is about avoiding potentially violent situations has been found more helpful than self defence training. Self defence techniques need to be regularly used to be remembered, and use of these techniques could result is a situation escalating. It's better a staff member leaves than stands their ground thinking "I have been trained in self defence!'" This illustrates that an organisation doesn't need to do everything possible. There has to be an evaluation of what works and what is beneficial even in this area of work (HSE, Internet).

If a service user has behaviour that challenges or they start to develop behaviour that challenges, it is important the person's needs are re-assessed, and a new or more appropriate care plan should be agreed.

Workers may contribute to the day to day application of the care plan or risk assessments. However, once risks are identified, workers then need to:

➤ arrange for risk assessment to be completed and risk management plans to be put in place

➤ evaluate the quality of the risk assessment and the risk management plan

Five or ten years ago services struggled to get any risk assessment and management plan in place. Whilst services have improved in this respect many services still need to look at the quality and appropriateness of the plan. Plans should balance:

➤ the views, opinions and rights of the service user

➤ the risks to the service user

➤ the quality of life in terms of risks and benefits for the service user

➤ the risks to staff and colleagues

➤ the risks to others (such as other service users or members of the public)

There may be more than one way to strike a balance.

The general options include:

➤ Skill acquisition by the service user. Can they learn or re-learn a skill that reduces risks? This could also be seen as maximising independence.

➤ Environmental changes, the use of aids, adaptations or assistive technology. Potentially there are lots of adaptations available. Often public services have a limited number of options. If the service user is able and willing to pay they could have an increased range of options.

➤ Increased level of supervision or support. This should be focussed on key times or during activities when the risk is most significant.

Recording and Reporting

Accurate recording and reporting of health, safety and security matters is another key responsibility of workers. Whatever the service's setting, professional honesty is crucial.

For a variety of reasons there can be wide variations in the number of actual or potential incidents that are reported by services. Hence one care service may report that there were, say, 12 violent incidents in a six month period whilst another care service reports that there were 2 violent incidents in the same period. Assuming that the two services were similar (in size and the needs of service users) why is there such a difference? Possible reasons include:

➢ more accurate recording in one service compared to the other

➢ one staff team manage risk better than the other (so the number of incidents reported is accurate in both services)

Without wanting to sound cynical, it is likely that both care services are under recording and under-reporting the number of incidents. However, one service under-records more than the other. Workers need to have the professional strength to recognise that reporting incidents is not a bad reflection on themselves or their team. It is also a key component of evaluating the effectiveness of risk management procedures that have been put in place.

MESSAGES FROM RESEARCH: VIOLENCE AGAINST CARE STAFF

➢ Violence and abuse against staff are more common in the social care sector than for comparable professions

➢ Violence and abuse in social care is significantly under reported, because:

- Staff believe managers will not support them
- Staff feel they will be seen as incompetent
- There is a belief that verbal abuse and threats are "part of the job"
- Complex and inconveniently situated forms deter reporting

➢ Violence and abuse against staff needs to be taken more seriously by managers and the organisation as a whole

➢ Immediate support for staff after an incident is essential and valued by staff. Research indicates that effective support involves:

- Effective communication within the team
- The offer of counselling
- Recognition that everyone present might need support
- Provision of practical advice
- Calling specific debriefing meetings (if possible using an external facilitator)

Source: Osser (2000)

 In Summary

Violence and aggression towards social care workers is referred to in a range of social care qualifications. Staff need to understand the issues involved. Applying the principles of good practice can reduce the likelihood of violent incidents occurring. However, violence and aggression can and does occur in social care settings and staff need to be clear how they should respond.

SECTION G: EVIDENCE BASED PRACTICE

Evidence based practice is a key concept in social care. Originating in health, where it is commonly referred to as evidence based clinical practice or evidence based medicine, the concept of evidence based practice is now commonly applied in social work and associated fields, meaning that all social care workers need to develop their knowledge in this area.

48: THE BASICS OF EVIDENCE BASED PRACTICE

The Canadian medical group at McMaster University, who first used the term evidence based practice, defined it as a process which considers

"the conscientious, explicit and judicious use of current best evidence in making decisions about the care of individuals."

(Sackett, Straus, Richardson, Rosenberg and Haynes 1997)

The Government says of evidence based practice:

"Although there are many complex definitions of evidence-based practice, it can be succinctly described as the systematic use of the best available evidence of what works when reaching decisions about how best to treat, care for or support patients and clients. Crucially, evidence-based practice involves the integration of the individual practitioner or clinician's expertise with the best available evidence from research, as well as with the preferences of the individual client or patient."

(Department for Children, Schools and Families 2008)

Evidence based practice is often taken to refer to the use of research in practice. Strictly speaking, however, the term for this would be research minded practice. Evidence based practice is increasingly seen as using a range of evidence in practice - drawn not only from research, but also from knowledge of legislation, theory and practice. This is one of the main reasons that qualifications in social care require candidates to have an understanding of legislation, theory and research. If workers are committed to the principles of evidence based practice, then they should be able to easily identify the specific knowledge in relation to theory, legislation and research which is influencing their daily work.

This publication should enable readers to develop their knowledge about all three areas – since research, theory and legislation are regularly referred to. However, to show a true commitment to evidence based practice, candidates will need to take their learning about the three areas deeper. For example in terms of the concept of horizontal and vertical knowledge (see page 6) this book will provide largely vertical knowledge. Social care workers will need to take a proactive evidence based approach to develop their horizontal knowledge (the knowledge about specific service user groups / areas of work etc).

The process of evidence based practice is outlined in the following diagram:

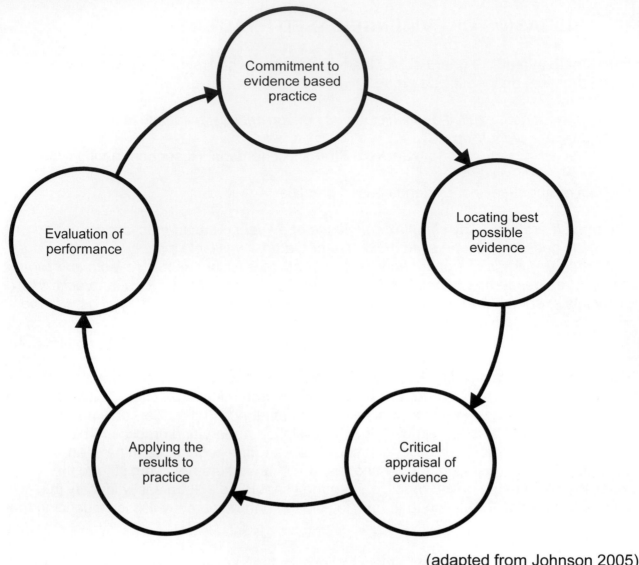

(adapted from Johnson 2005)

Commitment to evidence based practice

Evidence based practice is essential for a range of reasons:

➢ it can assist in developing best practice

➢ it assists in explaining process, practice and actions and therefore results in improved accountability for practice

➢ it helps to ensure that resources are effectively targeted – which leads to increased efficiency and possibly more resources to use elsewhere.

For these reasons, most social care professionals have a commitment to evidence based practice. Candidates for social care qualifications will also have the added incentive that they have to make use of evidence based practice to meet the standards of their Award.

Locating the best possible evidence

This is potentially one of the most challenging aspects of evidence based practice. There is a huge amount of research, legislation, policy and theory relating to the field – how do you find it? and how do you know you have found the "best possible information"?

Locating Research

There is a massive amount of research relating to the care sector. This can mean that there is almost "too much" for you to sift through to find some research which might be relevant to your practice. So here are a few ideas to help:

➤ *Conference Reports/Papers*
Recent research is often presented at Conferences – if you don't attend the Conference you may still be able to get hold of a copy of the papers presented.

➤ *Government Publications*
The Government produces a range of documents referring to research and often also publish their own research papers. The easiest way to access these is generally through the relevant Government department's website.

➤ *Research Reports*
Organisations generally publish their own research reports. If you are a member of an organisation like Action Against Elder Abuse or Values into Action, you will find out about these and may receive summaries. Alternatively, the reports are often available from the organisation's website.

Research Organisations

A number of specific research organisations exist in the field. They each have a website and most provide links or direct access to a range of research. For example:

➤ Social Care Institute for Excellent (SCIE) (www.scie.org.uk). SCIE also operate social care online – a fantastic website for research information (www.scie-socialcareonline.org.uk) and a people management website which will be particularly relevant for managers (www.scie-peoplemanagement.org.uk).

➤ Research in Practice for Adults (www.ripfa.org.uk)

➤ Economic and Social Research Council (ESRC) (www.esrcsocietytoday.ac.uk).

➤ National Centre for Social Research (NatCen) (www.natcen.ac.uk)

E Bulletins

A number of websites offer regular updates (including news on important research) through registration. These are well worth signing up to. For example:

➤ The Policy Hub (sign up at www.nationalschool.gov.uk/policyhub)

➤ The Social Policy and Social Work Subject Centre offer updates and has a number of research articles on its site. Sign up at www.swap.ac.uk

➤ Journals

Examples include:

➤ Journal of Social Service Research

➤ Journal of Health and Social Policy

There are also a host of regular magazines in the field, such as Community Care. These are now more regularly carrying summaries of recent research projects.

Critical Appraisal of Evidence

Critical appraisal is probably the key aspect of evidence based practice, but one which is often missed. The danger of skipping this stage is that evidence might be flawed or out of date, knowledge might not be relevant. It is not unknown for services to be making use of legislation which is not relevant to the country in which they are based, for example.

Critical appraisal in itself is a vast area and there are a range of published tools which provide comprehensive details on how to critically appraise research evidence in particular. This is too vast an area to consider in detail in this publication. However, what we would say is that it is vital to question whatever evidence (knowledge) is gathered. For example:

	Research	Legislation	Theory
Is it valid?	➢ What kind of research methods were used? ➢ Is it from a reliable source? etc	➢ Does it relate to this country? ➢ Has it been implemented? etc	➢ Is it widely tested? ➢ Is it widely used? etc
What are the implications?	➢ What are the results of the research? ➢ What are the recommendations? etc	➢ What "form" of legislation is this? ➢ Does it defer a 'power' (a can do) or a 'duty' (a must do)? etc	➢ What are the key principles? ➢ What does this mean for my practice? etc
What can I do with it?	➢ Can the results be applied to my area? ➢ How could I use or adapt the findings for use?	➢ What do I/we need to do? ➢ What changes do we need to make to policy and practice?	➢ How could I use this? ➢ What would this mean in terms of changes to practice? etc

It is important to note that these are basic questions for what is a complex process. When critically appraising research in particular, you will need to ask more detailed questions about the validity of the research, but the key to this stage of the process of evidence based practice is to take a questioning approach.

"It is important to note at this point that no research is perfect. However, through critically appraising what has been written in a paper, we can consider whether a study is good quality to use in our decision-making. Although it may be time consuming, it is essential to be able to distinguish a good piece of research from a poor one. This should prevent practice decisions being based on unreliable information, which could result in a poor decision being taken on the basis of unreliable evidence."

(RIPFA 2008)

Applying the result to practice

This is another absolutely key aspect to evidence based practice. There is no purpose to having a wealth of knowledge and not making any use of this in practice. The evidence which is generated must be shared with others and applied to practice. Evidence based practice isn't simply about having knowledge. It's about what workers do with their knowledge – how do they use it? After all, a walking encyclopaedia does not make a good social care worker.

Evaluation of Performance

When knowledge has been applied to practice, it is likely that changes have been made to service delivery in some way. It is important that the changes are reviewed or evaluated to ensure that they have been effective. This "evidence" then feeds back into the process of evidence based practice.

Evidence based practice is now a key concept in social care, with a great deal to offer the field. Evidence based practice is particularly important in improving decision making processes and supporting the continual development of staff and services. It is an area which no effective worker in social care can afford to ignore.

It is important that social care workers develop skills in evidence based practice. In terms of working towards qualifications, this will be partly about incorporating and demonstrating knowledge evidence with evidence of competent performance – knowledge and performance cannot be separated (i.e.: it's not just about what you do, but why you do it).

Reflective Practice and Evidence Based Practice

Evidence based practice and reflective practice are very closely linked as recognised by a number of writers (e.g.: Hamer and Collinson 1999). The process of evidence based practice presented in this chapter, in many ways reflects the process of reflective practice. Certainly practitioners need to take a critically reflective approach to choosing and appraising an evidence base. The final section of this book contains a chapter on reflective practice (chapter 53) which we could just as easily locate in this section because reflective practice is so closely linked to evidence based practice. To truly develop knowledge in terms of evidence based practice, it is important to also read the chapter on reflective practice.

In Summary

Evidence based practice is now seen as key in social care practice. As such social care workers need to develop their knowledge in this area.

49: THEORY INFORMED PRACTICE

What is a Theory?

Theories in social care are nothing more than an attempt to explain social relationships. Theories have been developed since it became clear that there were similar patterns or repeating cycles of behaviour both in an individual's life and in the lives of lots of different people.

Since theories have been expressed by academics and social scientists, they often use an academic language. Don't let that put you off. Theories are life dressed up! Many theories actually have a very simple message. Einstein who developed what is probably the most famous theory of all – the theory of relativity – said:

"A theory is the more impressive the greater is the simplicity of it's premises, the more different are the kinds of things it relates to and the more extended the range of it's applicability."

(www.thinkexist.com 2005)

There has been some debate about what actually constitutes a theory. Generally, a theory helps to explain a situation and perhaps how it came about. In science a theory is seen as helping to:

➤ describe (e.g.: what is happening?)

➤ explain (e.g.: why is it happening?)

➤ predict (e.g.: what is likely to happen next?)

Sometimes theories are also seen as helping to plan intervention and bring about change (e.g.: What can I do to bring about a change in this situation?). Social care workers need to be able to describe the situation they are working with, explain why they think this came about, what they can do to bring about some form of change etc. In doing so, they will be drawing on some form of theory. They may, however, not always be aware of this.

In social care, there are a range of different types of theory. An understanding of these different types or forms of theory can be helpful in recognising that all workers within social care do use a range of theories in any given situation.

Beckett (2006) separates theory into "formal" theory and "informal" theory. We have known some people use these terms inappropriately – formal theory being taken to mean theory which is presented more academically and informal theory taken to mean theory which is more accessible and understandable (and therefore not academic!) However, this is a misunderstanding. Formal theory is basically theory which can be named and traced back to a writer or an academic. Informal theory on the other hand, is the worker's own ideas about a situation. As this is often developed through experience – both practice experience and personal experiences, this type of "theory" is also referred to as practice wisdom (Doel and Shardlow 1992) or "common knowledge" (Beckett 2006).

Why do we need to apply theory to practice?

Whilst individual social care theories have different purposes, using all kinds of theory in our work offers social care professionals some important things:

➤ Theories can help make sense of a situation. Using theory, social care professionals can generate ideas about what is going on, why things are as they are etc.

➤ Using theory can help to justify actions and explain practice to service users, carers and society in general. The aim is that this will lead to social care becoming more widely accountable and ultimately more respected.

➤ In work with individuals, making use of the theories which may relate to their specific situation will give workers more direction in their work.

➤ Using theory can give a reason about why an action resulted in a particular consequence. This can help staff to review and possibly change their practice in an attempt to make the consequences more effective.

It is clear then, that theory is important in practice – both for work with service users and for social care to be more valued in society.

Recognising the importance of the term "theory" and what it can offer is part of the move towards the professionalisation of the social care workforce.

There is an old saying, started by Leonardo Da Vinci, *"Practice without theory is to sail an uncharted sea; theory without practice is not to set sail at all."* Imagine a boat setting out to sea in a good breeze, without a map or compass. This is like practice without theory – how will the crew know when they have arrived at their destination? If they do (by a remote chance) arrive safely in a port they like, how would they ever be able to repeat the journey? On the other hand, a boat might bob along tied to its bollard, safely in the harbour. It might well have every direction finding device known, but isn't going anywhere. This is like theory without practice. It's pointless.

"Practice without Theory is to sail an uncharted sea: Theory without practice is not to set sail at all."

How do we apply theory to practice?

There is no single approach to applying theory to practice. We all apply theory to practice every day – what we may not be able to do is name the theory and use the academic language that has built up around it. But theory "seeps in".

Some people will claim that they don't use theories, but that they work on common sense principles. But whose sense is common? Is your sense the same as everyone else's? Just because someone cannot imagine another way to view something this doesn't mean that they aren't using theory. It just means that their one or two theories are their entire world or "sense".

In applying theory to practice, it is helpful to remember the following points:

➤ No single theory can explain everything: When a person engages in an action (or inaction) the reason for their behaviour can be rooted in a range of causes or motives.

➤ Related to the first point, recognise that some theoretical approaches just don't work with some people.

➤ Take a critical approach to theory. If it doesn't "work", why not? Can you adapt aspects such that it is helpful?

> Always apply the value base to theory – much of the theory used in the sector is from outside of social care practice. Theory may have its roots in education, psychology or even industry and engineering. As such, it may not incorporate social care values and everyone in the field should take responsibility for applying these.

> Different professionals may draw on different theories given the same presenting situation. There is no right or wrong approach – just boundaries of good practice.

> Theories of different types may be used at different points in intervention in a situation.

> Some theories may compliment each other, others may clash and may therefore not be appropriate to use together.

> An anti-oppressive approach is always vital – any theory should be evaluated from an anti-oppressive standpoint.

 In Summary

Theory informed practice is essential to effective social care. Professional practice is practice which is informed by a knowledge of theory. This is what makes the difference between a professional and someone who acts on instinct or "gut feelings". A professional is someone who has knowledge about why they have made certain decisions and who can explain these to managers, other professionals, vulnerable people and their families.

50: LEGISLATION AND POLICY

It is worth firstly clarifying what is meant by legislation. Many people take legislation to mean Acts of Parliament. Actually, Acts of Parliament would be referred to as law and the word legislation is about much more than this.

The following diagram demonstrates how legislation is much wider than just Acts of Parliament.

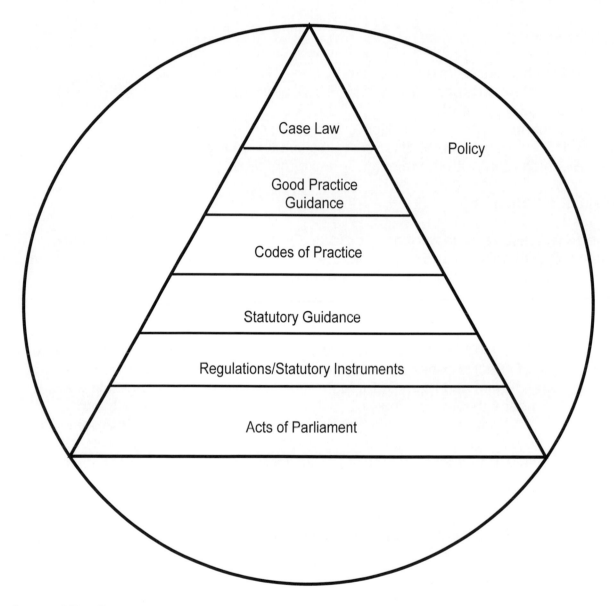

Acts of Parliament

There are potentially more than sixty Acts of Parliament which might have an impact on the provision of care services. Some of these are covered in this publication but for more information you should see *Social Care and the Law: An NVQ Related Reference Guide for Direct Care Staff,* by Siobhan Maclean and Mark Shiner.

Regulations/Statutory Instruments

Acts of Parliament often include a clause which gives the senior minister involved (usually the Secretary of State) the power to introduce regulations at a later date.

These Regulations detail more specific law on areas covered by the Act. This is done by means of a statutory instrument which goes before Parliament, but which is not usually debated. Regulations are used extensively around health and safety.

Statutory Guidance

Major Acts of Parliament may be followed at a later date by Guidance. These do not have the same force of law as Acts or Regulations, but they explain and clarify the law and offer guidance on best practice.

Codes of Practice

Some Acts of Parliament have an associated Code of Practice (for example the Mental Capacity Act 2005). The Care Standards Act 2000 placed a responsibility on the regulatory bodies for social care (for example the General Social Care Council) to issue Codes of Practice for social care. It is vital that all staff working in care are fully conversant with the relevant codes of practice.

Good Practice Guidance

The Government issues a range of good practice Guidance which changes regularly. Social care workers need to be familiar with the good practice Guidance relevant to their area of practice, and take active steps to keep up to date with developments.

Case Law

Case Law is the term used to describe the process by which the courts decide on matters of law as a result of specific cases presented to the courts. The wording in some Acts of Parliament is ambiguous, and many individual circumstances do not neatly fit in specific situations. This means that increasingly people are taking social care, health and educational organisations to court when they feel that a particular agency has come to a decision which they disagree with and which they feel does not uphold legal requirements. Some cases result in judgements that have implications far wider than the original case.

Policy

The diagram clearly shows policy as encircling all of the other forms of legislation we have covered. This is for two reasons:

➤ The Government publishes National Policy Guidance which essentially brings together the principles of all the forms of legislation covered and which often subsequently leads to new legislation and therefore changes in the "triangle".

➤ Organisational policies should reflect all of the legislation covered – changes in any area of the triangle should influence changes in organisational policy.

Social care professionals need to be able to identify what is law and what is policy. They need to keep up to date with changes in legislation and policy to ensure that their practice is legal and informed by policy and procedure.

A straightforward analogy of the relationship between law and policy is to think of a car.

Laws would be represented by the engine. Once in place laws and legislation are the main driving force. This is especially relevant where the particular law lays a duty onto service providers. The provider must move to fulfil its legal obligation. It's not unusual to find that some services have been driven to engage in various changes because of one law or another.

However, an engine on its own is not very useful – it can't go anywhere without wheels and bodywork.

Government policy is the chassis and bodywork. It dresses up the engine and mounts it on wheels. This means that the engine can move and get to where it wants to, or needs to go. Government policy adds depth to the law.

To pursue the analogy - organisational policy is the cabin within which the driver and passengers sit. The car's bodywork (Government Policy) establishes the amount of room (the boundaries) within which an individual social care organisation can work. The Government wants to cultivate diversity within service provision. Therefore it does not detail exactly how social care organisations should carry out the tasks that they are required or expected to do.

In theory it should be the service users who are in the driving seat. They are using the car to get them where they want to be. Often, however, managers of the service may need to take the driving seat to ensure that services get to where they need to be to provide the best possible outcomes for service users.

One of the main issues for social care workers is that just when they think they have worked out the engine (the law) it changes. It is essential that social care staff ensure they keep up to date with legislation and policy developments. This constitutes basic practice – after all you wouldn't drive your car unless you regularly checked your oil, water and brakes would you?

In Summary

Social care staff need to ensure that their practice is in line with legal requirements. Staff might feel that managers create policy almost for the sake of it, but everyone must follow policy and procedures to ensure that they are acting in line with legal requirements.

51: LEARNING LESSONS FROM FAILURES IN SOCIAL CARE PRACTICE

There have been a variety of serious failures in care and support in both health and social care settings in the 1990s and 2000s. Following such failures, inquiries are often set up to investigate the failings and to support people to "learn the lessons" such that similar failings do not happen again. A key element of evidence based practice is learning these lessons.

Inquiry reports have often highlighted the following issues:

Values

The attitudes that staff have (both direct care staff and managers) towards service users appears to be a key gateway as to whether the service will uphold the persons rights or dismiss their rights.

Attitudes held by staff towards some or all service users have included a sense of contempt and disrespectfulness. Staff perceive the person or people as not understanding what they are experiencing, that the person has a poor quality of life *"anyway"*, or that a harsh and positive punishment was *"good for them"* or *"they deserved it"*.

Added to this can be an attitude of laughing at service users.

These sort of staff attitudes are behind many situations where there is a serious failure in care practice.

Power

Related to values is the issue of power. Where there have been failures of practice there appears to have been an abuse or misuse of power – sometimes relating to a lack of understanding of power and where it lies. Many direct care staff feel relatively powerless in relation to their own organisation. However, direct care staff can have great power over the day to day experience of service users (see chapter 37).

Some staff who have felt powerless in their own work situation or life have used the power they can wield over service users in a manner that is egocentric and destructive towards the service user.

Isolation

Abusive situations have arisen in services that are isolated. Where service users:

➢ Receive all their support from within one service

➢ Are placed a long way from family members

➢ Have few or no visits from family

➢ Have little contact with other professionals

then there is increased risk of negligence, neglect or more active abuse.

Staff Team Culture

Where abuse or service failures have occurred it is not unusual to find that there are features of the staff team that raised concerns. Aspects include:

➢ Staff teams include family members within the team

➢ There is no or little interest in training and development

➢ There is resistance to advice or information from visiting professionals

➢ Some staff cultures can act as barriers to reporting poor or dangerous practices.

➢ Loyalty to colleagues is considered far more important than upholding the well-being of service users.

Failures to Follow Policy and Procedure

Many inquiry reports have identified that appropriate policies and procedures were in place within the organisation but these were not effectively followed. Clearly this reinforces the need for social care workers to follow policy and procedure.

Inquiry Reports

Whilst many inquiry reports are specific to Children's or Adult Services, it is important that we learn the lessons from all areas of social and health care work. If an inquiry report doesn't seem particularly relevant in terms of geography or user group, social care staff can still develop their practice by considering the findings. Many reports conclude with very similar findings and recommendations.

Staffordshire Pin Down (1991)

The experiences of over 130 children and young people in Staffordshire in the 1980s came to light in 1989. Children were found to have been removed from their peers, left in dark and empty rooms for long periods, deprived of all stimuli and forced to wear night clothes during the day. Some children were found to have been placed in these "pin down rooms" for periods of weeks or even months.

Lord Levy's inquiry (Levy and Kahan 1991) explained the context within which this situation and developed and criticised confused policies in Staffordshire at the time, inadequate staffing levels, poor and remote management, poor training and a disinterested and introspective culture of practice. Levy's view was that the wider context which allows poor practice to occur, including poor management practice, needed highlighting as much as the issues themselves.

Fatal Accident Enquiry into the Death of Miss Agnes McCabe (1994)

Miss Agnes McCabe, was admitted to hospital suffering from severe bedsores and malnutrition. Miss McCabe was living at the time in a small residential care home – she had been subject to considerable physical neglect and after a protracted period of warnings and appeals, the home was closed down by the Inspection Unit. A public inquiry (Convery 1994) found the following factors had contributed to the risk for residents:

> All the residents had lived previously in a long stay psychiatric hospital, their social networks had virtually broken down and there were few visitors to the home

> Most had dementia or at least the beginnings of dementia and may not have made very credible witnesses even if they had managed to raise the alarm

> The same GP dealt with all the residents, and he was also the owner of the home, so there was no independent medical expert coming in on a regular basis

> The manager of the home was the owner's wife

> The manager had no relevant qualifications and had been given a fixed amount of time to acquire these. Her deputy manager, the "fit person" at the time of registration, had relevant qualifications, but left after a few months, disgusted at the way things were being run

> Some staff members "blew the whistle", but working life was made so uncomfortable for them that they soon moved on and there was high staff turnover.

The Independent Longcare Inquiry (1998)

This reported that staff denied the adult residents of the care home their dignity and rights. Residents were viewed as children and were subject to a range of punitive punishments. Established staff encouraged new staff to hit or intimidate residents in order to establish control.

There was a staff culture that acted as a barrier to the reporting of concerns with intimidation, victimisation and threats being used to prevent residents and staff from complaining.

Standards of care were poor and there was rationing of essential items. Conditions were temporarily improved prior to inspection visits, and this included having a full staff team on duty the day the inspectors visited.

Lessons from Commission for Health Improvement Investigations 2000-2003 (Published 2004)

Between 2000 and 2003 the Commission for Health Improvement carried out 11 investigations into serious failures in the NHS. Findings from these investigations were published in this report.

The report found the following issues contributed significantly to the service failures:

> Lack of effective leadership

> Staff shortages

> Poor induction, training and supervision

> Poor team relationships

> Poor incident reporting and poor recording

> Poor information for service users

Rowan Report (2003)

Following allegations of abuse on Rowan Ward, a hospital ward for older people with mental health problems, the Commission for Health Improvement carried out an investigation. The investigation concluded that:

"The Rowan Ward Service had many of the known risk factors for abuse: a poor and institutionalised environment, low staffing levels, high use of bank and agency staff, little staff development, poor supervision, lack of knowledge of incident reporting, closed inward looking culture and weak management."

A range of recommendations were made including:

➢ Management and leadership must be strengthened

➢ All staff need to receive training on vulnerable adult procedures

➢ There is a need for robust information systems

➢ Multi-disciplinary working needs improvements

➢ Priority needs to be given to the continuing professional development of staff

➢ Work is required to raise expectations in terms of basic care standards

Victoria Climbié Inquiry (2003)

The public Inquiry was set up following Victoria's tragic death in February 2000 and the subsequent murder conviction of her carers in January 2001.

The Inquiry found that there were significant inter agency failings and failings within social services. As a result the Inquiry report recommended that:

➢ Where the child's first language is not English an interpreter must be used

➢ When social services place a child in temporary accommodation, an assessment must be made of the suitability of that accommodation

➢ All staff who work with children must receive appropriate training, receive a thorough induction in local procedures and receive continuing training to keep up to date

➢ When social workers are absent, there must be a system in place to ensure post and phone calls are checked and actioned as necessary.

(Lord Laming 2003)

Investigation into Child Protection in Eilean Siar (2005)

In Scotland, following a catalogue of abuse against three girls which was not sufficiently acted on, a report by the Social Work Inspection Agency recommended:

➢ All foster carers have training appropriate to their role. The needs of foster carers own children should be considered

➢ Staff who work directly with children must receive regular supervision

➢ The Scottish Executive should provide guidance for professionals on how to help children express their views

> ➤ The Scottish Executive should give all children involved in children's hearings and inter-agency meetings the opportunity to have an advocate

Joint Investigation Into the Provision of Services for People with Learning Disabilities at Cornwall Partnership NHS Trust (2006)

This is an inspection report into services provided by Cornwall Partnership NHS Trust for people with learning disabilities. It was jointly published by the Healthcare Commission and the Commission for Social Care Inspection (CSCI).

The Healthcare Commission was originally contacted by a Mencap service in Cornwall about complaints raised by a number of families and by the news that the NHS Trust was holding disciplinary proceedings towards seven staff in one service (five of whom were dismissed).

The Trust operated three assessment and treatment centres; 45 supported living services (most with 4 or 5 people in each service); one specialist service for a person detained under the Mental Health Act; and services for children (three respite services and one providing long term accommodation for two children).

The inspection report is focused on the assessment and treatment centres and the supported living services. The assessment and treatment services were all, at best, poor. One was over crowded and one had a ward that was appalling (and this ward has been closed). There were recorded accounts of 64 separate incidents from 2000 to 2005 involving staff hitting, kicking, dragging service users, withholding food, giving cold showers and using excessive restraint all on one ward. These are recorded incidents. Generally, the inspectors found recording to be chaotic and incomplete.

The supported living services were characterised by great variation in the quality of care provided. Some houses provided care that was at least adequate, but most provided care below acceptable standards. Institutional practices were common in many houses. Staff held keys and service users could not lock their own bedrooms. In fact, staff locked doors to restrict movement of service users. There was a general culture of risk aversion resulting in one house where all the taps were removed. There was no effective person centred planning process, no clear commitment to choice and control for service users. Recording was chaotic. Financial arrangements were irregular. Most service users had never had a community care assessment.

The main point made by the inspectors was that the services claimed to be "supporting people" services and not care homes. However, the CSCI viewed the services as unregistered care homes. Additionally, the local supporting people team reviewed the services and decided that it was not appropriate to provide supporting people funds to the service users.

Recommendations

The inspection report included a battery of recommendations, many of which are values based. For example:

> ➤ widen opportunities for service users to exercise choice and control over their own care

> ➤ provide external advocacy

> provide accessible information to service users about how the service is developing

Recommendations also included the importance of leadership and strategic vision. Other recommendations relate to more direct service delivery and include the following:

> Staff training should enable the delivery of care in accordance with the principles of Valuing People (Department of Health 2001)

> Care plans and risk assessments are to be holistic and used and updated regularly

> A unified system for compiling care records should be developed

> Staff should receive support and regular structured supervision

There are further recommendations relating to:

> Promoting best practice in the use of restraint

> Financial responsibility and accountability

> Protecting vulnerable adults

6 Lives: The Provision of Public Services to People with Learning Disabilities (2009)

Following a request from Mencap, the Local Government Ombudsman looked into complaints from family members of six adults with learning disabilities who died whilst in health and social care services between 2003 and 2005. The investigation *"illustrated some significant and distressing failures in service across both health and social care."* A range of recommendations were made, including:

> People must be treated as individuals

> Basic care must be well provided

> Leadership needs to be improved

> Policy, standards and guidance must be followed

> Workers should demonstrate empathy for service users

> Communication at all levels needs improvement

> There needs to be improvement in partnership working and multi agency co-operation

> Services need to find constructive and positive ways to work with families and informal carers

> Advocacy may provide additional support for service users and families and opportunities to work with advocates should be available

Investigation into West London Mental Health NHS Trust (2009)

This investigation by the Care Quality Commission was triggered by concerns about the Trust's responses to suicides within the Trust. The investigation found that:

> The Trust failed to properly investigate or report serious incidents

> The trust did not learn from previous incidents or implement all previous recommendations

> Some of the hospitals and wards were not a safe environment for care

➢ Some wards were overcrowded

➢ People had limited access to primary care services

➢ There was a shortage of staff with high rates of sickness absence

➢ Staff attendance at mandatory training was extremely low

The Inquiry into the Death of Baby Peter (2009)

The Serious Case Review into the death of Baby Peter in Haringey in August 2007 led to massive media criticism of staff across services for children, and to public concern about failures to protect vulnerable children. Lord Laming was commissioned by the Department for Children, Schools and Families to report on the progress made in implementing his previous set of recommendations, and to identify the key issues in children's services today.

This report scrutinises issues from the training of social workers to evidence based practice through to legal and financial implications around better safeguarding practices. There are some key areas which all social care workers need to be aware of:

➢ The need for better services when children are defined as "children in need". Laming recommends *"Local authorities must ensure that 'Children in Need', as defined by Section 17 of the Children Act 1989, have early access to effective specialist services and support to meet their needs"* (Laming 2009: 86). The focus in children's services on prevention and early intervention from the Children Act 2004 means that social care workers may often be involved in a "Team around the Child" working to ensure that services are coordinated and that children's needs are met as early as possible.

➢ Laming reports that thresholds for assessment of children in need by local authorities "have no statutory basis" (p. 29). This represents something of a "sea change" in current practices, as does the expectation that all professional referrals must be assessed by the local authority. Social care staff who make a referral for a vulnerable child may need this knowledge to make an effective challenge if this does not occur.

➢ The responsibility of all services is to understand their roles in safeguarding children and current practice around integrated working, common assessment, early intervention and the role of the lead professional. Linked to this is the need for integrated working tools and processes such as CAF and Contact Point to be used effectively. No evaluation of the impact of these tools will be possible until the "roll out" has had time to take effect. Therefore all workers who are involved in children's social care need to access relevant training, keep their knowledge around best practice up to date, and use these tools consistently in order to improve multi-agency working and information sharing. See www.everychildmatters.gov.uk for more information and the most up to date resources for professionals.

➢ There is a need for better planning, particularly where a child is the subject of a child protection plan. Laming states that plans need to identify clearer expectations around the improvements which need to occur, and when further action by local authorities may be necessary. Again, if social care workers are part of a child protection plan, they may need to be confident enough to challenge when this clarity is not achieved. All workers need to ensure that their role in any social work plan is clear, that timescales for change are identified, and that clear outcomes are planned with milestones agreed. It is not good practice for vague and undefined "support" to be offered to families as part of a plan as it is not easy to measure progress towards outcomes in this way.

In Summary

Inquiries into serious failures in both adult services and childrens services can provide social care workers with key learning as to how services should structure and improve their practices. Several of the Inquiries summarised in this chapter focus on learning around person centred planning, service user power and isolation and staff values and behaviours.

SECTION H: CONTINUING PROFESSIONAL DEVELOPMENT

The concept of continual professional development is vital in social care. Whatever qualifications and experiences a social care worker has they should never feel they have nothing further to learn. Social care and the evidence base for it are constantly changing and we therefore all have much to learn in order to provide the best quality service to the people we work with. In order to learn effectively and to facilitate the learning of others, it is useful to have at least a basic understanding of the principles and theories of adult learning. This section therefore begins by exploring these.

52: ADULT LEARNING THEORY

Whilst a knowledge of adult learning is particularly useful in ensuring continued professional development, this knowledge can also be very useful in actual social care practice. For example, knowledge in this area can be used to assist an adult with learning disabilities to develop their daily living skills; to assist a stroke survivor in relearning essential skills; in reablement or rehabilitation services etc.

Principles of Adult Learning

In exploring adult learning theory and literature, it is clear that a number of basic principles underpin most theories of adult learning. A quick review of these principles seems a good place to start this chapter:

The Law of Exercise

People learn most effectively by actually doing something. The phrase "practice makes perfect" is drawn from the law of exercise (although it is important to be aware that practice doesn't always make perfect!) Practising something away from the real environment will limit learning. Whilst we may believe that we are helping people to learn by giving them lots of opportunity to practice a skill, if the opportunities do not include practising the skill in the actual environment, with the real equipment etc, we may actually be hindering an adult's learning.

The Law of Association

Like a building, learning needs a foundation which can be built upon. New facts, new skills or new approaches are best learned if we can associate them with something we already understand or something we have previously experienced (our foundation).

The need to know motivation

It is clear that adults learn best when they feel that they *need* to know what they are called upon to learn. If an adult doesn't feel they need to know or need to be able to do something they are unlikely to learn ("What's the point?" is a common question). It is therefore important to outline clearly why a particular skill or a particular piece of knowledge is useful in order to motivate an adult to learn.

The need to be self directing

Responsibility for adult learning is predominantly individual. Adults therefore learn best when they are directing their own learning. An increased sense of ownership in the programme of learning will enhance learning.

Readiness to learn

Linking with other principles, adults will only learn effectively when they have a readiness to learn. This can relate to recognising what there is to learn and recognising why this is important and relevant. However, if these issues have been considered and an individual still has no "readiness" to learn, even the most effective teaching will probably not facilitate learning.

Learning empowerment

Adults learn best from a position of confidence. It is important therefore to recognise people's experiences and facilitate some degree of self confidence. If the "teaching" relationship is viewed as one where the learner is the "empty vessel" and the teacher the "full vessel" prepared to fill the learner with knowledge, then the learner will not learn effectively. It is preferable to view learning as a two way process – an approach which will empower the learner.

Learning curves and plateaux

We all learn at different rates and sometimes our learning curves are steep. It is not realistic to expect steady increases in learning patterns. There is more likely to be steep increases in learning at some points and a consolidation of learning (a plateau in the learning curve) at other stages. Learners do not always recognise or expect the plateau and may become anxious during these stages, so that reassurance is required.

Positive learning

If we receive positive reinforcement about a subject or experience, we are more likely to learn from it. This reinforces the need to provide constructive feedback to facilitate learning. Specific and realistic feedback is the most effective to facilitate learning.

Whole / Part / Whole Learning

Where a task is significant, it is easier to learn when it is broken down into its component (smaller) parts. However, individual parts of a task can only be assimilated when the whole is understood. Where a learner is responsible for part of a larger task, they need to understand how their part fits into the bigger picture.

Adult Learning Theory

These general principles appear in many theories of adult learning. Some of the most widely used theories of adult learning used in the social care sector are outlined in the remainder of this chapter.

Experiential Learning

Experiential learning theory is probably the most influential adult learning theory in social work and social care. David Kolb (1984) is the most well known writer in experiential learning circles, although the ideas can actually be traced back to 450BC when Confucius said:

> *"Tell me, and I will forget.*
> *Show me and I might remember.*
> *Involve me and I will understand."*

Perhaps because of this Confucius quote, experiential learning theory is sometimes misinterpreted as simply saying that people learn through experience. To some extent this is true but experiential learning theory asserts that it's not enough for people to have an experience – they won't learn from this unless they spend some time reflecting on the experience.

Experiential learning basically proposes that people learn based on an experience by going through a cycle of learning. Kolb breaks down this cycle into four stages:

1. Concrete Experience
2. Reflective Observation
3. Abstract Conceptualisation
4. Active Experimentation

People often feel that the jargon used in this theory is off putting, but the actual theory is really useful so it's worth trying to see beyond the initially off putting jargon.

Kolb's cycle is outlined in the following diagram:

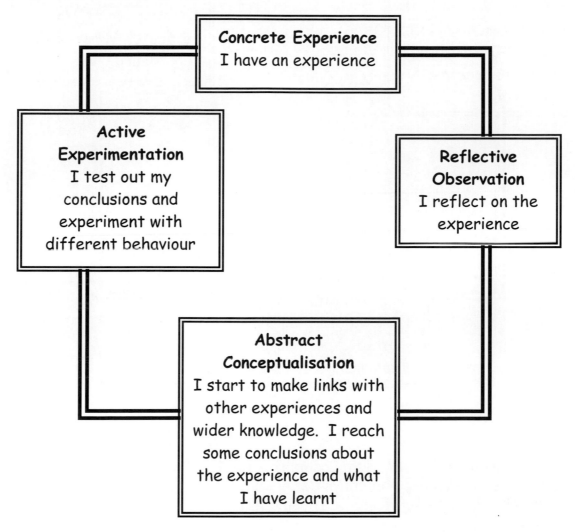

Concrete Experience
I have an experience

Reflective Observation
I reflect on the experience

Abstract Conceptualisation
I start to make links with other experiences and wider knowledge. I reach some conclusions about the experience and what I have learnt

Active Experimentation
I test out my conclusions and experiment with different behaviour

This theory of adult learning is particularly helpful in understanding continuing professional development, as it clearly demonstrates that it's not enough for someone to simply immerse themselves in a range of experiences. They won't necessarily learn from the experience unless they are supported to follow through the whole learning cycle.

In order to learn effectively, social care workers need to reflect on their experiences, make wider links, draw conclusions and plan any necessary changes to their practice.

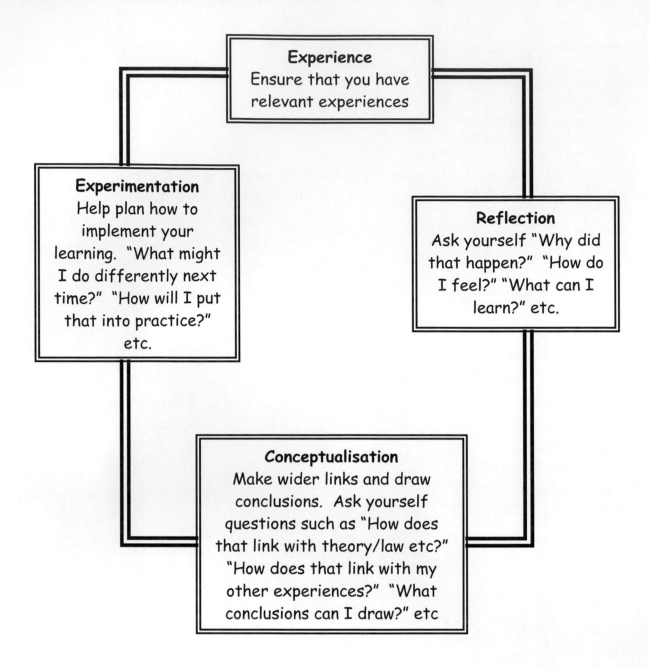

Learning Styles

Honey and Mumford (1982) report that people have different styles of learning. They have developed four different styles and have designed a learning styles questionnaire which identifies which style a person prefers. These questionnaires are widely available in social care services.

The four learning styles identified by Honey and Mumford are:

Activists

Activists are often open minded and enthusiastic – they like new experiences and want to get involved in the here and now. They enjoy getting involved and they learn by "doing". Activists can become bored when an activity stops and will want to quickly move onto the next challenge or activity, rather than dwell on reflection of the last activity.

Reflectors

Reflectors (do just what it says on the tin!) stand back, reflect, ponder and consider many perspectives before acting. Reflectors mull over things before reaching a conclusion. They observe, gather information and use plenty of time to think things over.

Theorists

Theorists are logical thinkers: they analyse, question and learn step by step in a logical way. Theorists question any new learning and want to ensure it fits and makes sense with their logical approach. Theorists are often perfectionists and don't appreciate a flippant approach to a subject.

Pragmatists

Pragmatists like to try out something new to see if it works in practice. They like experimenting with new ideas. They will often take a problem solving approach to learning and will seek to apply something that they have learnt straight away. However, if it doesn't work they are likely not to try the approach again. Instead, they will try to look for something new to try.

We all have a little of each style in us (and some of us are evenly matched across all four styles), but most of us favour one style more than the others. The learning styles questionnaires we referred to generally give a score in each of the four areas, identifying which of the styles a person has a preference for. It is vital to remember that no one style is "better" than another – they are simply different.

As a social care worker or a social care educator it is useful to have some understanding of these identified styles and approaches. However, it is important to remember that this is a theoretical approach. The styles are not scientifically set and it is vital to remember that there are other influences on how an adult learns. There is an argument that we tend to "teach" in our "own style" so it is important for social care educators to understand their own learning style and to ensure they consider the style of a learner in their 'teaching' approach.

Different social care educators use their understanding of learning styles in different ways. One common approach is to ask a learner to complete a learning styles questionnaire to identify their preferred style and to then select learning activities which suit their preferred style. For example, completing reflective journals will suit a reflector's preferred learning style. This is certainly an approach to using learning styles recommended in many texts. For example, Williams and Rutter state that *"A good match between the style of a learning activity and a learner's preferred style maximises learning potential."* (Williams and Rutter 2007:85)

We would argue, however, that if you link Kolb's experiential learning theory to an understanding of styles, this may not be the right approach:

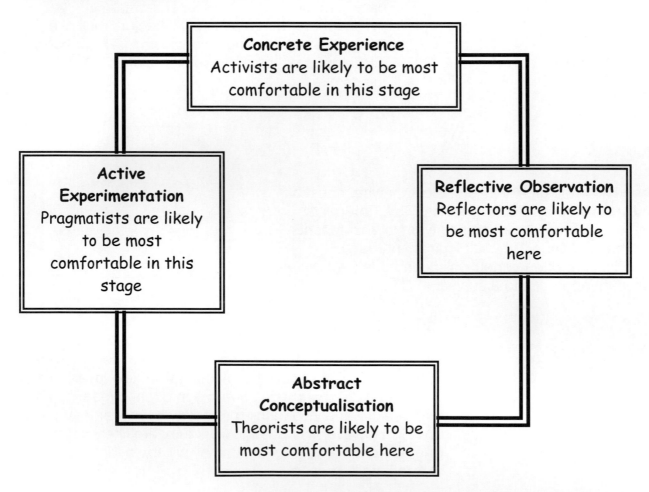

If Kolb's theory that we need to move round the full cycle in order to learn effectively is true, then we would argue that choosing learning activities to suit a person's learning style could impede learning. For example, asking a reflector to complete a reflective journal is likely to keep them in the phase of reflective observation where, according to the learning styles approach, they will spend most time naturally anyway. We would assert that social care educators need to support a learner through the whole cycle of learning identified by Kolb. Maybe, therefore, we should look to providing learning activities that encourage learners to move around the cycle, which may take them outside of their natural comfort zone. This, though, needs to be carefully planned with the learner being offered additional support where they are engaged in learning activities which are "outside" their preferred learning style.

Likewise, social care workers may need to think about this when choosing learning activities for themselves. An activist might want to choose a "doing" type activity, but if they don't reflect, then their learning is likely to be impeded.

Approaches to Learning

Honey and Mumford

Although they are most well known for devising learning *styles*, Honey and Mumford (1986) also assert that there are four different *approaches* to learning. These are different to the styles of learning they discuss. References are often made to learning styles and less commonly to approaches to learning. However, we find an understanding of approaches to learning very useful in understanding how adults learn. The approaches identified are as follows:

Intuitive Learning

We are not conscious of this, but we are learning by our experience. If we use the intuitive approach then we are making use of the experiences we have to learn and develop. Intuitive learners soak everything up and see learning as a kind of process of osmosis. If this approach is challenged we are able to refer to a variety of detail of experiences. However if questioned, the intuitive learner finds it difficult to articulate what they have learnt or how they have learnt it. People who are intuitive learners regularly see themselves as having attended the University of Life!

The Incidental Approach

This generally involves learning by chance from activities that force an individual to carry out a reflection of the situation. This can sometimes be borne out of frustration. If something happens to an incidental learner, e.g.: something in their plan goes wrong, they will often reflect over the incident in an unstructured informal way.

This can happen in less formal patterns such as travelling home, sitting in the garden or even lying in the bath. Incidental learners often use the "benefit of hindsight" as a way of rationalising what has happened.

Incidental learners will often discuss their experience with someone else and it is even more beneficial to discuss it with someone who was present at the time of the experience.

The Retrospective Approach

Similar to the incidental approach, the retrospective learner looks back over what has happened and then goes on to draw a specific conclusion from it. However, people using this approach will also tend to draw lessons from routines and successes. Therefore, in effect, they are learning from a diverse range of small and large, positive and negative experiences.

The process looks something like this:

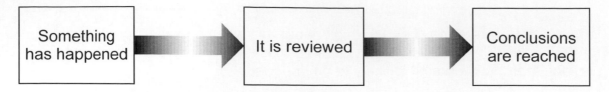

The Prospective Approach

This is similar to the above, except that there is another dimension included – this is the dimension of planning. The experience is planned for, set up and then reviewed with conclusions drawn. That means that future plans are seen as learning opportunities as opposed to just merely things to be done.

Social care workers will maximise their opportunities for continuing professional development if they adopt a prospective approach to learning. In fact, this approach is encouraged in many social care learning and qualification processes. Learners are expected to identify their learning needs, to participate in the development of a plan, to engage in the available learning opportunities, to keep their learning under review and to reach conclusions about their learning. Where learners have a tendency to follow one of the other approaches, they may need help to develop the prospective approach.

Surface and Deep Approaches to Learning

First identified in 1976 by Marton and Saljo, most people involved in adult learning and teaching have heard of the terms deep learning and surface learning as this is a widely used concept:

Surface approach

This approach focuses on acquiring and memorising information. An uncritical, unquestioning approach is taken to acquiring new knowledge and there is little reflection. Learning is motivated by external factors such as demands from employers or assessment requirements.

Deep approach

This approach involves critically analysing new ideas and linking them with existing knowledge. This approach means that a learner will understand and be able to apply the learning in new and different contexts. Deep learning assists with problem solving and making wider connections.

Encouraging a deeper approach to learning is an important aspect of continuing professional development. It is important to recognise that these approaches are not based on personality types, but can be encouraged and developed.

"We should not identify the learner with a fixed approach to learning,….. It is the design of learning opportunity that encourages students to adopt a particular approach… Very crudely: deep is good, surface is bad and we should teach in a way that encourages learners to adopt a deep approach."

(Houghton 2004:2)

Thinking Styles

Danbury (1994) identifies that people have two different thinking styles:

<u>Pictorial Thinkers</u>

Pictorial thinkers have pictorial memories. They think visually. They are attracted to visual images, they like flowcharts, diagrams, imagery etc.

<u>Verbal Thinkers</u>

Verbal thinkers have verbal memories. They think in words rather than pictures. Verbal thinkers will learn best through reading and discussion. Diagrams and imagery will have little meaning for them.

Cognitive Dissonance

This is a theory drawn from psychology and used widely in understanding people's behaviour and motivation. It was first written about by Leon Festinger (1957). We find it useful in understanding the process of adult learning as follows.

The idea is that we all go through four phases when we are called on to learn something new:

1. *Unconscious Incompetence*
   When asked to undertake a new task, we don't know what we don't know. It could be said that we're incompetent but that we are unconscious of this. In a way this is quite a comfortable stage – it could be seen as "blissful ignorance". We don't know that we can't do something. However, as we attempt to undertake the new task, we quickly realise that there is a lot more involved than we think and we move onto:

2. *Conscious Incompetence*
   Now we become aware of what we don't know – we realise that we can't do the new task. This is a very uncomfortable and potentially painful stage. Many people are socialised to believe "there's no such word as can't" and becoming conscious of our incompetence is distressing.

   At this phase, some people decide to concede the learning – give up on the task. People can develop quite sophisticated defence mechanisms to ensure that people around them aren't aware of their "incompetence". Think of the highly

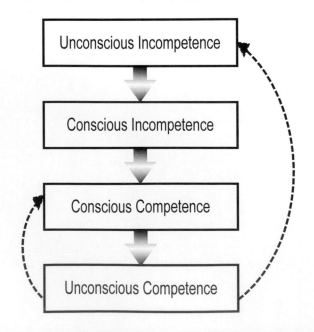

developed systems that some adults with literacy difficulties have developed.

Others seek out support and new and useful experiences in order to get through this stage, learn the task and move onto the next stage:

3. *Conscious Competence*
When we have recently learned a new task we are very aware or conscious about it. Think about that new driver who is saying "mirror, signal, manoeuvre" every time they go out in a car! Whilst we may be anxious to ensure we get things right, this is probably the most comfortable and safe stage to be in. We are aware of what we are doing, so we are likely to continue to question ourselves and are probably getting it right! The danger is that we will probably, at some point, move onto the next stage:

4. *Unconscious Competence*
This is where we have become so familiar with the task and confident about our abilities that we almost go onto an "automatic pilot". The potentially dangerous aspect of this is that when we are unconscious about something, how do we know that we are still doing it right? Think how many of us (if we are honest) wouldn't pass our driving test today if we just had an examiner sitting in the car on one of our usual journeys. When we are unconscious about something, we slip into bad habits, we take shortcuts – maybe we have actually slipped back to this first phase (unconscious incompetence). If we are unconscious, how do we know?

In many ways cognitive dissonance provides the whole back drop of continuing professional development. When people have been in a post for a while they may well have moved into unconscious competence – and as covered might well have slipped into 'bad habits'. Continuing to learn and develop means that staff are encouraged to revisit their skills and maintain themselves in the phase of 'conscious competence' which is the only place to be in terms of safe practice.

Social Learning Theory

One of the principle writers of social learning is Bandura (e.g.: 1977). Like so many theories, this is just describing a common life event. Social learning describes the way that we engage in a behaviour because we have seen another person engage in the behaviour and that other person benefited from the behaviour (or they avoided something unpleasant happening to them). Social learning is more likely to be successful if the role model has status or standing with the learner and the new behaviour can be rewarded. Arguably, much of what people learn is through role modelling. This is most apparent in a parent/child relationship, but there are lots of other examples.

Many teenagers and young adults learn social skills from their peers through social learning. Many adults have learned other skills (such as computer skills) through watching others succeed at the task (in relation to computer skills, it is often their young child!)

Behaviourist Learning Theory

Behaviourist approaches to adult learning focus on learning as a change in a person's behaviour. Initially developed by Skinner (e.g.: 1973), the belief is that behaviour is intrinsically linked to consequences. A learner will repeat desired behaviours as a result of positive consequences – for example, if positive feedback follows the behaviour. The "rewards" in behaviourist approaches are seen as external to the learner. Burns (1995) notes that many competency based training programmes are based on this theory. However, he argues that whilst it may be a useful theory in relation to repetitive tasks and work skills which require a great deal of practice, higher levels of learning are not involved. He criticises this approach as rigid and mechanical.

Humanist Learning Theories

Developed from the work of Carl Rogers (e.g.: 1980) this is sometimes referred to as facilitative learning. Opposing behaviourist approaches which see learning as a consequence of extrinsic (external) rewards, humanists argue that learning is a result of intrinsic (internal) rewards. The approach is based on the belief that people have a natural eagerness to learn and that people will learn in order to meet their needs for self actualisation. Self satisfaction is the motivating force for learning. Humanistic approaches are linked to the idea that adults are self directing in their learning.

A number of specific theories are drawn out of the humanistic approach. For example, Burns (1995:233) argues that andragogy is *"very much in the spirit of the humanist approach to learning and education."*

Andragogy

Malcolm Knowles (1978) believes that most adult teaching has consisted of teaching adults as if they were children. He argues that adults are different from children as learners in three critical ways:

1. In terms of their self concept. Whereas a child first sees themselves as a completely dependent personality, the adult has developed a concept of themselves which values a certain degree of autonomy. Adults have a need to be perceived as self directing. The deepest need an adult has is to be treated as an adult, to be treated as a self directing person and to be treated with respect.

2. In terms of their experience. Whereas a child defines his or her self identity by reference to their family, school, community etc, adults usually define themselves in terms of their experiences. Self identity is derived from what we have done. Accordingly adults are very jealous of the worth of our experience and wherever we find people devaluing our experience, not paying attention to it, or not incorporating it in the education plan, we feel rejected as people.

3. In terms of their time perspective. Whereas in most aspects of life, a child's time perspective is one of immediacy and therefore they find it hard to postpone the satisfaction of present desires, an adult is more accustomed to postponing immediate satisfactions. However, in regard to learning, the time perspectives of children and adults is reversed. Children become used to learning things that will not have immediate application, but will be accumulated into a reservoir of knowledge and skills that will/may be useful in adult life. On the other hand an adult's perspective in regard to learning is likely to be one of immediate application. According to Knowles, the reason an adult enters into education is to be able to better deal with some life problem about which they feel inadequate now.

Knowles refers to the approach of teaching children as pedagogy and says that the teaching of adults should be based on a different approach which he calls andragogy. Andragogy should take account of the differences outlined above.

Situated Learning Theory

Most approaches to learning in social care are based on the idea of situated learning theory – a term coined by Lave in the 1980s. He argues that learning needs to take place in the context and culture in which the activity ordinarily occurs (ie: where it is situated). Social interaction is an essential aspect of situated learning. Learners need to become involved in a "community of practice". As the learner moves from the edge of this community to its centre, they become more active and engaged in their learning. Lave and Wenger (1990) call this process "legitimate peripheral participation", they carried out an analysis of situated learning in five different settings (including midwives). In all five cases, they found that learners had a gradual acquisition of knowledge and skills as they learnt from 'experts' in the context of everyday activities. Others have developed the concept of situated learning further. Brown, Collins and Duguid (1989) emphasised the idea of "cognitive apprenticeship".

Many social care workers spend much of their time "lone working". This limits their opportunities to become involved in a "community of practice" and therefore may impede their learning. This demonstrates why lone workers need to attend regular activities with other social care practitioners – for example, team meetings, training courses etc.

 ## In Summary

It is particularly important for social care trainers to be informed about adult learning theory. However, it is also useful for all social care staff to have a basic level of knowledge about approaches to adult learning as this can assist in supporting service users to learn new skills and to promote active support.

53: REFLECTIVE PRACTICE

The experiential learning cycle shows the importance of learners reflecting on their experiences in order to learn. However, reflective practice is not just about learning. It's about continually monitoring and improving practice and outcomes for service users. As such, reflective practice is a vital aspect of social care practice. It is therefore vital that everyone involved in social care has at least a basic idea of the process of reflection and reflective practice.

Schön (1987) asserts that there are two types of reflection:

➢ Reflection IN action
➢ Reflection ON action

Reflection in Action

Reflection IN action is the process of reflection when you are engaging in an activity. Essentially it is working and being aware of what you are doing at the same time. Reflection in action involves:

➢ Thinking ahead *("Right if that's happened, then I need to .....")*

➢ Being critical *("That didn't work very well....")*

➢ Storing up experiences for the future *("I could have dealt with that better, so next time I will try....")*

➢ Analysing what is happening *("She's saying that to test me – I think I should....")*

Reflection in action is happening all the time – if your mind is on the task! We all know people who are planning their night out whilst carrying out a task and would all agree that this doesn't constitute good practice. Having your mind on the job is important. Not only is it good practice, but it constitutes reflection in action.

Whilst reflection in action is good practice and can help people to develop their practice, it does have drawbacks. The main problems with reflection in action are:

➢ You can only see things from your own perspective *("I think, I feel, I'm not sure....")*

➢ You will only have short term reflection. If your mind is on the task at hand, when the task changes so will your thoughts.

These drawbacks can be addressed by making sure that you also use reflection ON action.

Reflection on Action

This is the reflecting you do after an event. Reflection ON action refers to the process of thinking through and perhaps discussing the incident with a colleague or a supervisor.

Reflection on action is free from urgency and any pressures of the actual event. As such, it allows for longer term reflection. You can also ensure that by seeking feedback you use other people's perspectives in your reflection.

The main drawback of reflection on action is that because of time constraints we tend only to think in this way about more complex or critical work issues. Therefore in terms of more routine events and work practice, we tend only to "reflect in action". This can lead us to not making much improvement in our routine work practice. It is important therefore to plan reflection on action to ensure that it covers every aspect of practice.

Planning to reflect, rather than simply doing so when something has gone wrong or has been particularly difficult, is best practice. Planning to reflect, along with reflection in action and some spontaneous (or unplanned) reflection on action, constitutes reflective practice.

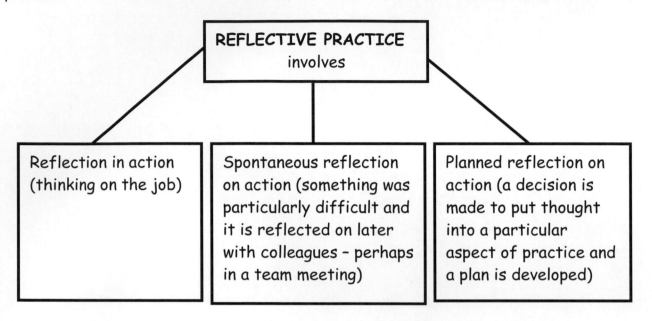

Schön argues that learning will take place if both reflection in action and reflection on action are used. Kolb refers to the stage of 'reflective observation' in the experiential learning cycle so it is clear that in order to learn effectively and to develop practice, we need to take a reflective learning approach.

Reflective Practice

Smith and Karban (2006: 4) argue that reflective practice is "accepted as being a key component of practice in health and social care." To clarify what they mean by reflective practice, they refer to a working definition based on Clouder (2000: 211):

"In its broadest sense reflective practice involves the critical analysis of everyday working practices to improve competence and promote professional development."

A number of frameworks have been developed to support reflective practice. The framework which is arguably used most extensively in health and social care is that of Gibbs (1988).

Gibbs Framework for Reflection

Gibbs (1988) suggests a six stage process as follows:

Stage 1:   **Description of the event**
What happened? Who did what? What were the results? etc.

Stage 2:   **Feelings and thoughts**
This stage is essentially about self awareness. The person reflecting needs to think about questions like:

- How were they feeling when the event began?
- How did their feelings change as the event unfolded?
- How did they feel about outcomes?
- How do they feel about it now?

Stage 3:   **Evaluation**
In this stage the person needs to think through what was good and bad about the experience. What went well? What didn't go so well?

Stage 4:   **Analysis**
This develops on from stage 3 but involves breaking the event down into component parts so that they can be explored separately. It may involve considering more detailed questions than those covered in Stage 3. For example:

- What went well?

could be followed up with:

- What did I do well?
- What did others do well?

and:

- What didn't go so well?

could be followed up with:

- What didn't turn out as it should have?
- In what way did I contribute to this?
- In what way did others contribute to this?

Stage 5:   **Conclusion**
Now that the event has been explored from a range of perspectives, the person reflecting should be able to draw some conclusions. This will involve the person asking themselves what they could have done differently and what impact this would have had on the outcome. If the

previous stages have not been fully and honestly explored, then the conclusions reached in this stage will be fundamentally flawed.

Stage 6:   **Action Planning**
During this stage, the person reflecting should think about what they would do if they encountered the event again. Would they do anything differently or take similar action?

Gibbs sees this process as a cycle, such that when the action plan is put into place the event should become the focus of further reflection, as follows:

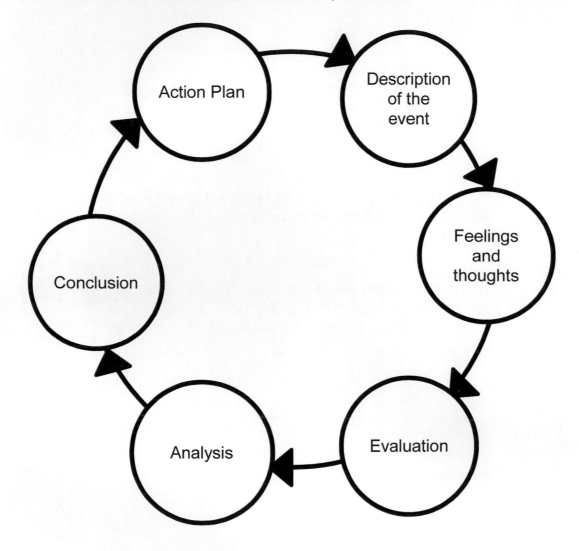

    Copyright © Kirwin Maclean Associates Ltd

Borton's Framework for Reflection

Another useful framework is proposed by Borton (1970). This is a straightforward model which proposes working through three questions – what? So what? And Now What? The following diagram provides an outline of how this might work:

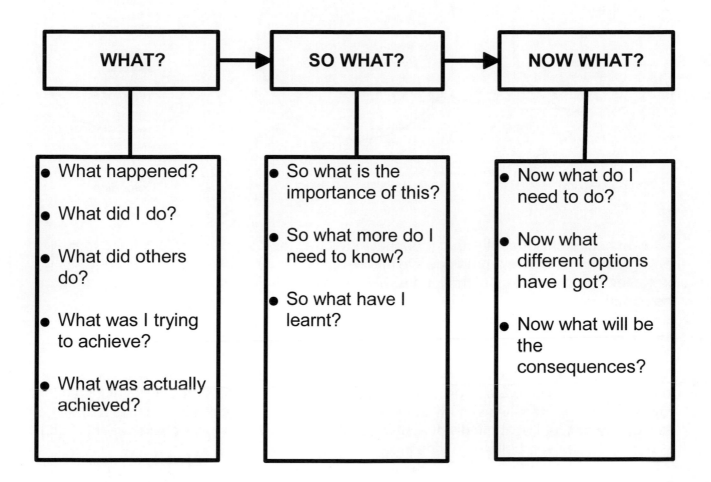

WHAT?	SO WHAT?	NOW WHAT?
• What happened? • What did I do? • What did others do? • What was I trying to achieve? • What was actually achieved?	• So what is the importance of this? • So what more do I need to know? • So what have I learnt?	• Now what do I need to do? • Now what different options have I got? • Now what will be the consequences?

Boud, Keogh and Walker's model of reflection

Boud, Keogh and Walker (1985) describe reflective practice as where a person:

➢ recaptures their experience
➢ thinks about it
➢ mulls it over (perhaps with others)
➢ evaluates it
➢ acts on the evaluation

They propose a model for this as follows:

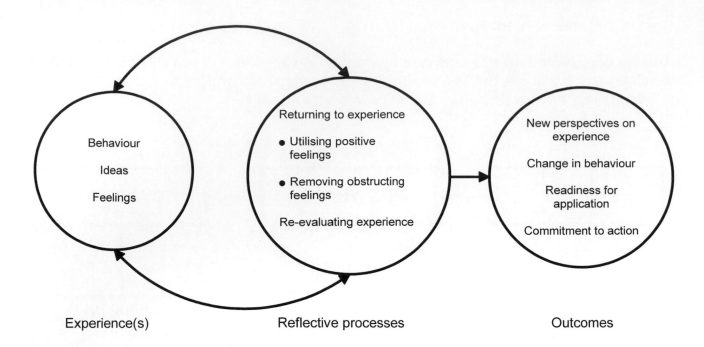

Experience(s) Reflective processes Outcomes

A key aspect of this model is that it refers to the need for the individual to "attend to their feelings" about the event, both positive and negative. In reflecting on the feelings prompted by an experience, the idea is that it is easier to draw conclusions and learn from the experience.

Self Awareness

Whatever model of reflection a person uses they need to be open and honest in their reflection. They also need to be self aware and willing to question their own values and attitudes. Atkins identifies self awareness as essential to the reflective process and defines the concept as the individual being well informed of their own character, including their own values and beliefs. (Atkins in Burns and Bulman 2000)

Reflective Writing

Reflective writing has a long history in academic qualifications, perhaps because reflection is widely acknowledged as a vital aspect of the learning process. Increasingly candidates for vocational qualifications are being encouraged to write reflective accounts which can be used as evidence. However, when candidates for particular awards are looking to meet specific standards in their accounts it can lead to a very descriptive "narrative" of an event. To demonstrate how knowledge, values and skills come together, then it is important to write in a truly reflective way. The following models for reflective writing can assist with this:

The Royal Melbourne Institute of Technology University (2007) produce some useful guidance for their students around a D-I-E-P formula:

D - Describe objectively what happened – Answer the question "What did I see and hear?"

I - Interpret the events – explain what you saw and heard. (Your new insights; your connections with other learning; your feelings; your hypotheses; your conclusions.) Answer the question "What might it mean?" or "What was the reason I did this activity?"

E - Evaluate the effectiveness of what you observed / learned – make judgements clearly connected to observations made. Evaluation answers the question "What is my opinion about what I observed or experienced? Why?"

P - Plan how this information will be useful to you. What are your recommendations? (Be concrete.) Consider: "In what ways might this learning experience serve me in my future?"

(RMIT University 2007)

Another model for reflective writing is for the writer to work through the cycle of experiential learning.

Concrete experience	-	What was the event?
Reflective Observation	-	What are your personal thoughts and feelings about the experience?
Abstract Conceptualisation	-	How can you draw on previous experiences and on your knowledge to help you 'make sense' of this experience?
Active Experimentation	-	If this event were to occur again, what would you do differently?
	-	What additional knowledge do you need to gain?

Williams and Rutter (2007: 141) offer the following model for reflective writing based on Gibbs (1998):

➢ Description: What happened?

➢ Feelings: What were you thinking and feeling?

➢ Evaluation: What was good and bad about the experience?

➢ Analysis: What sense can you make of the situation?

➢ Conclusion: What else could you have done?

➢ Action Plan: What was learnt? If it arose again, what would you do?

The University of York (2000) developed a collaborative model of direct observation. This involves using various areas for discussion between the observer and the candidate following the observation. The broad "headings" to be used in this discussion are:

➢ Surprises

➢ Satisfactions

➢ Dissatisfactions

➢ Learning

We feel that these four areas can be used to prompt useful reflection on any experience:

➢ What surprised me about this?

> ➢ What was I satisfied with?

> ➢ What was I not satisfied with?

> ➢ What have I learned?

> ➢ What might I do differently in future as a result?

We have added the final question because in reflective practice it is important to look at future planning. For example, Atkins and Murphy (1993) state:

"For reflection to make a real difference to practice, it is important that the outcome includes a commitment to action. This may not necessarily involve acts which can be observed by others, but it is important that the individual makes a commitment of some kind on the basis of that learning. Action is the final stage of the reflective cycle."

REFLECTIVE PRACTICE CHECKLIST

Roth (1989) summarised the basic elements of a reflective process as follows:

✓   Keeping an open mind about what, why and how we do things

✓   Awareness of what, why and how we do things

✓   Questioning what, why and how we do things

✓   Asking what, why and how other people do things

✓   Generating choices, options and possibilities

✓   Comparing and contrasting results

✓   Seeking to understand underlying mechanisms and rationales

✓   Viewing our activities and results from various perspectives

✓   Asking "What if....?"

✓   Seeking feedback and other people's ideas and viewpoints

In Summary

Reflective practice is a key aspect of contemporary social care practice. It is essential that social care workers develop skills in critically reflective practice to ensure that they keep their practice up to date and that they work towards achieving the best possible outcomes for service users.

54: THE IMPORTANCE OF FEEDBACK

Feedback is an essential aspect of continuing professional development. As covered in other chapters in this section, feedback forms an important part of adult learning and reflective practice. This chapter will cover both providing feedback and receiving feedback.

Providing Feedback

Many social care workers might think that developing their knowledge and skills in the provision of feedback isn't important – it's just something for managers and assessors to worry about. However, it is important for all social care workers to understand the basics of providing feedback, as it helps them to recognise whether they are receiving useful feedback. All social care workers will also be required to provide feedback at times too – to managers, to colleagues and to service users. Social care workers often shy away from providing feedback to service users, but this can be an important aspect of supportive social care practice. For example, providing feedback to service users can help them to maintain or develop their skills.

Feedback can be either positive (that is, reinforcing good practice) or negative (that is, feedback on poor performance). Both positive and negative feedback can be constructive. Where feedback is constructive it will enable the receiver to develop their practice. Where feedback is missing or destructive the receiver will not be able to develop effectively.

What Makes Feedback Constructive?

What makes feedback constructive is not whether you are being told you did a job well or whether you did a job badly. The way the feedback is given is what makes it constructive (or not!). The main differences between constructive and destructive feedback are outlined in the following table.

Constructive Feedback	Destructive Feedback
Solves problems	Intensifies problems
Concentrates on behaviour/work performance	Concentrates on personality
Strengthens relationships	Damages relationships
Builds trust	Destroys trust
Is a two-way process	Is one-way
Reduces stress and tension	Adds to stress and increases tension
Manages conflict	Creates conflict
Helps development	Hinders development
Is assertive	Is aggressive

Constructive feedback provides information about knowledge and performance in such a way that the person receiving it maintains a positive attitude towards themselves, their work and the person giving the feedback. It encourages people to commit themselves to a personal action plan to move towards the agreed standards. Constructive feedback is intrinsically linked to the process of learning. When you provide effective feedback you are helping the recipient to learn. The following guidelines will help you to think through what makes feedback constructive and therefore effective.

Constructive feedback should be:

Positive

Feedback should always start and finish with a positive. This is often referred to as the positive sandwich. The content of the sandwich gives the candidate something to work on, whilst the "bread" is the positive aspects. In this way the esteem and motivation of the person receiving feedback will be built on.

BE SPECIFIC

Specific

Deal clearly with particular instances and behaviour rather than making vague or sweeping statements. For example, "*when asking about mobility, you moved too quickly through the questions rather than allowing the person to fully answer*", rather than "*your listening skills were rubbish*".

Descriptive

Use descriptive rather than evaluative terms. For example, "*my perception was that when you repeated the same question several times the person became confused*", rather than "*your questioning technique was confusing*".

Actionable

Direct feedback towards behaviour that can be changed. For example, "*if you slowed down your delivery, it would probably be easier for the person to follow what you were saying*", rather than "*your accent is hard to understand.*"

Prioritised

Concentrate on the two or three key areas for improvement, preferably including those where the recipient can see a quick return. Break down a major problem into smaller, step-by-step goals. (This is the 'content' of the positive sandwich).

CONCENTRATE ON TWO OR THREE KEY AREAS

MAKE SURE THE FEEDBACK IS WELL-TIMED

Well Timed

The most useful feedback is given when the person is receptive to it and it is sufficiently close to the event to be fresh in their mind.

Facilitative

Rather than prescribing behaviour, feedback should help the recipient question their behaviour and make them aware of where they are going wrong. For example, "*How might that have been interpreted by the service user?*"

Clear

Avoid jargon wherever possible and ensure that your communication is clear. Always check feedback to ensure that the other person understands you.

When feedback is difficult

Giving feedback can be difficult for a range of reasons. Fears about the responses of recipients, particularly to negative feedback, can inhibit people in giving accurate feedback. However, it is vital to give honest feedback to others to enable them really to develop their practice.

<u>What do I do if the person disagrees with the feedback?</u>

If the recipient disagrees with the facts you are basing your feedback on then:

➢ Give detailed examples

➢ Check the areas of disagreement e.g.: "Do you think 'it' didn't take place or are you disagreeing about details of 'it'?"

➢ Clarify the recipient's version of events and have an open mind

If the recipient disagrees that a problem exists ("everyone makes mistakes") then explain the consequences of the action. Point out that making mistakes can constitute poor practice and that this needs to be addressed.

<u>What do I do if they start crying?</u>

If you ensure that your feedback follows the guidelines given, this is unlikely. However, if a recipient does cry when you are giving them feedback, then:

➢ Be empathic e.g.: "I understand you will be shocked if no one has talked to you about this before"

➢ Give permission for the person to cry (it can relieve stress)

➢ Talk about why the recipient is finding the feedback upsetting

➢ Try not to put off the session. It may be tempting to do so, but if you do, you will be leaving the recipient with the distress. Try to move on instead to finding solutions which will end the session on a positive note.

<u>What do I do if they get angry?</u>

A natural defence mechanism when a person feels under pressure is anger. If a recipient becomes angry, then:

➢ Be empathic e.g.: "I understand why you feel shocked/angry...."

➢ Find something to say that agrees with the recipient e.g.: "I know that you are working hard on this area in difficult circumstances."

Receiving Feedback

Accepting and receiving feedback is a vital skill which all social care workers are expected to have. In fact it is widely accepted that being able to *"receive feedback gracefully is a career enhancing skill which is greatly valued by employers"*. (King 2007: 1)

Receiving feedback is a fantastic learning opportunity. The learning though is maximised by the feedback being constructive. However, this isn't all about another person's responsibility. The feedback process will only be constructive if the person receiving the feedback has developed the necessary skills in receiving feedback. When receiving feedback at any stage, social care professionals should work towards the following:

➢ *Maintain an open attitude*
Don't be defensive or "defend" yourself. This may sound easy, but believe us it isn't easy to do. If you find yourself feeling defensive about a piece of feedback, you need to remind yourself that the reality is that a defensive reaction to feedback generally results from it being accurate!

➢ *Employ your active listening skills*
Listen actively, look at the person providing feedback and maintain an open body language.

➢ *Clarify the feedback*
Ask any questions you need to in order to make sure you understand the feedback.

➢ *Recognise the giver of the feedback*
Providing feedback is not an easy task. The person providing feedback is likely to have put a great deal of thought into the feedback. Believe us, it takes a great deal of time and effort to provide thoughtful feedback. It is advisable to thank the person giving you feedback – just something like "you've really given me something to think about there. Thanks", not only demonstrates your commitment to learning but also helps you to maintain that vital positive and open attitude.

➢ *Write down the feedback*
Try to write down what you can remember of what was said as soon as possible. You will find this assists with your reflection later.

TOP TIPS FOR RECEIVING FEEDBACK

➢ Be open and positive
➢ Listen actively
➢ Focus on your reactions
➢ Make sure you understand the feedback
➢ Make notes
➢ Don't take criticism personally
➢ Reflect on your learning
➢ Use the feedback to enhance your practice

➢ *Don't take criticism personally*
Feedback is a professional process. Recognise that part of being a professional is learning from how others perceive you.

➢ *Recognise learning*
Remember that simply because someone has picked up on an area of your practice which can be improved, this does not mean you are not a good social care worker. Even the very best worker can improve on some aspect of their practice.

➢ *Reflect*
If some aspect of the feedback puzzles you, take some time to reflect. How might the person's perception have been formed?

➢ *Focus*
Make sure that you are not distracted so that you can focus fully on the feedback. Stay "in the moment" and try to truly understand the meaning behind the feedback. Try to avoid framing a response in your mind until you have heard all of the feedback.

➢ *Recognise your reactions*
Notice your own reactions and how the feedback is making you feel. Sometimes it helps to partially disassociate yourself and imagine you are a "fly on the wall" witnessing feedback being given to someone else. This can help you to think the feedback through objectively, rather than emotionally.

Rich (2009) suggests that in receiving feedback, people take either a negative (closed) style or a positive (open) style. The following table summarises this:

Negative / Closed	Positive / Open
Defensive: defends actions, objects to feedback	Open: listens without frequent interruption or objection
Attacking: turns the table on the person providing feedback	Responsive: willing to truly "hear" what is being said
Denies: refutes the accuracy or fairness of the feedback	Accepting: accepts the feedback without denial
Disrespectful: devalues the person giving the feedback	Respectful: recognises the value of the feedback
Closed: ignores the feedback	Engaged: interacts appropriately seeking clarification where needed
Inactive listening: makes no attempt to understand the meaning of the feedback	Active listening: listens attentively and tries to understand the meaning of the feedback
Rationalising: finds explanations for the feedback that dissolve personal responsibility	Thoughtful: tries to understand the personal behaviour that has led to the feedback
Superficial: listens and agrees but does not act on the feedback	Sincere: genuinely wants to make changes and learn

When Feedback is Difficult

Receiving feedback can be difficult for a range of reasons. However, it is vital that social care workers receive honest feedback throughout their career and use it to enhance their practice.

<u>What do I do if I disagree with the feedback?</u>

If you disagree with the feedback then:

➢ Ask for specific detailed examples

➢ Clarify each other's version of events and have an open mind

➢ If you still disagree about the facts then you should discuss together as to what action will be taken in order to explore this further or how agreement can be reached

➢ Clarify exactly what you need to do about the feedback – what is expected of you in terms of action?

<u>What do I do if I feel upset by the feedback?</u>

Receiving negative feedback can be really hard, so if you feel upset:

➢ Try not to get angry as this will not help you or the person giving the feedback. Take a break and don't worry about crying as it can relieve stress

➢ Talk about why you find the feedback upsetting

➢ Try not to put off the session. Try to move on instead to finding solutions together which will end the session on a positive note.

 In Summary

Feedback is a vital aspect of continuing professional development. Social care practitioners will not be able to develop their practice unless they seek, accept and use feedback. "No news is good news" is certainly not the right approach!

55: LEARNING AND DEVELOPMENT OPPORTUNITIES

Not too long ago learning and development opportunities were viewed almost purely in terms of training courses. The learning and development plans which social care staff developed, appeared to be little more than a "shopping list" of training courses. However there is now an increasing level of understanding about the range of development opportunities which exist. If you consider Kolb's theory of experiential learning (see pages 298 – 300), then any experience can be viewed as a learning opportunity.

Some of the most widely utilised development opportunities in social care include:

➢ supervision

➢ mentoring

➢ coaching

➢ role modelling

➢ performance review or appraisal

➢ e learning

➢ assessment and feedback

➢ independent research around evidence based practice

➢ supporting others' learning (e.g.: working with students)

➢ team meetings

➢ support groups

➢ reading

➢ support from colleagues

➢ reflecting on, and learning from, your own practice

Social care professionals can utilise all of these opportunities to develop their practice. Supervision is such as a significant aspect of effective social care practice that the following chapter is dedicated to this area. The remainder of this chapter will consider some of the other development opportunities.

Mentoring

Mentoring has a long history. The term itself is drawn from ancient Greek mythology - when Odysseus went to Troy he left Mentor to be the trusted friend and adviser to his son. Since then, the term mentoring has been used to describe a relationship where one person who is more experienced than another takes on a role to assist, support and advise another. Traditionally, people have sought informal mentors. For example, when a person has joined a new team, they may approach a worker they trust and whose practice they respect, to ask questions etc. In this way they are seeking an informal mentor. Many organisations have begun to recognise the value of mentoring and have set up formalised mentoring schemes, where workers new to a role or task are linked with a more experienced worker who will act as a mentor.

Coaching

A coach could be formally matched or introduced to a worker or a coach could be informally approached by a worker who feels they would benefit from a supportive relationship. The main difference between coaching and mentoring is that generally a coach will support a person to develop in an identified area.

"A coach is an individual who helps another identify and remedy performance or skill deficit via modelling and rehearsal."

(Hay 1995)

A coach might use a range of tactics to support an individual to learn. For example:

➢ Modelling: this involves carrying out a behaviour/skill etc in what is considered to be the "correct" way whilst the "learner" is able to observe and ask questions. The coach may need to model the behaviour on a regular basis to enable the learner to develop.

➢ Rehearsal: this involves the coach supporting the learner to practice the skill or activity with the coach observing/supporting and then providing feedback. This is sometimes referred to as role play.

➢ Coaching conversation: this involves the coach talking to the learner using a questioning approach to enable the learner to work through the process and learn for themselves.

Mentoring and coaching are similar in many ways and are sometimes used as interchangeable terms. One of the main differences between mentoring and coaching and the supervisory relationship is that the process of mentoring and coaching is negotiable and should mostly focus on the learner's agenda. Supervision, on the other hand, has a number of functions including accountability.

Training

Not too long ago training in social care meant the worker going away from the workplace for a day or more to take part in a course. However, nowadays training opportunities are much more varied and might include:

➢ A traditional 'course'

➢ A presentation given to the team (maybe in a team meeting)

➢ A distance learning course

➢ On-line or computer-based training (often referred to as e learning)

➢ In-service training (e.g.: a supervisor showing a worker a new task)

Assessment and Feedback

Social care workers regularly undertake competence based qualifications. People can learn a great deal from being assessed and receiving feedback, not least because of the fact that being assessed encourages people to reflect on their practice.

Research and Evidence Based Practice

There is an increasing emphasis in social care on evidence based and research based practice. This basically means practice which draws on what is known – e.g. from research in the service area. Section G covers evidence based practice in more detail. Many staff learn a great deal and develop both their own practice and service delivery based on their reading and research in this area.

Job Enlargement or Enrichment

Concepts of job enlargement and enrichment are drawn from Porter et al's model (1982) which considers job characteristics. This model talks about the importance of job satisfaction and the way that different work roles motivate people in different ways. When people have been in a particular role for some time, their satisfaction with the role may reduce and their performance may be affected. The model describes how this can be addressed by changing jobs either through *enlargement* or *enrichment*.

Enlargement means extending the scope of the job by combining two or more jobs into one, giving greater variety and a more 'holistic' feel. *Job enrichment* means giving people more responsibility for setting their own pace, deciding their own methods, and correcting their own mistakes - resulting in greater autonomy.

Providing Support to Students / New Staff

Staff teams can learn a great deal from supporting learners in the workplace. Many social care settings offer practice placements to students and supporting their learning can assist staff to learn a great deal themselves. When new members of staff begin in a team, other team members may act as a mentor or supporter (for example, during induction). This can also assist the existing worker to develop their own practice. Adult learning is a two way process and everyone can learn from the experience.

Everything is a Learning Opportunity!

It is important that professionals recognise the whole range of opportunities that can be accessed in terms of learning and development. Some opportunities are formal and have formal access procedures – such as training. Other opportunities are informal, where everyday activities are undertaken in a reflective way in order to aid learning. Absolutely anything can be viewed as a learning opportunity and recognising this is, in many ways, what makes a worker a professional: what makes a job a career.

In Summary

In the not too distant past learning and development opportunities were viewed almost entirely in terms of training courses. Some more traditional (we could argue out dated) services may still take this approach. However, it is now widely recognised that in professional practice learning and development, opportunities are varied and where a worker has the "right" approach, anything can be viewed as a learning opportunity.

56: SUPERVISION

Supervision has a long tradition in social work, although its use in health care is less well established. The importance of good quality supervision is becoming more widely recognised in social care settings. However, since social care professionals often come from a range of different working backgrounds, there are often misunderstandings about the nature and purpose of supervision which can affect the way in which supervision is utilised. The dictionary definition of the word "supervision" is based on being watched and in industrial professions this may well be what supervision is all about. In social care, supervision can probably be best defined as:

"the process by which one worker is given responsibility by the organisation to work with another worker in order to meet certain organisational, professional or personal objectives which together promote the best outcomes for service users"

(Morrison 2005).

The functions of supervision

It is generally accepted that there are four functions (or purposes) of supervision, as follows:

Accountability

Sometimes called the managerial or normative function, this refers to the fact that the supervisor is responsible in various ways for the supervisee's work. The supervisor and supervisee will need to discuss the work which the supervisee is undertaking. Where this function is carried out well, it provides a safety net for the supervisee who will recognise and value the opportunities to share their work and the challenges they face with their supervisor. The supervisor can use this discussion to ensure that legal requirements are being met and that organisational policies and procedures are being followed.

Professional Development

Sometimes called the developmental, educational or formative function of supervision this involves the supervisor and supervisee discussing the supervisee's learning needs and how these can be addressed. Unskilled supervisors will think they have addressed this function simply by asking the supervisee "and are there any courses you want to go on?" As covered in the previous chapter, learning and development is about a great deal more than training. Skilled supervision discussion in itself should provide extensive opportunities for reflection and learning.

Personal Support

Sometimes this function of supervision is referred to as staff care or the supportive or restorative function. Supervision should always involve discussion about what support the supervisee needs. The roles and tasks which social care workers have can be very demanding. Thompson (1996: 51) recognised that *"there are many dangers in undertaking people work unsupported, not least because of the emotional demands of this type of work."* Supervision should allow time for social care workers to explore their feelings about the work they are undertaking. Discussions like these may involve the supervisee sharing aspects of their personal life which may impact on their professional functioning. However, it is important to remember that supervision is not a counselling session and the balance needs to be well managed with professional boundaries upheld.

<u>Mediation</u>

This function recognises the fact that the supervisor is in an *"intermediate position between the staff he or she supervises and the senior management hierarchy."* (Thompson 1996:52). As part of this, the supervisor needs to 'mediate' between the worker and the organisational management structure. The manager will need to, for example, support staff through any organisational changes and feed back staff concerns to managers etc.

This function involves the supervisor making clear what the policy, procedure and expectations of the agency are and why the supervisee needs to apply these to their practice. It might involve negotiation about dilemmas faced by the supervisee in relation to organisational requirements and how these can be managed.

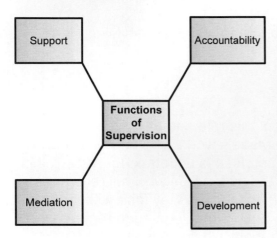

Very often agency supervision policies refer to the various functions of supervision. However, very often managers focus on one function at the expense of the others.

Good quality supervision balances all four functions such that social care workers have opportunities to explore their work, organisational requirements, their learning and the support they need.

Good practice in supervision is a joint responsibility and involves the following aspects being in place:

➢ Supervision should be planned and thorough

➢ The process of supervision needs to be explicit and there should be a clearly agreed working definition of supervision

➢ Past experiences of supervision should be acknowledged – in order to clarify current expectations

➢ Supervision should be accurately recorded and this should be shared – with both parties signatures included

➢ Power imbalances should be acknowledged and discussed. By virtue of the fact that one worker is accountable to the other in an arrangement formalised within the agency, the supervisor is in a more powerful position. However, it is important to remember that other general power imbalances may exist

➢ A written agreement (supervision contract) should be in place and this should be regularly reviewed

➢ A safe environment should be fostered. This basically involves all of the above points being covered.

(ILPS 1993)

Types / Forms of Supervision

There are a range of different types or forms of supervision and often a variety of these are used in social care settings.

Direct or Indirect?

Supervision can be described as direct or indirect. Direct supervision refers to supervision "on the job" – basically discussion, advice and guidance whilst a worker is actually undertaking a task. Indirect supervision is supervision which takes place in a private room away from the actual "jobs" at hand.

Whilst it is very valuable for social care professionals to receive some direct supervision, it is vital that indirect supervision takes place on a regular basis, to allow for time away from the tasks at hand and opportunities for reflection and private discussion.

Formal or Informal?

Informal supervision is unplanned. Basically, any discussion providing advice, guidance and answers to a supervisee's questions is informal supervision. Formal supervision on the other hand is planned and structured, has a formal agenda and should take place in a private environment with no interruptions. All social care workers must receive formal supervision but all workers, however experienced, will also need opportunities for informal supervision as and when the need arises.

Group or Individual?

Supervision is probably most often carried out on a one to one basis. However, it can also take place in groups. Group supervision is not simply a team meeting, but allows time for all four functions of supervision to be addressed.

Using these three subheadings, it is clear that all supervision can be categorised as either:

➢ Direct *or* indirect

➢ Formal *or* informal

➢ Individual *or* group

All social care workers should receive regular indirect, formal, individual supervision sessions (i.e.: the supervisor and supervisee meeting in a private room with a clear agenda). However, this can be supplemented by other forms of supervision to enhance learning and professional development.

Agency Practice

Some social care agencies have additional supervision arrangements. For example, some have peer supervision sessions (where groups of individuals working in similar roles consult about their work) or clinical supervision (where people with specific professional roles have supervision with someone with similar qualifications other than their line manager).

Appraisal

Supervision often fits in with a system of staff appraisal. Appraisals are less regular than supervision but will generally fit into the same working relationship. Appraisals are basically a review of a worker's practice and progress. All organisations will have their own systems in place for appraisal.

One of the basic principles of both supervision and appraisal is that they should involve the provision of constructive feedback and there should be a "no surprises approach". A worker should not go into an appraisal and hear for the first time that there is a major aspect of practice for them to work on.

In Summary

Supervision is a vital activity for all social care professionals. Unfortunately, some staff value supervision more than others – this includes supervisors and supervisees. Both parties need to value the process and be committed to it in order for it to be effective.

Supervision has a range of benefits for social care, including:

➢ supervision allows workers to share any concerns, dilemmas etc

➢ supervision provides opportunities for growth and professional development

➢ supervision can provide a safe forum for the provision of feedback

➢ supervision provides a useful forum for reviewing actions and monitoring progress against plans – providing a safety net for workers and organisations

Ultimately, good quality supervision leads to improved outcomes for service users.

57: PUTTING IT ALL TOGETHER: THE CPD PROCESS

The chapters in this section have explored some of the knowledge which is important in terms of continuing professional development. This knowledge should assist social care workers to work through the process of continuing professional development, as illustrated in this chapter.

Benefits of Continuing Professional Development

Where social care workers take an active approach to their own professional development there are a range of acknowledged benefits (Thompson 1996). For example:

➤ Increased job satisfaction. Learning can be stimulating and rewarding and can improve a worker's job satisfaction.

➤ Improved practice. Where a worker develops their knowledge and skills this will lead to improved practice and better outcomes for service users.

➤ Stress management and burnout prevention. Social care workers operate in complex and demanding situations. This can lead to stress and ultimately "burnout". Engaging in effective continual professional development can assist in avoiding burnout. This has been recognised in a range of studies, including international research on standards in social work practice (IFSW 2010).

➤ Recognition of change. Continuing to learn and develop can help social care workers to understand the need for change in the sector. This will enable them to adapt to change more effectively.

➤ Self awareness. Being "self aware" is an important aspect of good social care practice as covered in section A. Continual professional development will help social care workers to develop their self awareness.

➤ Improved relationships with colleagues and other agencies. Partnership working becomes easier and more enjoyable when workers can take opportunities to learn from other professionals about their roles, perspectives and ideas (see chapter 14).

➤ Workers who take active approaches to their own development may be more likely in some organisations to develop their careers further as more opportunities to enlarge or enrich roles may be offered to workers who are perceived by the organisation as open to change and development.

The CPD Process

One of the central themes of the knowledge drawn together in this book is that there are processes or systems which can assist workers in a range of areas. Continuing professional development is no different as the following process can be applied:

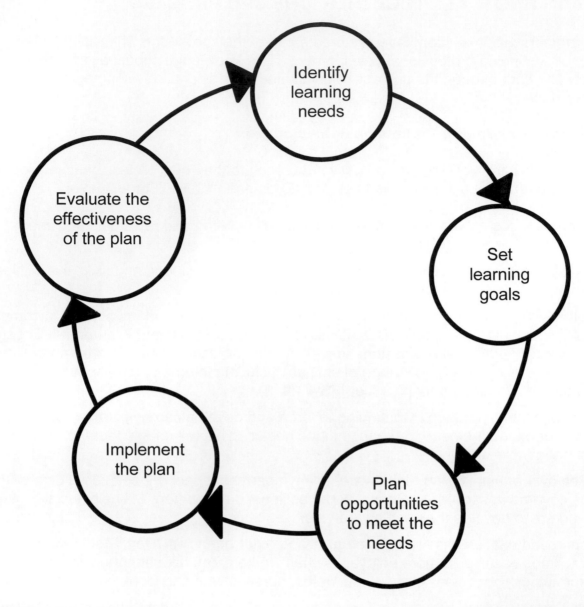

Identifying Learning Needs

In order to take a proactive approach to their continuing professional development social care workers need to identify their learning needs so that they can plan learning and development opportunities which will address these needs.

"The more time you invest in planning your programme of learning, the more likely it is that you will focus your learning effectively. You will then spend the precious time you have learning about topics that are relevant for your job, and the needs of your practice."

(NHS 2006:1)

Combining the processes of evidence based practice and reflective practice should enable social care workers to identify their personal learning needs. However, many staff find answering the question "What are your learning needs?" difficult. This could link into the process of cognitive dissonance (see pages 306 – 307) after all you don't really know what you don't know! Maclean and Lloyd (2008) propose the idea of a worker thinking through their learning needs by using a "bring and buy" approach. This involves the worker thinking about what experience, skills and knowledge they "bring" to their work and what further skills, knowledge and experience they would like to "buy" to enable them to do their job more effectively.

In order to create an accurate set of learning needs, social care workers should take into account:

> any specific issues as a result of changes in role and responsibilities

> any forthcoming changes in their employing organisation

> the future direction of social care

> the needs of the service users they work with

> aspirations for the future (perhaps in terms of career goals, improvements in practice etc)

Identifying gaps in knowledge and weaknesses in practice can be particularly challenging and so it is important for a worker to draw on feedback and to seek additional feedback in order to create a truly accurate picture of their learning needs.

Setting Learning Goals

As covered in chapter 38, a goal can be defined as the point to which operations are directed or the point to be reached. If you think about setting a goal as planning a journey then this can be helpful. The learning need is the starting point whilst the goal is the destination you want to get to.

To illustrate this, a worker might identify that they have a need to learn how to use a hoist safely. They could set the goal as being confident and safe in using the hoist to assist a service user to get out of bed.

Planning Opportunities to Meet the Needs

This will become the worker's professional development plan (sometimes referred to as a PDP). As previously stated, when planning development opportunities, it is important to think more widely than simply training opportunities. The worker needs to think about the whole range of development opportunities available to them. These opportunities then need to be accurately matched to their learning needs. For example, if a person wants to develop a particular skill they may feel it would be useful to ask a colleague who is skilled in this area to assist them by talking them through the skill, observing them and providing feedback etc.

Implementing the Plan

The worker needs to engage in the opportunities they have planned. In doing so they will find it helpful to consider the following questions:

> What do I want to learn?

> What are my expectations?

> How will I know when I have learned it?

> How will I use what I learn?

Thinking through questions such as these will help the worker to take a proactive and reflective approach to their learning. It might be useful for the worker to make some notes on their responses to the questions and on their experiences as they implement the learning plan. This will assist with the next stage of the process:

Evaluating the Effectiveness of the Plan

Once the plan has been actioned and the worker has effectively engaged with all the planned opportunities, it is vital that they evaluate what they have learnt. A key aspect of the evaluation will be in revisiting the originally identified learning needs and associated goals, then considering to what extent they have been met by the plan.

If the needs haven't been met, are there different opportunities which could be used? Would a different approach help? Where the learning needs have been met, this won't be the end of the process as it is likely that the learning will have highlighted some further needs and so the cycle continues – hence the name <u>continuing</u> professional development.

Keeping a Record

Keeping a record of professional development is a requirement for those staff who are registered with a regulatory body. Even though not all care staff are currently required to be registered, it is good practice for all professionals to keep track of their professional development in a systematic way. There are a range of benefits to this, including:

> the record can be used as evidence for a range of professional qualifications

> the record can be used in appraisal systems

> continued professional development records can be used to update CVs or provide useful information in job interviews

> reflection will be easier with a record to base thoughts on

Some organisations provide a system for recording professional development – which makes it much easier for staff who simply need to complete the documentation. Other staff can choose how to record their professional development. Whatever system is used it should be easy to identify the following:

> the workers learning needs and their associated goals

> the activities undertaken to address these

> progress towards the goals

 In Summary

Continuing professional development is a vital aspect of all professional practice. The importance of CPD is increasingly acknowledged in the social care sector. All social care staff need to develop a learning or development plan and keep this under regular review. Recording professional development activities and associated learning is useful for social care practitioners in a range of ways.

BIBLIOGRAPHY

About Equal Opportunities (2009) *Confronting Sexism and Sex Discrimination.* Available online at: www.aboutequalopportunities.co.uk/confronting-sexism.html (accessed 25.10.09)

Alzheimer's Society (2009) *Communicating* (factsheet). Available online at: http://www.alzheimers.org.uk/factsheet/500?gclid=CM3gt4HGmZ4CFdBb4wodTygJmQ (accessed 20.11.09)

Arnold, L. (1995) *Women and Self Injury: A Survey of 76 Women.* (Bristol) Bristol Crisis for Women.

Association of Directors of Social Services (1995) *Safeguarding Adults: A National Framework of Standards for good practice and outcomes in adult protection work.* (London) ADSS.

Atkins, S. and Murphy, K. (1993) *Reflection: a review of the literature.* Journal of Advanced Nursing, 18, pp. 1188-1192

Bailey, G. (1998) *Action Against Abuse: Recognising and preventing abuse of people with learning disabilities: Support workers pack.* (Chesterfield) Association for Residential Care.

Bandura, A. (1977) S*ocial Learning Theory.* (Eaglewood Cliffs, New Jersey) Prentice Hall.

Barber, M., Jenkins, R. and Jones, C. (2000) *A survivors group for woman who have a learning disability.* The British Journal of Developmental Disabilities, 46, pp. 31-41.

Barford, R. and Wattam, C. (1991) *Children's Participation in decision making.* Practice 5(2), pp. 93-102

Barnard, C.I. (1968) *The Functions of the Executive.* (Cambridge, MA) Harvard University Press.

Barrett, G. Sellman, D. and Thomas, J. (eds) (2005) *Interprofessional Working in Health and Social Care: Professional Perspectives.* (Basingstoke) Palgrave MacMillan.

Base, E. and Davis, L. (1988) *The Courage to Heal: A Guide for Women of Childhood Sexual Abuse.* Cedar Press.

Basnett, F. and Maclean, S. (2000) *The Value Base in Practice: An NVQ Related Reference Guide for Staff Working with Older People.* (Rugeley) Kirwin Maclean Associates.

Beckett, C. (2006) *Essential Theory for Social Work Practice.* (London) SAGE.

Bercovitch, J. and Jackson, R. (2009) *Conflict Resolution in the Twenty-first Century: Principles, Methods and Approaches.* (Michigan) University of Michigan Press.

Berne, E. (1978) *A Layman's Guide to Psychiatry and Psychoanalysis.* (London) Penguin.

Biestek, F. (1961) *The Casework Relationship.* (London) George Allen and Unwin.

Boddy, J. and Statham, J. (2009) *European Perspectives on Social Work: Models of Education and Professional Roles.* (London) Thomas Coram Research Unit, Institute of Education, University of London.

Borton, T. (1970) *Reach, Teach and Touch* (London) McGraw Hill.

Boud, D., Keogh, R. and Walker, D. (1985) *Reflection: Turning Experience into Learning.* (London) Kogan Page.

Bradshaw, J. (1972) *The Concept of Social Need.* New Society 496. pp. 640-643.

Brandon, D. (1997) *The Trick of Being Ordinary.* (Cambridge) Anglia Polytechnic.

British Association of Learning Disabilities (2009) (factsheet) C*ommunication.* Available online at http://www.bild.org.uk/pdfs/05faqs/communication.pdf (accessed 20.11.09)

Brown, H. and Stein, J. (2000) *Monitoring adult protection referrals in 10 English local authorities.* Journal of Adult Protection, 2, pp.19-31.

Brown, H., Stein, J., and Turk, V. (1995) *The sexual abuse of adults with learning disabilities: report of a second two year incidence survey.* Mental Handicap research 8, pp. 3-24.

Brown, J.S., Collins, A. and Duguid, S. (1989) *Situated Cognition and the Culture of Learning.* Educational Researcher, 18(1), pp. 32-42.

Buckinghamshire County Council (1998) *Independent Longcare Inquiry.* (Buckingham) Buckinghamshire County Council.

Bundy, C (2004) *Changing Behaviour: Using Motivational Interviewing Techniques.* Available online at: www.eatsmartmovemorenc.com/MotivationalInterviewing/Texts/changingbehavior.pdf (accessed 22.12.09).

Burns, R. (1995) *the Adult Learner at Work.* (Sydney) Business and Professional Publishers.

Burton, J. (ed) (1990) *Conflict: Human Needs Theory.* (London) Macmillan.

Caldwell, P. (2000) *You Don't Know What It's Like.* (Brighton) Pavilion.

Cameron, C. (2007) *Social Pedagogy and the Children's Workforce.* Available online at: www.communitycare.co.uk/Articles/2007/08/08/105392/social-pedagogy-and-the-childrens-workforce.htm (accessed 19.1.10).

Cameron, C. and Boddy, J. (2006) *Knowledge and education for care workers: What do they need to know.* In Boddy, J. Cameron, C. and Moss, P. (eds) *Care Work: Present and Future.* (London) Routledge.

Care Quality Commission (2009) *Investigation into West London Mental Health NHS Trust.* (London) CQC.

Carson, D. (1996) *Risking Legal Repercussions.* in Kemshall, H. and Pritchard, J, (ed) Good Practice in Risk Assessment and Risk Management (Volume 1). (London) Jessica Kingsley Publishing pp. 3-12.

Cass, E., Robbins, D. and Richardson, A. (2009) *Dignity in Care.* (London) Social Care Institute for Excellence.

Clemens, E. and Hayes, H. (1997) *Assessing and Balancing elder risk, safety and autonomy: Decision making practices of healthcare professionals.* Home Health Care Services Quarterly, 16, pp. 3-20.

Clouder, L. (2000) R*eflective Practice: Realising its potential.* Physiotherapy 86(10), pp. 517-521.

Commission for Health Improvement Investigations (2003) *Investigation into Matters Arising from Care on Rowan Ward, Manchester Mental Health and Social Care Trust.* (London) The Stationery Office.

Commission for Health Improvement Investigations (2004) *Lessons from CHI Investigations 2000-2003.* (London) The Stationery Office.

Commission for Social Care Inspection (2006) *Time to Care? An overview of home care services for older people in England 2006.* (London) CSCI.

Convery, D. (1994) *Fatal Accident Enquiry into the Death of Miss Agnes McCabe, Aged 79 at Glenglova.* (Glasgow) Glasgow Sheriff Court.

Cousins, N. (1989) *Head First: The Biology of Hope* (New York) E.P. Dutton.

Crisps, B., Anderson, M., Orme, J. and Lister, P. (2003) *Knowledge Review OI : Learning and Teaching in Social work Education: Assessment.* (London) Social Care Institute for Excellence.

Crosby, G., Clarke, A., Hayes, R., Jones, K., and Lievesley, N. (2008) *The Financial Abuse of Older People: A Review from the literature carried out by the centre for Policy on Ageing on behalf of Help the Aged.* (London) Help the Aged.

Dalrymple, J. and Burke, B. (1995) *Anti-Oppressive Practice: Social Care and the Law.* (Milton Keynes) Open University Press.

Danbury, H. (1994) *Teaching Practical Social Work.* (Third Edition) Arena Press.

Day, J. (2006) *Interprofessional Working: An Essential Guide for Health and Social Care Professionals.* (Cheltenham) Nelson Thornes.

Department of Health and Home Office (2000) *No Secrets: Guidance on developing and implementing multi-agency policies and procedures to protect vulnerable adults from abuse.* (London) Department of Health.

Department of Health (2001) *A National Service Framework for Older People.* (London) Department of Health.

Department of Health (2001) *A Safer Place – Combating Violence Against Social Care Staff.* (London) Department of Health

Department of Health (2001) *Valuing People: A New Strategy for Learning Disability for the 21st Century.* (London) Department of Health.

Department of Health (2002) *The Single Assessment Process: guidance for local implementation.* (London) Department of Health.

Department of Health (2003) *Confidentiality: NHS Code of Practice.* (London) Department of Health.

Department of Health (2007) *Independence, Choice and Risk: a guide to best practice in supporting decision making.* (London) Department of Health.

Department of Health (2007) *Self Audit tool: Introduction and overview.* Available online at: www.dh.gov.uk/en/managingyourorganisation/Humanresourcesandtraining/NationalTaskforceonViolence/Selfaudittool/DH_4052375. (accessed 13.10.08)

Department of Health (2009) *Safeguarding Adults – Report on the Consultation on the review of No Secrets: Guidance on developing and implementing multi-agency policies and procedures to protect vulnerable adults from abuse.* (London) Department of Health.

Department of Health (2009) *The Dignity in Care Campaign.* Available online at: www.dhcarenetworks.org.uk/dignityincare (accessed 17.10.09)

Department for Children, Schools and Families (2008) *Evidence Based Practice.* Available online at: www.everychildmatters.gov.uk/deliveringservices/multiagencyworking/glossary (accessed 2.9.08)

DeShazer, S. (1985) *Keys to Solution in Brief Therapy.* (New York) Norton.

Doel, M. and Marsh, P. (1992) *Task Centred Social Work.* (Aldershot) Ashgate.

Douglas, A. (2008) *Partnership Working.* (Abingdon) Routledge.

Dutt, R. and Phillips, M. (2000) *Assessing black children in need and their families.* In Assessing Children in Need and their Families: Practice Guidance, Department of Health (London) The Stationery Office.

Eraut, M. (1994) *Developing Professional Knowledge and Competence.* (London) Falmer Press.

Festinger, L. (1957) *a Theory of Cognitive Dissonance.* (Stanford) Stanford University Press.

Fiedler, F.E. (1994) *Leadership Experience and Leadership Performance.* (Alexandria) US Army Research Institute for the Behavioural and Social Sciences.

Focus (2000) *Self Injury.* Internet. Source Unknown.

Freechild Project (2008) *Challenging Adultism.* Available online at: www.freechild.org/adultism.htm (accessed 25.10.09).

General Social Care Council (2002) *Codes of Practice for Social Care Workers and Employers* (London) GSCC.

Gibbs, G. (1998) *Learning by Doing: A Guide to Teaching and Learning Methods.* (Oxford) Further Education Unit Oxford Polytechnic.

Glasby, J. and Dickinson, H. (2008) *Partnership Working in Health and Social Care.* (Bristol) Policy Press.

Goldsmith, L. (1999) *Recording with Care: Inspection of Case Recording in Social Services Departments.* (London) SSI and DoH.

Greenbaum, H. W. (1974) *The Audit of Organisational Communications.* Academy of Management Journal 17. pp. 739-754

Growney, T. (Ed) (1998) *Sometimes You've Got to Shout to be Heard: Stories from Young People in Care* (London) VCC – Voice for the Child in Care.

Hamer, S. and Collinson, G. (1999) *Achieving Evidence-Based Practice: A Handbook for Practitioners.* (Edinburgh) Harcourt.

Harris, T. (1970) *I'm OK – You're OK.* (London) Pan.

Harris, J., Foster, M., Jackson, K. and Morgan, H. (2005) *Outcomes for Disabled Service Users.* (York) SPRU. University of York.

Hawamdeh, S. (2009) *Knowledge Management: Competencies and Professionalism.* (London) World Scientific Press.

Hay, J. (1995) *Transformational Mentoring* (London) McGraw Hill Publications.
Healthcare Commission/Commission for Social Care Inspection (2006) *Joint Investigation into the Provision of Services for People with Learning Disabilities at Cornwall Partnership NHS Trust* (London) Healthcare Commission.

Health and Safety Executive (2006) Five Steps to Risk Assessment. Available online www.hse.gov.uk/pubns/raindex.htm (accessed 9.9.08).

Higham, P. (2005) *What is Important About Social Work and Social Care?* Available online at: www.ssrg.org.uk/assembly/files/patriciahigham.pdf (accessed 26.10.09).

Honey, P. and Mumford, A. (1982) *Manual of Learning Styles.* Peter Honey Publications.

Honey, P. and Mumford, A. (1986) *Using Your Learning Styles.* Peter Honey Publications

Houghton, W (2004) *Engineering Subject Centre Guide.* Available online at: www.engsc.ac.uk/er/theory/learning.asp (accessed 18.01.08)

HM Government (2007) *Putting People First: A shared vision and commitment to the transformation of Adult Social Care.* Available online at: www.dh.gov.uk/prod_consum_dh/groups/dh_digitalassets/@dh/@en/documents/digitalass et/dh_081119.pdf (accessed 19.1.10)

HSE (Internet undated) Work-Related Violence Case Studies. www.hse.gov.uk/violence/hs/casestudies/westlothian.htm (accessed 4.10.06).

Hylton, C. (1997) *Family Survival Strategies.* (London) Exploring Parenthood.

IFSW (2010) *Social work Standards Meeting Human Rights.* (Berlin) International Federation of social Workers European Region.

Inner London Probation Service (1993) *Working with Difference: A Positive and Practical Guide to Anti-Discriminatory Practice Teaching.* (London) ILPS.

Jacobs, M. (1999) *Psychodynamic Counselling in Action.* (London) SAGE.

John Moores University (2009) *Fact and Information Sheet about Heterosexism.* Available online at: www.jmu.edu/safezone/wm_library/Heterosexism%20Fact%20Sheet.pdf (accessed 25.10.09).

Johnson, M. (2005) *Evidence Based Practice in the Social Services: Implications for organisational change.* (University of California) School of Social Welfare.

Kemshall, H. (2002) *Risk Assessment and Management.* In Davies, M. (ed) The Blackwell Companion to Social Work (Oxford) Blackwell.

Knowles, M. (1978) *the Adult Learner: A Neglected Species* (Second Edition) (Houston) Gulf Publishing.

Kolb, D.A. (1976) *The Learning Style Inventory: Technical Manual* (Boston) McBer.

Kolb, D.A. (1984) *Experiential Learning.* (Englewood Cliffs, NJ) Prentice Hall.

Lave, J. and Wneger, E. (1990) *Situated Learning: Legitimate Peripheral Participation.* (Cambridge) Cambridge University Press.

Local Government Ombudsman and Parliamentary and Health Service Ombudsman (2009) *6 Lives: The Provision of Public Services to people with learning disabilities: Second Report.* (London) The Stationery Office.

Lord Laming (2003) *The Victoria Climbié Inquiry* (London) Command Paper 5730.

Limandri, B. and Sheridan, D. (1995) *The prediction of intentional interpersonal violence.* In J. Campbell (ed) Assessing Dangerousness: Violence by Sexual Offenders, Batterers and Child Abusers. (London) SAGE.

Loewenberg, F. and Dolgoff, R. (1996) *Ethical decisions for social work practice.* (Itasca) Peacock.

Logan, J., Kershaw, S., Karban, K., Mills, S., Trotter, J. and Sinclair, M. (1996) *Confronting Prejudice* (Aldershot) Arena.

Lord Laming (2009) The *Protection of Children in England: A Progress Report.* (London) Available online at www.publications.everychildmatters.gov.uk/eOrderingDownload/HC-330.pdf (accessed 8.1.10).

Macdonald, K. and Macdonald, G. (1999) *Perceptions of risk.* In Parsloe, P. (ed) Risk Assessment in Social Work and Social Care. (London) Jessica Kingsley.

Maclean, S. and Caffrey, B. (2009) *Developing a Practice Learning Curriculum: A Guide for Practice Educators.* (Rugeley) Kirwin Maclean Associates Ltd.

Maclean, S. and Harrison, R. (2009) *Theory and Practice: A Straightforward Guide for Social Work Students* . (Rugeley) Kirwin Maclean Associates Ltd.

Maclean, S. and Lloyd, I. (2008) *Developing Quality Practice Learning in Social Work.* (Rugeley) Kirwin Maclean Associates Ltd.

Maclean, S. and Maclean, I. (2005) *Supporting You: Supporting Others. Health and Social Care (Adults) Level 3.* (Rugeley) Kirwin Maclean Associates Ltd.

Macpherson, W. (1999) *The Stephen Lawrence Enquiry.* (London) The Stationery Office.

Mansell, J., Elliot, T., Beadle-Brown, J., Ashman, B. and Macdonald, S. (2002) *Engagement in meaningful activity and 'active support' of people with intellectual disabilities in residential care.* Research in Developmental Disabilities, 23(5) pp. 342-352.

Martin, F. and Saljo, R. (1976) *On Qualitative Differences in Learning: 1. Outcome and Process.* British Journal of Educational Psychology, 46. pp. 4-11

Maslow, A. (1970) *Motivation and Personality.* (New York) Harper Collins.

Maxwell, S. (2010) *Social Care Processes need Improving not the System.* BJHC and IM. Available online at www.bjhcim.co.uk/news/2010/n1001008.htm (accessed 17.1.10.)

McCreadie, C. (2001) *Making Connections: Good Practice in the Prevention and Management of Elder Abuse.* (London) Department of Health.

Mehrabian, A and Ferris, I. *Inference of attitudes from non verbal communication in two channels.* The Journal of Counselling Psychology. Vol 31 (1967) pp. 248-252.

Mencap (2008) *Advocacy.* Available online at www.mencap.org.uk/document.asp?id=2113. (accessed 21.09.08.)

Miller, S. (2003) *Personal Communication Passports: Guidelines for Good Practice.* (Edinburgh) Communication Aids for Language and Learning: University of Edinburgh.

Milner, J. and O'Byrne, P. (1998) *Assessment in Social Work.* (Basingstoke) MacMillan.

Monahan, J. and Steadman, H. (1994) *Violence and Mental Disorder: Developments in Risk Assessment.* (Chicago) University of Chicago Press.

Morris, J. (1989) *Able Lives: Women's Experience of Paralysis* (London) The Women's Press.

Morrison, T. (2005) *Staff Supervision in Social Care: Making a Real Difference for Staff and Service Users.* (Brighton) Pavilion.

Moss, B. (2007) *Communication Skills for Health and Social Care* (London) Sage Publications

Mowlam, A., Tennant, R,. Dixon, J, and Mc Creadie, C. (2007) *UK Study of Abuse and Neglect of Older People: Qualitative Findings.* Available online at http://assets.comicrelief.com/cr09/docs/older_people_abuse_report.pdf (accessed 27.1.10).

Neufeldt, A. (1990) *Celebrating Differences.* Journal of Practical Approaches to Developmental Handicap, 15, pp. 3-6.

NHS (2006) *Learning Needs Assessment.* Working in Partnership Programme, Crown Copyright.

NHS (2008) *What is Clinical Governance?* Available online at www.cgsupport.nhs.uk/About_CG (accessed 1.10.08).

O'Callagahn, A., Murphy, G. and Clare, C. (2003) *The impact of abuse on men and women* with severe learning disabilities and their families. British Journal of Learning Disabilities, 31, pp. 175-180.

O'Keeffe, M., Hills, A., Doyle, M., McCreadie, C., Scholes, S., Constatine, R., Tinker, A., Manthorpe, J., Biggs, S., and Eren, B. (2007) *UK Study of Abuse and Neglect of Older People: Prevalance Survey Report. Available online at http://www.elderabue.org.uk/AEA%20Services/Useful%20downloads/Prevalence/Prevalence%20Report-Full.pdf (accessed 27.1.10).*

Orris, M. (2004) *Karpman Drama Triangle.* Available online at www.coachingsupervisionacademy.com/our_approach/karpman_drama_triangle.phtml accessed 22.12.09.

Osser, D. (2000) *Violence against social care staff: Report on qualitative research among Social Care professionals.* (London) Department of Health.

Owusu-Bempah, K. and Howitt, D. (1999) *Even their soul is defective.* The Psychologist 12.

Phillipson, J. (1992) *Practising Equality: Women, Men and Social Work.* (London) CCETSW.

Pillemer, K. and Finkelhor, D. (1998) *The prevalence of elder abuse: a random sample survey.* The Gerontologist, 28, pp. 51-57.

Playfield Institute, Barnardo's Scotland, Scottish Government, University of Dundee and Heads Up Scotland (2008) *Hands on Scotland: Self Harm.* Available online at www.handsonscotland.co.uk/topics/self_harm/general.htm (accessed 5.2.09).

Porter, L., Bingley, G. and Steers, R. (1982) *Motivation and work Behaviour* (New York) McGraw Hill.

Prochaska, J. & DiClemente, C. (1983) *Stages and processes of self change of smoking: Toward an integrative model of change.* Journal of Consulting and Clinical Psychology 51, pp. 390-395

Rafferty, A. (1996) *The Politics of Nursing Knowledge.* (London) Routledge.

Raven, N. (1993) *The bases of power: origins and recent developments.* Journal of Social Issues, 49, pp.227-251.

Reddington, A. and Wasltham, P. (1995) *Intermediate Health and Social Care,* (Surrey) Thomas Nelson and Sons Ltd.

Rich, P. (2009) *Giving and Receiving Feedback.* Available online at: www.selfhelpmagazine.com/articles/growth/feedback.html (accessed 10.9.09).

RMIT University Study and Learning Centre (2007) *Reflective Journal Help.* Available online at: www.dlsweb.rmit.edu.au/lsu/content2_AssessmentTasks/assess_pdf/Reflective%20journal.pdf (accessed 12.1.08).

RIPFA (2008) *Critical Appraisal Skills.* Available online at: www.ripfa.org.uk/aboutus/archive/skills.asp?TOPcatID=6&TOPcatsubID=4&id=4 (accessed 12.10.08)

Rogers, C. (1980) *Freedom to Learn for the 80s.* (New York) Free Press.

Roth, R. (1989) *Preparing the reflective practitioner: Transforming the apprentice through the dialectic.* Journal of Teacher Education, 40, pp. 31-35.

Royal College of Nursing (2006) *RCN Principles: A Framework for evaluating health and social care policy.* (London) RCN.

Royal College of Nursing (2008) *Principles to Inform Decision Making: What do I need to know?* (London) RCN.

Royal College of Psychiatrists and Princess Royal Trust for Carers (2004) *Carers and Confidentiality in Mental Health: Issues Involved in Information Sharing.* Available online at: www.carers.org/data/files/carersandconfidentiality-13.pdf (accessed 23.10.09).

Royal College of Speech and Language Therapy (2006) *Communicating Quality 3.* (London) RCSLT.

Royal National Institute for Deaf People (2009) *Communication Tips* (factsheet). Available online at http://www.rnid.org.uk/information_resources/factsheets/communication/factsheets_leaflets/communication_tips.htm (accessed 20.11.09)

Rushland Poets (1997) *Sticks and Stones* (Bristol) Living Magically Press.

Rushton, A., Beaumont, K. and Mayers, D. (2000) *Service and client outcomes of cases reported under a joint vulnerable adults policy.* Journal of Adult Protection, 2, pp. 5-17.

Sackett, D.L., Strauss, S.E., Richardson, W.S., Rosenberg, W. and Haynes, R.B. (1997) *Evidence-based Medicine: How to practice and teach EBM. (2nd edition)* (Edinburgh) Churchill-Livingstone.

Safe and Sound in Partnership with the NSPCC (1995) *So Who are we Meant to Trust Now? Responding to Abuse in Care: The Experiences of Young People* (London) NSPCC.

Saleebey, D. (1996) *The strengths perspective in social work practice: extensions and cautions.* Social work 41, pp. 296-305.

Schön, D. (1987) *Educating the Reflective Practitioner.* (San Francisco) Jossey Bass.

Shardlow, S. (Undated). *Inspecting Social Work Values.* Available online at www.scie-socialcareonline.org.uk/repositiry/fulltext/0005992.pdf (accessed 30.8.08).

Skinner, B.F. (1973) *Beyond Freedom and Dignity.* (Hammondsworth) Penguin.

Smale, G., Tuson, G., Biehal, N. and Marsh, P. (1993) *Empowerment, Assessment, Care Management and the Skilled Worker.* (London) HMSO.

Smith, S. and Karban, K. (2006) *Developing Critical Reflection within an Interpersonal Learning Programme.* (Leeds Metropolitan University). Available online at: www.leeds.ac.uk/medicine/meu/lifelong06/papers/P_suesmith_kate_karban.pdf accessed (6.2.10)

Social Platform (2010) *Briefing Number 33: Annual Theme 2010 on Care.* (Brussels) Social Platform.

Social Services Inspectorate and Department of Health (1991) *Care Management and Assessment – Practitioner's Guide.* (London) HMSO.

Stancliff, R., Jones, E. and Mansell, J. (eds) (2008) *Special Issue of Journal of Intellectual and Developmental Disability.* 33(3).

Sutton, C. (1999) *Helping Families with Troubled Children.* (London) Wiley.

Sutton, J. (1999) *Healing the Hurt Within.* How to Books.

Taylor, B. and Devine, D. (1993) *Assessing Needs and Planning Care in Social Work.* (London) Arena Press.

ThemPra Social Pedagogy Community Interest Society (2009) *Social Pedagogy: Theory meets Practice. Available* online at: www.socialpedagogy.co.uk/concepts.htm (accessed 19.1.10)

Thomas, M and Pierson, J. (Eds) (1995) *Collins Dictionary of Social Work* (London) Collins.

Thompson, N. (1996) *People Skills: A Guide to Effective Practice in the Human Services* (Hampshire) Macmillan Press Ltd.

Thompson, N. (1994) *The Value Base of Social and Health Care.* Prospects Training Publications.

Thompson, N. (1998) *Promoting Equality.* (Basingstoke) Macmillan.

Thompson, N. (2005) *Anti-Discriminatory Practice.*   Third Edition (Basingstoke) Palgrave.

Thompson, N. (2005) *Understanding Social Work: Preparing for Practice.* (Basingstoke) Palgrave Macmillan.

Timms, N. (1983) *Social work Values: An Enquiry.* (London) Routledge and Kegan Paul.

Tizard Centre (2008) *What is person-centred active support?* Available online at www.personcentredactivesupport.com/aboutperson-centredactivesupport. (Accessed 10.10.08)

Topss England (2004) *National Occupational Standards for Social Work.* (Leeds) Topss England.

Topss England (updated 2005) *Induction Standards.* (Web edition) Topss England.

University of York (2000) *Facts, Feelings and Feedback: A Collaborative Model for Direct Observation* (York) University of York.

Vanier, J. (1988) *The Broken Body.* (London) Darton, Longman and Todd Limited.

Walker, S. and Beckett, C. (2005) *Social Work Assessment and Intervention.* (Dorset) Russell House Publishing.

Weightman, J. (1990) *Managing Human Resources.* (London) Istitute of Personnel Management.

White, C., Holland, D., Marsland, D. and Oakes, P. (2003) *The identification of environments and cultures that promote the abuse of people with intellectual disabilities. A review of the literature.* Journal of Applied Research in Intellectual Disabilities, 16, pp1-9.

Williams, P. (1978) *Our Mutual Handicap: Attitudes and Perceptions of others by people with a mental handicap.* (London) CMH.

Williams, P. (2006) *Social Work with People with Learning Difficulties.* (Exeter) Learning Matters.

Wolfensberger, W. (1988) *Common assets of mentally retarded people that are commonly not acknowledged.* Mental retardation, 26, pp. 63-70.

Wolfensberger, W. and Thomas, S. (1983) *PASSING (Program Analysis of Service Systems' Implementation of Normalisation Goals): Normalisation criteria and ratings manual.* (Toronto) National Institute on Mental Retardation.

Wolfensberger, W. (1983) *Social role valorisation: A proposed new term for the principle of normalisation.* Mental Retardation, 21, pp. 234-239.